Who Returns to Work & Why?

International Social Security Series

In cooperation with the
International Social Security Association (ISSA)

Neil Gilbert, Series Editor

Targeting Social Benefits:
International Perspectives and Trends
Neil Gilbert, editor

Social Security at the Dawn of the
21ˢᵗ Century: Topical Issues and New Approaches
Dalmer D. Hoskins, Donate Dobbernack, and
Christiane Kuptsch, editors

Activating the Unemployed: A Comparative
Appraisal of Work-Oriented Policies
Neil Gilbert and Rebecca Van Voorhis, editors

Recent Health Policy Innovations in
Social Security
Aviva Ron and Xenia Scheil-Adlung, editors

Who Returns to Work and Why: A Six-Country
Study on Work Incapacity and Reintegration
Frank S. Bloch and Rienk Prins, editors

Who Returns to Work & Why?

A Six-Country Study on Work Incapacity & Reintegration

Frank S. Bloch
Rienk Prins
editors

International Social Security Series
Volume 5

Transaction Publishers
New Brunswick (U.S.A.) and London (U.K.)

Library of Congress Catalog Number: 00-062886
ISBN: 0-7658-0770-X
Printed in the United States of America

Library of Congress Cataloging-in-Publication Data

Bloch, Frank S.
   Who returns to work and why : a six-country study on work incapacity and reintegration / Frank S. Bloch & Rienk Prins, editors
      p. cm.— (International social security ; v. 5)
   Includes bibliographical references.
   ISBN 0-7658-0770-X (alk. paper)
   1. Workers' compensation—Case studies. 2. Vocational rehabilitation—Case studies   I. Bloch, Frank S. II. Prins, Rienk. III. Series.

HD7103.6 .B56 2000
368.4'1—dc21   00-062886

Contents

Foreword   xvii
Preface   xix
Note to Readers   xxv

1. Work Incapacity and Reintegration:
   History and Aim of the WIR Project
   Frank S. Bloch & Rienk Prins   1

   Background and Central Research Goals   1
   Participating Countries and Institutions   2
   Common Core Research Design   3
   Interventions, Incentives, and Disincentives   4
   Measurement of Outcomes   5
   Organization of the Project   5
   Implementation of the Project   5
   Presentation of Data and Results   6
   References   8

2. Social Security, Work Incapacity,
   and Reintegration
   Rienk Prins & Frank S. Bloch   9

   Background of the Problem   9
        Labor Market Considerations   9
        The Health Perspective   10
        Social Security Concerns   11
   Sickness and Disability Benefit Schemes:
       Similarities and Differences   12
        Eligibility   16
        Payment Levels and Replacement Rates   16
        Administration and Determination of
         Eligibility   17
        Rehabilitation Services   18
   Job Protection   20
   Selected Incentives and Disincentives:
       A Comparative Overview   21
   Placing the Project's Research Questions
       in Context   23
   Notes   25
   References   25

3. Work Incapacity and Reintegration:
    A Literature Review
      Jan Høgelund   27

    Introduction   27
    Clinical Studies   28
          Return to Work in Chronic Low-back
            Pain Patients   29
          Effects of Interventions   31
    Economic Studies   33
          Economic Incentives and Return to Work   33
          Effects of Vocational Rehabilitation   36
    Public Policy Studies   37
          The Importance of Benefit Schemes   38
    Sociological Studies   42
          The Micro Approach   42
          The Macro Approach   43
    A Theoretical Model of Work Incapacity and
      Work Resumption   47
    Summary and Conclusions   49
    Appendix 3.1: Selected Literature from
      the Review   51

4. Research Design and Methodology
      Jockel Wolf   55

    Background and Aim of Research Design   55
    Operationalizing the Research Design   57
          Inclusion Criteria and Cohort Creation   57
          Cohort Characteristics, Interventions,
            and Outcomes   58
          Observation Period and Measurement Points   60
          Standardized Measurements   60
    The National Cohorts   61
          Non Response at T1   61
          Cohort Sizes   61
    Data Collection Methods   61
    Data Analysis Methods   63
    International Database   63

5. Cohorts Compared: Cross-national
    Similarities and Differences
      Andreas Weber   65

    Introduction   65

Demographic Characteristics   66
Work Characteristics   70
Subjective Health Status   71
Subjective Work Prognosis   73
Non-response Analysis   74
Comparison with Working Population   75
Comparability of Cohorts   77
Summary and Conclusions   84
Reference   84

6. Work Status and Benefit Status
      Theo J. Veerman   85

    Work Status and Benefit Status after One
      and Two Years   86
          Work Status   86
          Benefit Status   88
    Work Status at T3 and Demographic, Health,
      and Work Characteristics   91
    Conclusions   95

7. The Role of Medical Interventions
      Tommy Hansson & Elisabeth Hansson   99

    Introduction   99
    National Health Care Systems and the
      Back Patient   101
          Denmark   101
          Germany   102
          Israel   102
          The Netherlands   102
          Sweden   102
          The United States   103
    Medical Interventions and their Providers   103
          Caregivers   103
          Imaging Techniques   104
          Hospitalization, Surgery, and Bed Rest   105
          Treatments   106
          Medication and Injections   107
          Braces and Supports   107
    Back-related Health within the National
      Cohorts   108
    Medical Interventions   111
          Consultation with Physician   111

	Consultation with a Physiotherapist or Other Caregivers	113
	Imaging the Lumbar Spine	115
	Treatments	117
	Health Indicators and Return to Work	124
	Back Function	124
	General Health	125
	Social Functioning	125
	Vitality	126
	Mental Health	128
	Pain Intensity	129
	Summary and Conclusions	131
	Note	132
	References	132

8. Vocational and Other Non-medical Interventions
   Sisko Bergendorff & Dalia Gordon — 135

	Scope and Provision of Interventions	136
	Repertoire of Vocational and Other Non-medical Interventions	136
	Actors, Timing and Procedures in the Work Incapacity Process	137
	Conclusions	143
	Training and Education	143
	Training and Education Measures	144
	When Training and Education Started	145
	Relationship to Work Resumption	145
	Work Accommodations and Employer Motivators	147
	Work Accommodations	148
	When Work Accommodations were Applied	150
	Transportation to Workplace and Sheltered Workshops	151
	Employer Motivators: Wage Subsidy and Exemption of Wage Payment	151
	Combinations of Training, Education, and Work Accommodations	152
	Relationship to Work	154
	Employee Motivators: Disciplinary Actions and Labor Relationships	155
	Warning of Dismissal and Dismissal	155
	Contacts With Colleagues/Employer	157

Relationship to Work Resumption 158
Work Incapacity Assessment, Benefit
  Withdrawal, and Rehabilitation 159
    Medical Examinations for Sickness Benefit
      Eligibility 159
    Threat and Actual Withdrawal of Sickness
      Benefit 160
    Rehabilitation Inquiry and Plan 161
    Test of Vocational Capacity 162
    Assessment of Eligibility for Disability
      Benefit 163
    Capitalization of Benefit 165
    Relationship to Work Resumption 165
Job Services and Other Services 166
    Job Counseling 167
    Job Search 167
    Job Offer 168
    Job Club 169
    Change in Day Care Arrangements
      for Children 170
    Counseling 170
    Reduction of Waiting Periods for
      Health Care 171
    Relationship to Work Resumption 172
Summary and Conclusions 173
    Rehabilitation Inquiry and Plan 173
    Education and Training 173
    Work Accommodations 174
    Threat and Actual Loss of Work, and
      Job Services 174
    Return to Former Work 175
    Disability Benefit 175
    Relevance of Policy Context and Timing
      of Interventions 177
Reference 178
Appendix 8.1: Vocational and Other Non-medical
  Interventions in the Six Cohorts 179
Appendix 8.2: Summary of Work Incapacity
  Procedures 186

9. A Closer Look at Work Resumption
      John Kearney 193

Characteristics of Work Resumption 193

Type of Employer 194
Occupation 195
Changes in Hours Worked, Wages, and
Occupation 198
Work Resumption and Vocational and
Other Non-medical Interventions 199
Work Resumption and Medical Interventions 201
Type of Medical Provider 201
Medical Treatments 203
Work Resumption Patterns 204
"Continuous" Versus "Late Resumers" 204
"Continuous Resumers" Versus
"Relapse" 206
Late Resumers" Versus "Non-resumers" 206
Work Resumption and Selected Baseline
Characteristics 209
Reasons Reported for Not Working 211
Summary and Conclusions 211
Employer and Occupation 211
Vocational and Other Non-medical
Interventions 212
Reasons for Non-resumption 212
Medical Providers and Treatments 212
Patterns of Work Resumption 213
Indications of Successful Interventions 213
Technical Note 214
Appendix 9.1: Additional Data on Work
Resumption Patterns 215

10. Work Resumption and the Role of Interventions
    Theo J. Veerman & Edward Palmer

Introduction 223
Work Capacity 225
Overview of the Model and Strategy for Analysis 228
Medical Interventions and Health in the
First Year 229
Baseline Characteristics, Vocational and
Other Non-medical Interventions, and Work
Status in the First Year 234
Baseline Characteristics 235
Vocational and Other Non-medical
Interventions 239

Baseline Characteristics, Vocational and Other
Non-medical Interventions, and Work Status
in the Second Year   240
    Work Status at T2   243
    Baseline Characteristics   244
    Vocational and Other Non-medical
      Interventions   245
The Cohorts Compared   247
Conclusions: Major Determinants of Work
Resumption   250
    Personal and Work Characteristics
    ("Baseline Characteristics")   251
    Medical Interventions   252
    Vocational and Other Non-medical
      Interventions   253
    Interventions, Incentives, and
      Disincentives   253
Notes   255
References   256
Description of the Statistical Analysis Used   257
Appendix 10.1: Full Results of Statistical
Analysis   258

11. Factors Influencing Work Resumption:
A Summary of Major Findings
Boukje Cuelenaere & Rienk Prins   273

Aim and Background of the Study   273
Ambitions and Restrictions   274
Striking Differences in Work Resumption Rates
and Patterns   275
The Role of Demographic, Health and
Vocational Factors   276
Health Condition, Medical Treatments and
Work Resumption   277
Vocational and Other Non-medical Interventions   279
Resumers, Non-resumers and Benefit Receipt   280
Health Condition, Interventions and Work
Resumption Reconsidered   281
Additional Conclusions from National Studies   282
    Denmark   282
    Germany   283
    Israel   283
    The Netherlands   283

Sweden 284
United States 284
Outlook for Future Research 284
References 285

Addendum A: Overview of Variables 287
Addendum B: List of Project Publications 296

Contributors 305

List of Tables and Figures

Table 2.1:	Main Dimensions of Sickness and Disability Benefit Schemes (1994-1997)	14
Table 2.2:	Main Features of Administration and Rehabilitation (1994-1997)	19
Table 2.3:	Incentives and Disincentives on Work Incapacity	23
Table 3.1:	Selected Clinical Studies on Socio-Demographic, Medical, Psychological, Job Related, and Lifestyle Variables on Return to Work of Work Incapacitated Employees with Low-Back Pain	30
Table 3.2:	Selected Economic Studies on Economic Incentives for Labor Market Reintegration of Work Incapacitated Employees	35
Table 3.3:	Selected Public Policy Studies on The Organization of Benefit Schemes and Provision of Benefits	40
Table 3.4:	Selected Sociological Studies on Social Support and Socialization into the Role as Disabled	44
Table 3.5:	Selected Studies on Working Conditions and Labor Market Conditions for Return to Work of Long-Term Work Incapacitated Employees	46
Figure 3.1:	Theoretical Model of Work Incapacity and Reintegration	47
Table 4.1:	Non-Response (%) and Cohort Size at T1	61
Figure 4.1:	Number of Subjects (T1, T2, T3)	62
Table 4.2:	Methods of Data Collection Applied	62
Table 5.1:	Mean Age at T1	66
Table 5.2:	Age Distribution at T1 (%)	67
Table 5.3:	Gender Distribution at T1 (%)	67
Table 5.4:	National Language as Mother Tongue at T1 (%)	68
Table 5.5:	Educational Level at T1 (%)	69
Table 5.6:	Household Composition at T1 (%)	70
Table 5.7:	Working Hours per Week at T1 (%)	71
Table 5.8:	Physical Job Demands at T1	71
Table 5.9:	Mental Health at T1	72
Table 5.10:	Pain Intensity at T1	72

Table 5.11:	Back Function (Hannover ADL) at T1	73
Table 5.12:	Work Prognosis, Long-Term at T1 (%)	73
Table 5.13:	Cohort Size and Non-Response Rates at T1, T2, T3	74
Table 5.14:	Results of Drop-out Analysis at T2 and T3	76
Table 5.15:	Age Distribution in Cohorts at T1 and in Labour Force (1997) (%)	78
Table 5.16:	Gender Distribution in Cohorts at T1 and in Labour Force (1997) (%)	79
Table 5.17:	Educational Level in Cohorts at T1 and in Labour Force (1997) (%)	80
Table 5.18:	Household Types in Cohorts at T1 and in Labour Force (1997) (%)	81
Table 5.19:	Working Hours per Week in Cohorts at T1 and in Labour Force (1997) (%)	82
Table 5.20:	Outcomes of Cluster Analysis	83
Table 5.21:	Similarities of Cohorts, T1	83
Table 6.1:	Work Status at T2 and T3 (% of cohort Working)	86
Table 6.2:	Work Resumption Patterns (% of cohort)	87
Table 6.3:	Benefit Status: Subjects Receiving Sickness, Disability, or Work Injury Benefit at T2 and T3 (%)	88
Table 6.4:	Combination of Work and Benefits: Working Respondents Receiving (Additional) Sickness, Disability, or Work Injury Benefits (%)	89
Table 6.5:	Non-Resumers at T3: Benefit Status (%)	90
Table 6.6:	Development of Total Personal Net Income from T0 to T3, in Non-Workers at T3 (%)	90
Table 6.7:	Significance of Associations between Work Status at T3 (Working/Not Working) and Selected Demographic, Health, and (Former) Job Characteristics as Measured at T1	91
Table 6.8:	Demographic Characteristics and Respondents Working at T3 (%)	93
Table 6.9:	Health Indicators (at T1) and Respondents Working at T3 (%)	94
Table 6.10:	Job Characteristics and Respondents Working at T3 (%)	95
Table 7.1:	Back Function (Hannover ADL) (Mean) at T1, T2, and T3	108
Table 7.2:	Social Function (Mean) at T1, T2, and T3	109
Table 7.3:	Vitality (Mean) at T1, T2, and T3	109

Table 7.4:   Mental Health (Mean) at T1, T2, and T3   109
Table 7.5:   Pain Intensity (Mean) at T1, T2, and T3   110
Table 7.6:   Response to the Question: When Did the
              Health Complaints Start? (%)   110
Table 7.7:   Visit to Physicians (%) at T1, T2, and T3   112
Table 7.8:   Visit to Physiotherapist and/or Other
              Caregivers (Chiropractor, Homeopath)
              (%) at T1, T2, and T3   114
Table 7.9:   Examinations by X-ray, CT and/or MRI
              (%) at T1, T2, and T3   116
Table 7.10:   Treatment with Hospitalization, Surgery,
              and/or Bed Rest (%) at T1, T2, and T3   117
Table 7.11:   Treatment with Heat or Cold; TENS,
              Ultrasound, and/or Short-Wave; Acupuncture;
              Massage; Manipulation, Traction, and/or
              Zone Therapy; Mud-Packing and/or Medicinal
              Baths (%) at T1, T2, and T3   119
Table 7.12:   Treatment with "Active Treatment":
              Physical Activities and/or Back School/
              Pain School (%) at T1, T2, and T3   122
Table 7.13:   Treatment with Pain Relieving Injections
              or Medications (Analgetics, Tranquilizers,
              Sleeping Pills, etc.), Walking Aids (Crutches),
              and/or Brace (%) at T1, T2, and T3   123
Table 7.14:   Back Function (Mean) and Work Status at T2   125
Table 7.15:   Surgery, Work Status, and Back Function
              within the Swedish Cohort at T2   125
Table 7.16:   Social Function (Mean) and Work Status at T2   126
Table 7.17:   Surgery, Work Status, and Social Function
              for the Swedish Cohort at T2   126
Table 7.18:   Vitality (Mean) and Work Status at T2   127
Table 7.19:   Surgery, Work Status, and Vitality for the
              Swedish Cohort at T2   127
Table 7.20:   Surgery, Work Status, and Vitality for the
              German Cohort at T2   128
Table 7.21:   Mental Health (Mean) and Work Status at T2   128
Table 7.22:   Surgery, Work Status, and Mental Health
              for the Swedish Cohort at T2   129
Table 7.23:   Surgery, Work Status, and Mental Health
              for the German Cohort at T2   129
Table 7.24:   Pain Intensity (Mean) and Work Status at T2   130
Table 7.25:   Surgery, Work Status, and Pain Intensity
              for the Swedish Cohort at T2   130

Table 7.26:   Surgery, Work Status, and Pain Intensity
                for the German Cohort at T2   130
Table 7.27:   Surgery, Work Status, and Pain Intensity
                for the US Cohort at T2   131
Table 8.1:   Vocational and other Non-Medical
                Interventions in Participating Countries   138
Table 8.2:   General Education, Vocational Education,
                and Job Training at T2 and T3 (%)   144
Table 8.3:   Timing of Education: Number of Months
                after Reporting Sick before Interventions
                Started (Median) at T2   145
Table 8.4:   Work Accommodations (% of Working
                Respondents) at T2 and T3   148
Table 8.5:   Timing of Work Accommodations: Number
                of Months after Reporting Sick before
                Interventions Started (Median) at T2   150
Table 8.6:   Wage Subsidy and Exemption of Wage
                Payment (% of Working Respondents) at
                T2 and T3   152
Table 8.7:   Major Combinations of Training, Education,
                and Work Accommodations (% of Working
                Respondents) at T2 and T3   153
Table 8.8:   Warning of Dismissal and Dismissal (%)
                at T2 and T3, and Timing (Median) at T2   156
Table 8.9:   Contacts with Colleagues/Employer (%)
                at T2 and T3   158
Table 8.10:   Medical Examinations for Sickness Benefit
                (%) at T2 and T3   159
Table 8.11:   Threat of Withdrawal of Short-Term Benefit
                (%) at T2 and T3, and Timing (Median) at T2   160
Table 8.12:   Withdrawal of Short-Term Benefit (%) at T2
                and T3   160
Table 8.13:   Rehabilitation Inquiry and Plan (%) at T2
                and T3, and Timing (Median) at T2   161
Table 8.14:   Test of Vocational Capacity (%) at T2
                and T3, and Timing (Median) at T2   162
Table 8.15:   Testing of Eligibility and Qualifications
                for Disability Benefit (%) at T2 and T3,
                and Timing (Median) at T2   164
Table 8.16:   Capitalization of Benefit (%) at T2 and T3   165
Table 8.17:   Job Counseling (%) at T2 and T3, and
                Timing (Median) at T2   167

Table 8.18:   Job Search (%) at T2 and T3, and Timing
              (Median) at T2   168
Table 8.19:   Job Offer (% of Job Searchers) at T2 and T3   169
Table 8.20:   Job Services – Correlations   170
Table 8.21:   Social/Psychological Counseling (%) at T2
              and T3, and Timing (Median) at T2   171
Table 8.22:   Reduction of Waiting Periods (%) at T2
              and T3   171
Table 8.23:   Main Characteristics of Vocational and
              other Non-Medical Interventions   176
Table 8A2.1: Summary of Work Incapacity Procedures
              (Denmark)   186
Table 8A2.2: Summary of Work Incapacity Procedures
              (Germany)   187
Table 8A2.3: Summary of Work Incapacity Procedures
              (Israel)   188
Table 8A2.4: Summary of Work Incapacity Procedures
              (Netherlands)   189
Table 8A2.5: Summary of Work Incapacity Procedures
              (Sweden)   190
Table 8A2.6: Summary of Work Incapacity Procedures
              (United States)   191
Table 9.1:   Work Resumption by Type of Employer
              (%) at T3   194
Table 9.2:   Rates of Work Resumption by Occupation
              (%) at T3   195
Table 9.3:   Change in Occupation by Occupational
              Group (%) at T3   196
Table 9.4:   Change in Hours Worked, Wages and
              Occupation for Resumers (%), T0 – T3   198
Table 9.5:   Rates of Work Resumption for Subjects
              Receiving Vocational and Other
              Non-Medical Interventions (%) at T3   200
Table 9.6:   Consultation of Medical Providers and
              Work Resumption (%) at T3   201
Table 9.7:   Consultation of Medical Providers and
              Working at Old or New Employer (%) at T3   202
Table 9.8:   Work Resumption at T3 for Subjects Receiving
              Medical Treatments (%)   203
Table 9.9:   Continuous vs. Late Resumers: Patterns of
              Work Resumption and Selected Characteristics
              (Significant Associations)   205

Table 9.10:	Continuous Resumers vs. Relapse Group: Patterns of Work Resumption and Selected Characteristics (Significant Associations)	207
Table 9.11:	Late Resumers vs. Non-Resumers: Patterns of Work Resumption and Selected Characteristics (Significant Associations)	208
Table 9.12:	Patterns of Work Resumption (Continuous/ Late Resumer/Relapse/Non-Resumer) and Selected Characteristics (Significant Associations)	210
Table 9.13:	Reason for not Working (%) at T3	211
Table 9A1.1:	Demographic Characteristics (%) of Continuous Resumers	215
Table 9A1.2:	Health Indicators (%) at T3 of Continuous Resumers	216
Table 9A1.3:	Job Characteristics(%) of Continuous Resumers	216
Table 9A1.4:	Demographic Characteristics (%) of Late Resumers	217
Table 9A1.5:	Health Indicators (%) at T3 of Late Resumers	218
Table 9A1.6:	Job Characteristics (%) of Late Resumers	218
Table 9A1.7:	Demographic Characteristics (%) of Relapse Resumers	219
Table 9A1.8:	Selected Health Indicators (%) at T3 of Relapse Resumers	220
Table 9A1.9:	Job Characteristics (%) of Relapse Resumers	220
Table 9A1.10:	Demographic Characteristics (%) of Non-Resumers	221
Table 9A1.11:	Health Indicators (%) at T3 of Non-Resumers	222
Table 9A1.12:	Job Characteristics (%) of Non-Resumers	222
Figure 10.1:	General Model for the Analysis	224
Figure 10.2:	Factors Influencing Work Ability	227
Table 10.1:	Percent of (Additional) Variance Explained by Back Function (ADL) and Other Health Measures on Work Status at T2	230
Table 10.2:	Prediction of Back Function Scores (ADL) at T2 by ADL-T1, Baseline Characteristics (T1) and Medical Interventions	232
Table 10.3:	Prediction of Work Status T2 by Baseline Characteristics and Vocational Interventions T0-T2	236

Table 10.4:   Prediction of Work Status T3 by Work
               Status T2, Baseline Characteristics and
               Vocational Interventions   241
Table 10.5:   Outcomes at Two Years and Baseline
               Indicators of the Work Capacity of the Country
               Cohorts   248
Table 10A.1:   Results of Multiple Regression Model
               Predicting Back Function Scores (ADL) at T2   260
Table 10A.2:   Results of Logistic Regression Model Predicting
               Work Status (Non-Working /Working) at T2   264
Table 10A.3:   Results of Logistic Regression Model Predicting
               Work Status (Non-Working/Working) at T3   268

Foreword

It is with pleasure and pride that the International Social Security Association (ISSA) presents the publication *Who Returns to Work and Why? A Six-Country Study on Work Incapacity and Reintegration*, which presents the results of the first longitudinal research project undertaken under the auspices of the ISSA.

Sound and relevant policy research is an indispensable tool for social security organizations in order to provide them with the basis to formulate policies adapted to the rapidly changing circumstances in which they operate. This publication demonstrates that what was frequently referred to as the "Dutch disease" in the late 1980s—rising rates of dependency on social benefits, especially among disability beneficiaries—is indeed prevalent in other industrialized countries as well, and that these countries are all seeking ways to effectively diminish this dependency. If successful, these approaches could ease the burden that these benefits represent for social security programs and increase the work participation rate of the overall population. And, as one of the key findings of the study suggests, the prospect of actually returning to work is for the individual one of the most critical factors leading to successful rehabilitation and reintegration.

On behalf of the ISSA, the participants in the project as well as those who will benefit from the results, I wish to acknowledge the central role played throughout this project by Mr. Dik Hermans, formerly Chair of the ISSA Research Advisory Board, for his insight when he initiated this project and for his commitment in seeing it through to conclusion.

This study paves the way for ISSA empirical research projects that deal with key issues and provide social security policy makers with insights for improving benefits in the best interests of their clients and of society as a whole.

Dalmer D. Hoskins
Secretary General
International Social Security Association

Preface

Without doubt, disability is a major social problem in most industrialized countries. What was first described in the 1980s in the Netherlands as a "Dutch disease" has struck most industrialized countries, sometimes with a delay, but with the same consequences: increasing social expenditures and decreasing work participation rates. It is not certain, however, that politicians and social security policy makers all perceive that modern social policy requires better solutions for work resumption. Consequently, it is essential to increase our knowledge about the types of work reintegration measures that are effective. This was the objective of the ISSA comparative study on work incapacity and reintegration (WIR Project) that lies behind this book.

In the early 1990s, the Advisory Board on Social Security Research—a consultative body of the ISSA charged with steering the Association's research activities and, more generally, with promoting research activities in social security—decided to become more active in comparative research. The idea was not only to support or sponsor projects, but to be directly involved in empirical research by taking advantage of the unique perspectives and resources available to the Advisory Board. Members of the Board are internationally recognized researchers, many of whom manage social security research programs. The Board wished to demonstrate how the results of empirical research could benefit social security institutions and help improve the effectiveness of their operations. Furthermore, a major empirical study as ambitious as the WIR Project would test the ability of the ISSA to function as a platform or network and to create the motivation, energy and means to undertake the project. Today, it can be affirmed that the ISSA, and in particular its Research Advisory Board, passed the test—and that this success should encourage the ISSA to undertake similar studies in the future.

When they set up the Project in 1993, members of the Board considered the question of work resumption for beneficiaries of social benefits to be a major challenge for social security programs. In retrospect, it is clear that the Board had considerable foresight, as in recent years work resumption has become a priority concern not only of social security programs, but of several international organizations. For example, the International Labor Organization and the OECD have initiated projects dealing with work resumption, and this has become an important issue in the deliberations of the European Commission.

The WIR Project, which was managed by a Steering Committee comprised of representatives from each of the participating countries, was unique for a number of reasons. In the first place, in the spirit of the ISSA, each country participating in the project not only assumed responsibility for the cost and the organization of its national research, but also supported the international coordination of the project. Second, each national team developed its own research project, and thus projects varied from country to country. A prerequisite was that each national research project should incorporate the "core design" established for the overall project. Last, in addition to their competence, the diversity of the researchers involved in the project was noteworthy: institutional and academic researchers from disciplines ranging from medicine to sociology, including statistics, law and social administration. This diversity, and the differing national situations, demanded considerable understanding and attention on the part of all participants in order to bring the project to fruition. The experience has been enriching both for the participants and for the Project.

The WIR Project was also unique in that it provides a model for undertaking a comparative research project without centralized financing. Financial support from each national partner requires the sincere interest and commitment of every participant. This provides the motivation to ensure the continuity and eventual realization of the project. Despite the extension of the Project time frame, all but one of the original seven countries involved in the Project participated in the Project until its completion. The coexistence of a project at the national and international comparative levels permitted an exchange of information; the national experiences providing the basis for the international study, and the latter providing the necessary framework for the design of the national studies. The Project also enabled the participants to compare their own national provisions with those of other countries, which was a major contribution to the enhancement of the national studies.

The enthusiasm and commitment of the participants at numerous meetings with sponsors and national research teams during the course of the Project was evident, and it was one of the essential factors contributing to the success of the Project. This enthusiasm was attributable in part to the interest of researchers in each country to discover whether national measures led to the return to work of the subjects included in the national study. At a meeting of researchers, sponsors, and external experts held in December, 1999, in Copenhagen in order to review the results of the research and the manuscript of this book, in-depth discussions took place on the policy implications of the research findings. Chapter 11 shows ample evidence of how stimulating these discussions were. To take only one striking example: in some countries, results of the WIR project could result in a shift in the focus of national policy from reintegration to greater emphasis on a preventive approach, as the findings clearly show that insufficient attention to early intervention and prevention are major problems.

A distinguishing feature of this publication is that it is not merely a compilation of separate case studies from the six participating countries—Denmark, Germany, Israel, the Netherlands, Sweden and the United States. Rather it is a truly comparative study wherein national experience and results have been totally integrated in the chapters comprising the report.

In addition to this international project report, numerous other documents—national and international—have been published. (A listing of existing publications at the time this book went to press can be found at Addendum B.) In addition, the international database put together for this project can lead to numerous other publications. In order to enable and encourage researchers who were not involved in the Project, the Board is making the project database available to the public at the end of the year 2000. This international project report is thus only the beginning of investigations into the numerous aspects of the WIR Project, which has already generated so much interest. Evidence of this interest also comes from the 6th European Congress on Research in Rehabilitation held in Berlin in 1998, where initial results from the national studies were presented and the session was awarded a prize for the best contribution.

Such a project could only have been accomplished through the cooperation of numerous individuals. The Steering Committee for the WIR Project, which took the initiative and guided the Project, included:

Ms. Inger Koch-Nielsen and Mr. Niels Ploug for Denmark (The Danish National Institute of Social Research)

Mr. Ferdinand Schliehe for Germany (Federation of German Pension Insurance Institutes, VDR)

Mr. Shlomo Cohen for Israel (National Insurance Institute)

Mr. Dik Hermans (Social Security Supervisory Board and Chair of the Project) and Mr. Bernardus Boekraad (Ministry of Social Affairs and Employment) for the Netherlands

Ms. Inger Marklund for Sweden (National Social Insurance Board)

Mr. Peter Wheeler for the United States (Social Security Administration)

The crucial international coordination of the Project was handled by the AS/tri Research and Consultancy Group, Leiden, the Netherlands, under the responsibility of Dr. Rienk Prins, together with an ISSA consultant, Prof. Frank Bloch, Vanderbilt University, United States. The international database was managed by the IEA Data Processing Center, Hamburg, Germany, under the responsibility of Mr. Jockel Wolf and Mr. Dirk Hastedt. General supervision and secretarial support for the project were provided by the ISSA, under the direction of the head of the ISSA Research Program, Mr. Roland Sigg.

The heart of the WIR Project was the numerous researchers who were involved in the day-to-day conduct of the national studies. The principal researchers were:

Denmark: Jan Høgelund (team leader), The Danish National Institute of Social Research; Jens Modvig, University of Copenhagen and The International Rehabilitation Council for Torture Victims in Denmark.

Germany: Andreas Weber (team leader), University of Lübeck and Working Group of Rehabilitation Research, Hamburg; Heiner Raspe, University of Lübeck.

Israel: Dalia Gordon (team leader), National Insurance Institute.

Netherlands: Theo Veerman (team leader), Boukje Cuelenaere, Anneke van der Giezen, Rienk Prins, AS/tri Research and Consultancy Group.

Sweden: Sisko Bergendorff, National Social Insurance Board (team leader); Hanna Arneson, Department of Health and Environment, Linköping University; Pia Carlberg, National Social Insurance Board; Ulla Gerner, Social Insurance Office in Stockholm; Parviz Ghaemian, National Social Insurance Board; Christina Goede, National Social Insurance Board; Elisabeth Hansson, Department of Orthopaedics at the Sahlgrenska University Hospital; Tommy Hansson, Department of Orthopaedics at the Sahlgrenska University Hospital; Carl Zetterberg, Department of Orthopaedics at the Sahlgrenska University Hospital; Edward Palmer, National Social Insurance Board and Department of Economics, Uppsala University; Mats Westin, National Social Insurance Board.

United States: John Kearney (team leader), Carolyn Harrison, Paula Laird, Kay Merrick, Scott Muller, Nelson Rambath, Evan Schechter, Social Security Administration; Sarah Higgins, Francina Kerr, Richard Schwartz, Bureau of the Census.

We have benefitted from the comments on preliminary drafts of this publication by the following distinguished experts whose assistance we gratefully acknowledge:

Prof. Monroe Berkowitz, Rutgers University, United States
Mr. Stephen Duckworth, Disability Matters Ltd, United Kingdom
Mr. Esko Kalimo, Social Insurance Institution, Finland
Prof. Ulrich Laaser, University Bielefeld, Germany
Ms. Nancy Lawand, Human Resource Development Canada
Ms. Susan Parker, ILO, Geneva
Ms. Monica Queiser, OECD, Paris
Dr. Gunnar Schioler, National Board of Health, Denmark
Ms. Patricia Thornton, University of York, United Kingdom
Mr. Barry Wight, Department of Family and Community Services, Australia
Ms. Ilene Zeitzer, Social Security Administration, United States

We acknowledge the National Insurance Administration of Norway and the contribution of the Norwegian research team, led by Prof. Holger Ursin, University of Bergen. Norway participated actively during part of the Project; however, due to unforeseen circumstances Norway could not participate in the Project up to its completion.

We also wish to acknowledge Ms. Cathy Drummond, the current Chair of the ISSA Research Advisory Board on Social Security, who gave her full endorsement to this project. Ms. Drummond is a strong advocate for the ISSA's involvement in comparative and policy-relevant social security research.

Last, but not least, we would like to express our sincere thanks to the persons who worked so hard to produce this publication: Linda Harvey at Vanderbilt Law School in Nashville, Boukje Cuelenaere at AS/tri in Leiden, and Evelyne Verdu of the ISSA Secretariat in Geneva.

This successful and wide-ranging project proved that informative comparative studies are possible, that an operational basis exists, and that there is the necessary motivation in countries to support such an endeavor. Examining international experience on a comparative basis is essential for informed formulation of domestic policy. One has to look externally in order to better understand and find solutions to national problems.

Dik Hermans
Director, Social Security Supervisory Board
Netherlands
Chair, WIR Project Steering Committee

Roland Sigg
Head of Research
International Social Security Association
Geneva

Note to Readers

This book is a truly collaborative project of the researchers who conducted the six national studies that provided the data for the Work Incapacity and Reintegration (WIR) Project. The pattern for creating this book flowed from the manner in which the research was conducted for the Project. Six national research teams cooperated and collaborated throughout the national studies, with the assistance of two international coordinators; the authors of this book are the same researchers, and the international coordinators are the co-editors.

A key element of the Project's research design was its dual tracks of common, standardized core elements and independent, albeit coordinated, separate national components. The editors followed a similar approach for this book, and, as a result, it falls somewhere between a fully integrated multi-authored book and a selection of related essays. The editors, together with the authors, sought to identify the most important themes that emerged from the Project and its results, and to organize these themes into coherent and logically flowing chapters. Researchers were then paired with the chapters, depending on their expertise in the relevant fields. Outlines for each chapter were circulated and discussed among all of the participants. Because of differing perspectives on the Project among the researchers/authors, there was considerable variation in the scope and style proposed for the various chapters—which was welcomed by the editors. The editors' task was to guide the authors toward a maximally unified product without sacrificing the individuality called for in realizing the separate ambitions for each chapter.

At a practical level, the editors often had to chose between imposing uniformity and allowing greater autonomy—in terms of both content and style. A certain degree of uniformity was maintained in the form and style of the chapters; again, perhaps less than is found in most fully edited, multiple-authored books, but more than with many collections of essays. Notes and references follow a uniform style. The use and format of tables and figures, appendices, lists, and other addenda follow a more individualized pattern.

In balancing these considerations, the authors and editors sought to achieve a reasonably uniform but fully readable text, illustrated with a reasonable number of helpful tables and figures.

One aspect of editorial uniformity deserves special mention. As explained in various contexts throughout the book, subtle, and sometimes not so subtle, differences among the six participating countries in their relevant benefit programs and interventions led to serious difficulties in terminology. In an effort to maintain a level of consistency in describing key concepts most relevant to the Project's research goals, groups of substantively related terms were clustered together and then referred to in the text, for the most part, with one term. These groupings are listed below.

Groupings of terms, and term used generally in the book for the group of terms

Terms: sicklisted; sicklister; sicklisting; long-term sicklisted; afflicted; disabled; work incapacitated; temporary disabled.
Term used generally: "work incapacitated," when referring to someone who cannot work due to sickness or injury.

Terms: sick leave; short-term sick leave.
Term used generally: "sick leave," when referring to status of being off work due to sickness or injury.

Terms: work incapacity; work disability; work inability.
Term used generally: "work incapacity," when referring to the inability to work due to sickness or injury.

Terms: sickness benefit/program/scheme; short-term sickness benefit; short-term income replacement.
Term used generally: "sickness benefit/program/scheme," when referring to benefits available immediately upon onset of work incapacity. (See also Chapter 1, page 2.)

Terms: disability benefit/program/scheme; permanent disability; invalidity.
Term used generally: "disability benefit/program/scheme," when referring to long-term benefits available only some time after onset of work incapacity. (See also Chapter 1, page 2.)

Terms: workers' injury benefit; workers' compensation benefit.
Term used generally: "work injury benefit."

Terms: vocational interventions; non-medical interventions; social interventions; vocational and other non-medical interventions.
Term used generally: "vocational" or "vocational and other non-medical" interventions, as appropriate.

Terms: patients; clients; employees; workers; subjects.
Term used generally: "subjects," when referring to participants in the studies; other terms, as appropriate, when describing people in general.

1

Work Incapacity and Reintegration: History and Aim of the WIR Project

Frank S. Bloch & Rienk Prins

Background and Central Research Goals

This book reports on the Work Incapacity and Reintegration (WIR) Project, a major cross-national study of work incapacity and return to work. The Project, initiated by the International Social Security Association (ISSA) in 1993, was prompted in part by large increases in long-term social security benefit payments based on work incapacity in many industrialized countries throughout the world (ISSA Secretary General, 1996; Aarts & De Jong, 1996; Bonner, 1995; U.S. General Accounting Office, 1994). Despite different national contexts and different forms of benefit schemes, many of these countries share common concerns over work incapacity, benefit payment, and return to work. Moreover, these countries have tended to seek similar solutions, typically focusing on the definition and onset of incapacity, eligibility and initial payment of benefits, continuing eligibility for benefits and availability of treatment and rehabilitation services, and options and expectations for return to work.

Although this project drew on various elements of the problem of work incapacity and reintegration in constructing its theoretical model and its research design, including eligibility requirements and benefit payments, it concentrated on interventions, incentives, and disincentives aimed at returning beneficiaries to work. Thus, the Project's research goals were stated follows:

- *Do the various interventions (by social security and health care systems) found in different countries make a difference as to work resumption patterns?*

- *If so, what are the best interventions?*

This focus on interventions, incentives, and disincentives carried over to all aspects of the Project's development and implementation.

Differences in benefit schemes present difficulties for any cross-national social security research project. In this project, there were special problems of terminology because the studies followed beneficiaries over a two-year period. As a result, subjects could be receiving different types of benefits at different times; because different countries may provide different types of benefits at different times, subjects at the same stage of work incapacity could well be receiving different types of benefits. In an effort to standardize the description of benefit programs across the countries included in the Project, benefits available immediately upon onset of work incapacity, regardless of how long they can be paid, are referred to as sickness benefits; long-term benefits paid only some time after onset, whether or not preceded by sickness benefits, are referred to as disability benefits.

Participating Countries and Institutions

The original concept for the Project was to conduct a multi-national prospective study of the timing and effects of various measures used to regain health and work capacity for persons receiving sickness or disability benefits. The idea was to study a broad range of interventions, including medical treatment and rehabilitation and vocational and other non-medical interventions, by taking repeated measurements of diagnosis-homogeneous sets of subjects with standardized measurement instruments. A group of countries, through appropriate social security institutions, was invited to carry out feasibility studies to evaluate the opportunities for such a common cross-national research design. These studies indicated that there was a substantial basis for comparisons among different national schemes according to the basic research plan. The feasibility studies also contributed insight into conceptual, methodological, and organizational matters that had to be clarified, such as the selection of an appropriate cohort, the variables and interventions that should be covered, as well as measurement and evaluation strategies.

Sponsoring institutions in six of the seven countries that carried out feasibility studies—Denmark, Germany, Israel, the Netherlands, Sweden, and the United States—agreed to commit to the Project. As part of this process, each sponsoring institution identified its own national research goals as well; the understanding was the Project's research design would address the question of work incapacity and reintegration from both national and cross-national perspectives.

Common Core Research Design

Drawing on shared elements of the various national research goals, the group of participating sponsors and researchers developed a common core research design in which the social security-treatment-rehabilitation-reemployment history of subjects receiving sickness and/or disability benefits was followed over a period of two years. The sponsors and research teams also reaffirmed that the aim of the Project was to learn how social security, labor, and health care systems operate in different countries in this context, and to measure and evaluate the effectiveness of various interventions, incentives, and disincentives on return to work. National studies based on the common core research design were then developed and implemented by national research teams from each participating country.

Six features emerged as key to the Project's core research design. *First*, each national study had to be prospective. This allowed for an analysis of the timing of interventions and their impact. The focus of the analysis would be the dynamics of interventions. It was important that comparisons not be static, as had been the case with most existing comparisons of social security arrangements. *Second*, the cohorts of subjects had to be homogeneous across all countries regarding the basic medical condition that accounted for work incapacity. This requirement was intended to avoid variations in work resumption patterns due to differences in major medical conditions. Low back disorders was chosen as the medical selection criterion for the cohorts due to its high prevalence among social security sickness and disability benefit recipients in all of the participating countries. *Third*, the cohorts had to be composed of persons who were either employed or employed immediately before work incapacity, and who had been work incapacitated for three consecutive months when entering the cohort. These criteria were intended to focus on the persons most likely to be offered interventions to return to work. *Fourth,* the studies had to cover a full range of interventions and incentives applied by the several actors in the fields of social security, health care and employment. This aspect of the design allowed for simultaneous study of actions aimed at recovery and work resumption, rather than a more limited focus on medical treatments or rehabilitation measures in isolation. A *fifth* characteristic of the core design was that these interventions would be evaluated in the light of critical social security indicators, such as work resumption and/or receipt of benefits and services. *Finally*, the observation period was set at two years, with at least three measurements during that period, in order to allow for a valid evaluation within available research and budgetary conditions.

Together, these features reflected the common goals of the core research design shared by all of the national research teams. They constituted a minimum package that each participating team was bound to include; however, the Project's research design deliberately allowed for national variations in national studies within the framework of its core research design. As a result, each national team could pursue its own national research objectives while it carried out its national study as part of the common project. At the same time, each participating research team benefitted from pooling its expertise and resources with teams from other countries involved in essentially similar studies.

Interventions, Incentives, and Disincentives

The feasibility studies conducted before the Project began showed that there was considerable variation within and between countries in terms of which interventions are applied to a work incapacitated person with a low back disorder. For these purposes, and throughout the Project, a distinction was drawn between interventions and incentives and disincentives. Specifically, interventions were defined as actions in response to the particular situation facing an individual; incentives and disincentives were defined as system-wide characteristics that may affect an individual's behavior and decisions.

A conceptual classification of the domestic repertoire of interventions in each participating country was prepared to assure full coverage in the questionnaires and to allow valid cross-national comparisons. Based on information gathered from the national teams, 26 vocational and other non-medical interventions, incentives, and disincentives were identified and classified into five categories: 1) training and education (general, vocational); 2) work accommodations (e.g. adaptations in work place, transportation, working hours); 3) motivators (e.g. wage subsidies, negative sanctions); 4) assessment of work capacity/incapacity (including rehabilitation inquiry); and 5) services (e.g. job search, daily care of children). These interventions are discussed fully in Chapter 8, including Appendix 8.1. Medical interventions are discussed in detail in Chapter 7. Social security system-based incentives and disincentives are discussed briefly in Chapter 2.

Measurement of Outcomes

As indicated earlier, a two-year observation period was chosen to monitor interventions and their outcomes for each subject. Because the Project was intended to examine return-to-work initiatives for persons receiving social security benefits, the subjects' benefit status was identified as a relevant outcome in addition to the obvious measures of full or partial work resumption. Therefore, the outcomes covered during and at the end of the observation period included: doing paid work (timing, type, duration, etc.); receipt of benefit (type of program, duration, etc.); participation in a rehabilitation program (timing, etc.); and others (e.g. deceased). Changes in health conditions and functional limitations were measured as well, in order to assess the impact of medical interventions.

Organization of the Project

Although the national research teams differed in many respects, including the disciplines of the researchers, the organizational setting, and the size of the team, they all included researchers who had experience with complex health care or social security research projects. The researchers and institutes that participated in the project are presented in the Preface.

The international coordination of the project was organized on two levels. At the operational level, the national project leaders met regularly to plan the studies and to report on national implementation. These meetings, as well as other on-going coordination and oversight of the national studies, were the responsibility of the ISSA Secretariat, including ISSA Head of Research Roland Sigg and ISSA consultant Prof. Frank Bloch of Vanderbilt University (Tennessee, United States), and the scientific coordinator of the project, Dr. Rienk Prins and the AS/*tri* Research and Consultancy Group (Leiden, the Netherlands). Final authority on shared matters of concern to the Project as a whole rested with a Steering Committee consisting of representatives of each of the national sponsors. The Chair of the Steering Committee was Dik Hermans, Social Security Advisory Board (the Netherlands). This committee approved all general policies and expenditures relating to the cross-national aspects of the Project, and it also monitored the international coordination and the overall progress of the Project.

Implementation of the Project

Preparations for the implementation of the Project started in 1994, after the national sponsors decided to carry out their national studies according to the Project's core design. One of the first tasks was to develop selection criteria so that similar cohorts would be created in each country. To qualify for inclusion in the cohort, subjects had to meet four sets of entry criteria relating to medical diagnosis, employment conditions, work incapacity, and demographics. The inclusion criteria are discussed in detail in Chapter 4.

National research teams started the preparations for filling their cohorts from Autumn, 1994. This work took place over a period of over six months, due to various difficulties in planning and data collection in some countries. Cohort construction and first measurement (T1, as soon as possible after three months of work incapacity) lasted from May, 1995 until September, 1996. The second measurement (T2, about one year after the onset of work incapacity) was completed in August, 1997. The final measurement (T3, two years after the onset of work incapacity) was completed in September, 1998. Information on cohort characteristics, interventions, and outcomes were measured by a variety of techniques. The main sources were client interviews and questionnaires, as well as documentation from social security administrators. The research process followed for the Project is described in greater detail also in Chapter 4.

Presentation of Data and Results

The WIR Project provided a unique opportunity to assess the application and outcome of interventions applied to stimulate resumption of work for persons receiving sickness or disability benefits. The research design took into account many sources of variation among national approaches to work incapacity and reintegration that usually restrict the cross-national comparability of information in this field.

The separate national studies have contributed already to a better understanding of the conditions that affect successful reintegration for persons receiving sickness or disability benefits. The Project's multi-national framework, in which largely independent national research teams carried out national studies with a shared core research design, allowed the sponsors to gain greater insight into the problems of work incapacity and reintegration than they would have from a series of fully independent national studies. Reports and other publications resulting from the various national studies are listed in Addendum B at the end of the book.

Because of their common design, the results from the national studies can be compared relatively easily to assess different national approaches to the problem of work incapacity and return to work. Moreover, the data compiled in the various national studies have been collected in an international database and made available for cross-national analysis. This database is described in Chapter 4. The Project's experience in running its unique research design will also assist others interested in cross-national social security research and, hopefully, will stimulate future collaborative studies of this type.

In the remainder of this book, authors from the various national teams present a review of related literature on determinants of work resumption, describe the methodology applied in the Project, and discuss the outcomes of various analyses on interventions and incentives. All researchers involved in the projects, including the organizer of the international database, participated as authors of this book. Depending on their expertise, each national researcher or research team covered one or more aspect of the project; however, this book is the product of a fully collaborating international team, whose participants all share the responsibility for the final product.

The next chapter presents an overview of the problem of work incapacity and reintegration. It also reviews some basic similarities and differences among the participating countries as to their social security programs. Chapter 3 reviews the relevant literature on the impact of medical treatments and vocational and rehabilitation measures on work resumption. It also relates that literature to the theoretical model on return to work used in the Project's research design. Chapter 4 describes the Project's core research design and the methodology applied in the national studies. It also describes the creation of the international database. Chapter 5 reports on the comparability of the cohorts created in each country, including issues raised by non-responses. Chapter 6 compares the cohorts as to their work resumption rates and benefit status after the two-year observation period. It also offers a preliminary insight into the role of age, household composition, and health indicators. Chapter 7 presents an overview of the medical interventions provided to the subjects in the various national cohorts. It also examines the impact of medical treatment on work resumption across cohorts. Chapter 8 focuses on the wide variety of vocational and other non-medical interventions that can be taken by social security, employers, or rehabilitation services. It also explores the relationship between various interventions and work resumption across cohorts. Work resumption patterns are analyzed further in Chapter 9, as to the role of work characteristics, medical care, etc. The chapter also contrasts different work resumption patterns (e.g. permanent resumers, late resumers). Chapter 10 presents a multivariate analysis to identify the role of interventions and various subject characteristics relative to work status and benefit receipt. It also interprets the outcomes in light of the theoretical model developed at the onset of the Project. Chapter 11 summarizes the major outcomes of the study, including both striking differences and similarities across cohorts.

References

Aarts, L. J. M. & De Jong, P. R. (1996). European Experiences with Disability Policy. In J. L. Mashaw, V. Reno, M. Berkowitz and R. Burkhauser (eds.), *Disability, Work, and Cash Benefits*. Kalamazoo: W. E. Upjohn Institute for Employment Research.

Bonner, D. (1995). Incapacity for Work: A New Benefit and New Tests. *Journal of Social Security Law*, 1995, 2, 86.

ISSA Secretary General (1996). Employment and Reintegration Measures for Disabled or Unemployed Workers. *International Social Security Review*, 49(2/1996), 111.

U.S. General Accounting Office (1994). Social Security Disability Rolls Keep Growing While Expectations Remain Elusive. Washington: Government Printing Office.

2

Social Security, Work Incapacity, and Reintegration

Rienk Prins & Frank S. Bloch

Background of the Problem

As noted in Chapter 1, the WIR Project was prompted in part by high levels of expenditures on sickness and disability benefits and low rates of return to work by beneficiaries. Among the important concerns raised by these circumstances were increased expectations for benefit programs, financing problems in times of slowing economic growth and rising unemployment, ineffectiveness in meeting new social needs, and unintended side effects on power structures and work motivation (Ploug, 1994; ISSA, 1994). Problems of work incapacity and reintegration arise generally in the context of broader socio-economic policy, as did the questions about interventions and return to work that were the focus of the Project. Three sets of issues particularly relevant to understanding current problems of work incapacity and reintegration are the labor and economic setting, the health perspective, and the social security context. Each is discussed briefly below in the context of the design and implementation of the Project.

Labor Market Considerations

Although data show considerable variations among countries, on average approximately seven to eleven percent of the insured population leave the work force—on a temporary or permanent basis—due to health

9

related restrictions (Einerhand et al., 1995). In many countries, work incapacity, rather than unemployment, is the major reason that persons over
the age of 55 do not participate in the labor market. Moreover, with the exception of Germany, in all countries included in the Project the numbers of
disability benefit recipients had been increasing.

There are serious short- and long-term implications of increased rates
of work incapacity and greater numbers of disability benefit recipients. Social security systems face high expenditures and decreasing numbers of insured workers that pay social security contributions (Zeitzer, 1994a). In
many countries, concern centers on the small number of persons leaving
the benefit rolls and returning to work. Consequently, better insight is
needed into the processes that affect the utilization of sickness and disability benefits to withdraw from the labor market, as well as factors and instruments that may prevent work incapacity.

Social security institutions and social policy experts have tended to focus on the income compensation purpose of these benefits. More recently,
greater attention has been given to rehabilitation policies and return-to-work strategies (Thornton, 1998; Sim, 1999). Moreover, in some
countries, employers have been charged with greater responsibility for
preventing work incapacity, including initiating rehabilitation measures
(e.g. rehabilitation plans) or work place adaptations. Increasing awareness
of the rights of persons with disabilities to work under appropriate conditions and pressures against discrimination on the grounds of disability have
also served to stimulate new policies and measures for job retention and return to work.

The Health Perspective

Work incapacity rates are affected directly by various medical factors
that influence the ability to work. Research in this area includes descriptive
epidemiology of diseases (Raspe, 1992), and medical statistics are available on the prevalence, incidence, trends, and regional differences in diseases. Risk factors, as well as environmental factors, such as working
conditions, education, and income, are often assessed not only in relation
to health conditions, but also in relation to work incapacity behavior and
entry onto the disability benefit rolls.

Health care is highly developed in the countries involved in the Project.
Medical treatments that were unknown or applied only to a small category
of patients in the recent past are now standard, and are being used regularly. However, resumption of work is not treated generally as an essential
criterion of successful treatment. Rehabilitation research has focused its attention on the development and success of treatments and interventions,
and patient- or working-conditions-related determinants of rehabilitation.

The administrative processes related to rehabilitation programs, their relationship to sickness and disability benefit schemes, and the role of the labor market in reintegration have not received much attention.

In particular, the transfer from completion of medical rehabilitation to return to work is recognized as a weak point in rehabilitation and social security. It has been observed in several countries that often, in spite of optimal recovery (from a medical point of view), work resumption is only partially realized. Badura refers to a "medical paradox" when describing the discrepancy between the expectations of work resumption according to scientific medical criteria and the actual work resumption rates and behavior of the patient (Badura & Waltz, 1993). The main influences on disappointing work resumption rates seem to be psychological factors, employer personnel policies, and sufficient income replacement by benefit schemes. In some countries, such as Germany and the United States, greater efforts have been made in the past decade to improve the processes and organizational structures related to medical and vocational rehabilitation and to work resumption (Zeitzer, 1990; Häussler, 1991). Other countries, including the Netherlands, are focusing on waiting periods and waiting lists in health care, which tend to prolong work incapacity, and are attempting to reduce those delays by allowing employers to pay for earlier treatment of their employees. More policy makers are now taking the relationship between health care and work incapacity seriously.

Social Security Concerns

The primary goal of social security sickness and disability programs is to alleviate the disruptive effects of work incapacity. Short- and longer-term sickness benefits and temporary and permanent disability benefits are all intended to replace—to one degree or another—income loss due to an incapacity for work. Over the long term, these programs have been reasonably successful in achieving their primary goal; large numbers of sick and injured workers have received timely benefits which have allowed them and their families to avoid serious financial crises.

There is, however, another side to the operation of sickness and disability benefit programs in terms of their effect on their target populations. The availability and payment of these benefits can, in certain circumstances, lead to counterproductive results. Sick or injured workers who might otherwise push through a period of work incapacity in order to hold onto a job may be diverted onto a path of benefit dependency; persons eligible for and receiving sickness or disability benefits may be discouraged from seeking reemployment or rehabilitation. In recent years, laws, rules, and regulations suspected of leading to such results have come under increasing fire by lawmakers and commentators alike. For example, in the Netherlands,

Sweden, and the United States, various changes have been introduced in regulations and administrative procedures over the past few years to stimulate the outflow of persons from the benefit rolls (Ploug & Kvist, 1994; Zeitzer, 1994a; Bonner, 1995).

Most social security systems address work incapacity by setting three interrelated goals: compensation, prevention, and rehabilitation. Most programs focus on providing compensation, whereas prevention has had a secondary role. The inclusion of rehabilitation measures into social security schemes is well known in various European countries; in Australia and the United States, however, rehabilitation is more in the domain of the labor market authority (Prins et al., 1993; Zeitzer, 1994b). The WIR Project focuses most directly on the effects of compensation and rehabilitation; it touches on prevention only indirectly, through data collected on work place conditions and some medical treatments.

More specifically, the national studies examined interventions intended to reintegrate work incapacitated persons into the work force. Each of the studies sought to identify key interventions and to measure their effectiveness on work resumption. The national and international data from the Project have been, and continue to be, analyzed in order to assess the effectiveness of the various interventions directed at persons receiving sickness and disability benefits, with some key cross-national results reported on in later chapters of this book. However, the social security context in which the interventions take place—the various rules and regulations through which these programs actually operate—must be taken into account to see if they create their own incentives or disincentives to return to work. The most important elements of the programs for these purposes are income replacement schemes and job protections. Both of these elements are discussed below. Another related system context for the national studies is health care, aspects of which are covered in Chapter 7.

Sickness and Disability Benefit Schemes: Similarities and Differences

The various benefit programs and services in place in the participating countries at the time of the national studies (1994-97) provide a major dimension of the contextual background for the Project. In most of the countries included in the Project, the longer periods of work incapacity targeted by the research design, that is, those lasting three months up to two years or more, are covered by both sickness benefits and disability benefits. Sickness benefit programs may cover only the earliest days of work incapacity, or they may carry over for a full year or more. In Israel, for example, where the subjects were drawn from persons eligible for a work injury benefit, those benefits are available for a maximum period of 90 days. By contrast, subjects from other countries in the Project may have received sickness benefits for up to one year (the Netherlands) or even longer (Denmark, Germany). Sickness benefit eligibility had lasted considerably longer in Sweden for many persons, but has since been limited in most instances to one year.

Depending on the country's sickness benefit scheme and the duration of the period of work incapacity, a subject's sickness benefits may then be superseded by some form of temporary or permanent disability benefit. In most countries, this takes place only at the end of a period of eligibility for sickness benefits, which usually is about one year after the onset of work incapacity. The exceptions among the countries participating in the project are Israel, where the General Disability Insurance Law takes over generally after 90 days, but is flexible in case of work injury, and Germany, where the transfer to the disability benefit program can take place without completion of a fixed waiting period. Circumstances are also different in the United States, where there is no national sickness benefit program. Subjects were chosen in the United States from two of the five states with their own sickness benefit programs—New Jersey and California—in order to conform to the Project's core research design. At a later point some of those subjects could be eligible for benefits under the federal Disability Insurance Program, which covers only persons whose incapacity has lasted, or can be expected to last, at least one year.

This section highlights key provisions of the sickness and disability programs from which the subjects in the national studies received benefits that may create incentives or disincentives to work resumption. The discussion focuses on four aspects of these programs: eligibility; payment criteria; administrative structure, including procedures for determining eligibility; and the provision of rehabilitation services. Differences among the national programs that may be relevant to the data on interventions for each of these aspects are noted briefly as well.

Because the Project focused specifically on interventions for long-term work incapacitated persons with an absence from work lasting several months, some additional background can be helpful relative to the operation of longer-term sickness benefit and disability benefit programs in the six participating countries. As a multi-national project, it involved various benefit systems, each providing benefits and rehabilitation measures according to their own criteria. A full explication of these programs is not necessary; indeed, some of these arrangements changed during the Project's observation period, and since then some arrangements may have changed again. Instead, an overview of major characteristics of these benefit schemes at the time the studies were undertaken is presented in Table 2.1.

TABLE 2.1
Main Dimensions of Sickness and Disability Benefit Schemes (1994-1997)

	Sickness benefit			Disability benefit			
	Start of benefit payment	Benefit level (% of gross wage)	Max. duration (weeks)	Min. degree of disability	Degrees of disability applied	Start of benefit payment	Benefit level (% of gross wage)
Denmark	After 2 weeks of wage payment[1]	100% (with a ceiling)[2]	52	50%	3: 50%, 67%, 100% (full)	Flexible	About 65% (in case of full disability)
Germany	After 6 weeks of wage payment	80%	78	50%	2: 50%,100%	Flexible	Varies from 15 to 70%
Israel[3]	After 1 waiting day	75%	26	5%	Ranging from 5 to 100%	Flexible	75% (in case of full disability)
Netherlands	After 2 or 6 weeks of wage payment	70%[4]	52	15-25%	7	After 52 weeks of benefit payment	Varies from 14-70%[6]

	Sickness benefit			Disability benefit			
	Start of benefit payment	Benefit level (% of gross wage)	Max. duration (weeks)	Min. degree of disability	Degrees of disability applied	Start of benefit payment	Benefit level (% of gross wage)
Sweden	After 2 weeks of wage payment	Days 2-14: 75%, days 15-365: 80%, days 366 on: 70%	No maximum	25%	4	Flexible	65%
US[5]	N.J.: After 1 week; Cal.: After 1 week	N.J.: Flat rate Cal.: Wage related with fixed min./max.	N.J.: 26 Cal.: 52	100%	1	After 5 months	Based on varying percentage of taxable wages

[1] All employees are entitled to sickness benefit from the first day; some employees are entitled to wages during the sick leave. In both cases, the employer finances the benefit for the first two weeks.
[2] Due to this low ceiling, very few insured receive 100% wage replacement.
[3] Regards occupational injury scheme.
[4] In collective labor agreements: 100%.
[5] N.J.: New Jersey; Cal.: California.
[6] In collective labor agreements: maximum, 100% for restricted period.

Eligibility

The threshold standard for eligibility is particularly important when considering the operational effect of disability benefit programs. Programs with relatively liberal eligibility requirements are more likely to attract and retain a larger number of beneficiaries who might, if faced with stricter eligibility requirements, continue with or return to work. Difficult labor markets accentuate this tendency; the harder it is to find work, the more appealing it becomes to qualify as unable to work. There were substantial differences in eligibility criteria for sickness and disability benefits among the benefit programs in place in the six countries that participated in the Project at the time the national studies were run.

Typically, insured workers can qualify for sickness benefits relatively easily. This is true especially early in a period of work incapacity. By contrast, the eligibility standard for disability benefits usually is quite strict. In most countries, eligibility for benefits is based on an incapacity for gainful work, although this baseline is modified, to one degree or another, by individual circumstances affecting the likelihood of reemployment, such as old age, limited education, and limited prior work experience.

In the Netherlands, for example, eligibility under the Sickness Benefits Act was measured relative to the employee's ability to perform the work "normally done" and no medical certification was required; by contrast, the standard for long-term benefits under the Disablement Insurance Act was an inability to earn. This strict standard was softened, however, by the use of seven degrees of qualifying incapacity, beginning at 15 to 25 percent. Eligibility for disability benefits in Sweden and for work-related disability benefits in Israel were also regulated by degrees of incapacity for work. In Sweden, there were four equal steps beginning with 25 percent; there were finer gradations in Israel. The disability benefit standard in the United States, by contrast, was fixed at near total incapacity: the inability to engage in substantial gainful activity.

Payment Levels and Replacement Rates

Another important operational characteristic is the benefit payment level. Most social insurance programs, such as the sickness and disability benefit programs relevant to this project, base benefit payments to some degree on past earnings. The closer the benefits are to a worker's wages, or the wages a worker could hope to earn in a slow economy, the more attractive they become. There were significant differences in payment levels among the six national programs, which were recorded and considered directly in the analysis of the data.

Benefit amounts were set in Sweden and the Netherlands at a percentage of prior wages. In Sweden, the percentage applied in the sickness benefit program ranged for most persons from 65 percent to 80 percent, plus an additional 10 percent during the first three months for many workers through collective bargaining agreements.[1] Disability benefits were set in Sweden usually at 65 to 70 percent for fully disabled persons, with most group insurances augmenting the benefit to 80 to 90 percent. In the Netherlands, sickness benefit payments were 70 percent of wages, with a maximum benefit amount, but that benefit often was supplemented by collective bargaining agreements to 100 percent; disability benefit payments were 70 percent of wages, also sometimes supplemented by collective labor agreements. In Israel, the benefit amount was 75 percent in cases of work-related disability, but general disability benefit amounts were based on a percentage of minimum income levels. In the United States, the single level of payment was set according to a formula that used percentages of wages but also weighed earnings to account for high earnings years and recent earnings, up to a maximum amount. The net result cannot be stated in terms of gross wages, as only wages subject to social security taxes were used; the practical effect was a higher percentage of gross wages for lower income workers.

Administration and Determination of Eligibility

There were some fundamental differences among the countries participating in the Project with respect to the administration of their sickness and disability benefit programs. In some countries, such as Denmark and Sweden, decentralized community social welfare offices exercised considerable local control over the administration of benefit claims, including the provision of rehabilitation and other return-to-work services. Sick funds and various trade associations played important roles in Germany and the Netherlands, with different associations becoming involved depending on the employment status of the beneficiary and the nature of the benefit or service. In the United States, sickness benefits were available in only a few states and were administered through state agencies; disability benefits were administered by the federal Social Security Administration with some assistance from state agencies operating under its direction. Responsibility for rehabilitation and other related services was spread across federal, state and local authorities.

Differences in forms or methods of administration can, of course, affect the distribution of benefits and services (Bloch, 1994a). For the most part, however, these differences should not influence the analysis of the results of the national studies, as they were designed to identify and chart the use of interventions aimed at reintegration. Although the involvement of social security institutions in this process is important to assess their role, as opposed to the roles of other relevant actors, the source of their authority in a particular country's social security scheme is not. The one effect of administration that is particularly important to this study, delays in receipt of services, was measured independently. Delays can result from disparities in utilization and/or funding, or from structural inefficiencies originating from the competence and responsibilities of several actors and agencies involved (e.g. medical rehabilitation provided by the sickness benefit or the disability benefit agency, or vocational rehabilitation supplied by the social security or labor market agency) (Prins et al., 1993; Zeitzer, 1994a).

Differences in methods for determining eligibility are more likely to touch on the subject matter of long-term work incapacity. Indeed, determination (and redetermination) of eligibility for benefits is one of the interventions that was measured in the studies. The evaluation of work incapacity for purposes of disability benefits was quite rigorous in each country included in the Project. The process typically included a series of examinations and assessments by medical, vocational, and social security experts, although there were differences in administrative structures and approaches to questions of proof (Bloch, 1994b).

Eligibility decisions for sickness benefits necessarily are made more quickly and with less information than eligibility decisions for disability benefits. In the Netherlands, for example, certification was not required to support a claim for sickness benefits; however, recent legislation moved forward the obligation of longer-term recipients to undergo the full medical and vocational assessments required for disability benefit eligibility. Sweden required certification for sickness benefits lasting more than one week. In the Netherlands, employers were obliged to send in a rehabilitation plan after 13 weeks to stimulate reintegration. In Denmark, a recipient of sickness benefits had to be assessed for treatment, rehabilitation, or transfer to disability retirement within three months, and every three months thereafter; from April 1997, this was changed to within two months and every month thereafter.

Rehabilitation Services

The social security context of the Project varied also with respect to the provision of rehabilitation services. In one sense, these services make up more than context; they are among the key components of the work incapacity-reintegration histories that were recorded and analyzed in the national studies. Nonetheless, certain broad characteristics of different national approaches to the delivery of rehabilitation services, particularly to recipients of benefits based on work incapacity, should be noted.

TABLE 2.2
Main Features of Administration and Rehabilitation (1994-1997)

	Documenta-tion of work incapacity	Evaluation of work incapacity	Initiation of rehabilitation measures	Determination of eligibility for benefit
Denmark	Certificate from treating physician at latest after 2 months of work incapacity	Social services department in municipality	Social services department in municipality	Evaluation of pre-pension by social services department in municipality
Germany	Medical certificate from treating physician on first or third day of work incapacity	Medical service engaged by sick funds	Disability pension agency	Disability benefit agency
Israel	Occupational doctor	Work injury branch of national insurance institute	Client, rehabilitation department of national insurance institute	Work disability branch of national insurance institute
Netherlands	No certificate prescribed, sometimes self-certification	Social security agency	Social security agency	Social security agency
Sweden	Medical certificate after 8 days of work incapacity	Medical and non-medical experts at social security agency	Social security agency, client, employer	Independent committee related to social security agency
US	N.J., Cal.: Medical certificate from treating physician when applying for benefit	Private treating or consulting physicians	Client, referral from social security agency	State agency under contract to Federal social security agency

Historically, there has been a surprising separation of administration for rehabilitation services and for social security benefits (Berkowitz, 1990). Sometimes, this results from passivity; in Israel, for example, rehabilitation services were available generally, but mainly at the initiative of the social security recipient. Or, it can result from historical divisions of responsibility, as happened in the United States. Despite recent efforts by the federal Social Security Administration to become more active in the area of rehabilitation, primary responsibility for rehabilitation services remains with the states (Rupp et al., 1994). Germany was a clear exception to this rule, where pension insurance institutions also provided rehabilitation services. Following a "rehabilitation first" philosophy, persons who apply for disability benefits in Germany should be evaluated for rehabilitation suitability before disability benefit eligibility is addressed. Sweden and the Netherlands moved strongly to integrate these services. In Sweden, authority over both benefit payments and rehabilitation services has existed for many years in local social security offices. In the Netherlands, employers were legally obliged to use occupational health and safety services to support the employer's policy towards work incapacitated employees, to develop rehabilitation plans for work incapacitated employees relatively early in a period of incapacity, and to report the plan to the relevant social security institution (Beljaars & Prins, 1996).

Job Protection

Short- and long-term absence from work due to work incapacity are affected not only by the health status of the employees, their working conditions, or the procedures used in the operation of the benefit schemes. The employer's employment strategy and job protection arrangements may also affect the attendance behavior of employees, and consequently create important features of the context of work incapacity behavior.

For example, an employer will not easily use the disciplinary measure of dismissal in countries where job security is extended in case of sickness. In Denmark, the United States, and Israel, the employer was allowed to dismiss an employee during the employees period of work incapacity. In Denmark, the employer had the right to dismiss several categories of employees after 120 days of work incapacity in a year.[2]

A related situation involves dismissal due to a high frequency of sickness. This situation was covered by protective regulations only in some countries. In other countries, an employer could dismiss frequently sicklisted personnel. There was considerable variation among the countries involved in the Project in this regard. In Germany, an employer could include regulations in the labor contract that specified when dismissal due to sickness absence would be applied. In the Netherlands, the public employment service was responsible for examining the legitimacy of such a planned dismissal; the main acceptable criterion, "disturbance of the production process," considered the organizational and economic consequences of frequent absences. Dismissal was allowed in Sweden also only under certain conditions, when "all" reintegration measures taken by the employer and other partners involved in rehabilitation (e.g. medical services, social insurance bodies) proved to be unsuccessful in returning the employee to work. By contrast, in the United States and Israel, workers lacked job protection related to frequent or long-term work incapacity.

Finally, it should be noted that some variation in these descriptions may arise when the employee has a special status within the work force. In Germany, for example, workers with the status of severely disabled person (*Schwerbehinderte*) were legally protected against dismissal. Certain workers in the United States classified as "disabled" were protected under the Americans with Disabilities Act.

Selected Incentives and Disincentives: A Comparative Overview

The preceding sections of this chapter discussed generally the sickness and disability benefit schemes in the countries involved in the Project, including actors, procedures, and services provided, as well as some issues of job protection. This section identifies how selected systemic incentives and disincentives that could affect work incapacity behavior differed across the six countries. It also assesses some similarities and differences for work incapacitated persons who are absent from work for several months.

There were substantial differences in the financial incentive of income loss among the countries included in the Project. Whereas Dutch workers hardly experienced income loss in case of work incapacity, at least up to one year, Swedish and German workers faced a loss of income of about 10 to 20 percent. For workers in the other countries, income may have been reduced even more. In half of the countries, the initial days of work incapacity were not compensated; this waiting period varied from one day (Israel, Sweden) to one week (United States). In the other countries, income replacement started at the first day of work incapacity.

Each benefit program has administrative obstacles that should filter inappropriate claims for sickness benefits or wage payment, such as certification procedures. Again, there was significant variation among the countries in the Project regarding certification of work incapacity. These procedures were quite strict in Germany, where the medical statement had to be provided by the employee on the first or third day of work incapacity. Certification procedures were less strict in most other countries. In Sweden and the United States, for example, a certificate was due after one week. In

Denmark, a certificate was due after two months of work incapacity; however, the employer and the municipality could have asked for a certificate much earlier, even as early as after four days of absence from work. Certification by a treating physician was not required in the Netherlands, due to a refusal in principle by the health care sector.

In those cases where work incapacity becomes a long term or permanent status, workers may apply for a disability benefit. Here again, eligibility criteria affect entry into the respective schemes. The Project did not examine closely the concepts of work incapacity applied in each scheme; instead, it focused on the minimum degree of work incapacity needed to be eligible for full or partial disability benefits. Comparisons show that only in the United States was full work incapacity required to qualify for benefits. In the other countries, the minimum degree of work incapacity was five percent (Israel, but only with regard to work injuries), 15 to 25 percent (the Netherlands), 25 percent (Sweden), or 50 percent (Denmark, Germany). The lack of an "all or nothing" standard in most countries was reflected in the variation in the number of categories or degrees of work incapacity: the Dutch scheme used seven categories; most other countries used two, three, or four categories. The Dutch, Israeli, and Swedish schemes had the lowest thresholds for eligibility, where claimants could have qualified for a partial benefit with only a small degree of work incapacity.

In all of the countries except Israel and the United States, the employer was obliged to continue partial or full wage payment in case of work incapacity; therefore, employers were among the main actors that played a role regarding work incapacitated employees and return to work. The employer had a formal role with respect to rehabilitation and reintegration in only two countries; in the Netherlands and Sweden, the employer sent a rehabilitation plan to the social security agency after a fixed period of work incapacity. In all other countries, initiatives on work resumption and reintegration were solely in the hands of the social security agency.

The rules on job security in case of sickness also differed considerably in the six countries. Whereas there were few or no legal obstacles in Denmark, Israel, and the United States to dismissing long-term work incapacitated employees, the other countries had significant job protection measures for workers who reported sick.

Table 2.3 summarizes the main similarities and differences regarding the presence of selected incentives and disincentives on work incapacity in the countries under study. It shows how the presence of incentives and disincentives to report sick or to stay for a long period on sickness or disability benefits varied considerably across the countries included in the Project. The country with the greatest number of disincentives to report sick and to

TABLE 2.3
Incentives and Disincentives on Work Incapacity

	Denmark	Germany	Israel	N'lands	Sweden	US
Financial disincentives						
Income loss (sickness)	+ +	+	+ +	–	+	+ +
Waiting day(s)	–	–	+	–	+	+ +
Administrative disincentives						
Certificates	+/–	+ +	+	–	+	+
High minimum degree of disability required	+	+	–	–	–	+ +
Job protection						
Risk of dismissal	+	–	+	–	+	+

Legends:
+ +   strongly present   +   weakly present   –   absent

be on the benefit was the United States, followed by Denmark; the country with the least number of disincentives was the Netherlands, followed by Germany and Sweden.

Placing the Project's Research Questions in Context

Reduced to its bare essentials, the central problem addressed by the WIR Project was the high number of long-term sickness and/or disability benefit recipients in the targeted countries, and the low rate of their return to work. This central problem consists of three key component parts, each of which is reflected in the theoretical model for the national studies discussed in Chapter 3.

First, there is the problem of entry onto the benefit rolls. Who can claim work incapacity? What are the standards for benefit eligibility, and how are those standards enforced? Second, there is the problem of continuing receipt of benefits. For how long and at what level of payment are benefits awarded? What actions are taken to return beneficiaries to work? Finally, there is the problem of reintegration into the work force. What sort of work, or work opportunity, signals the end of work incapacity?

As discussed in more detail in Chapter 3, there is considerable literature on both work incapacity and reintegration drawn from such disciplines as medicine, sociology, economics, political science, and law. The core problems of work incapacity and reintegration that led to the initiation of this project are also well-covered in the literature. Many studies document the high number of work incapacity benefit recipients in various countries, as well as the failure of beneficiaries to return to work (U.S. General Accounting Office, 1996). Some attempt to explain these phenomena on the basis of such factors as economic and market conditions, deficient benefit schemes and/or social service delivery, and inadequate health care systems (Emanuel, 1994; Prins, 1993; Soeters & Prins, 1985). Most often these studies are based on national experience; however, there is a growing interest in these subjects from a cross-national perspective (Mashaw et al., 1996; Lonsdale, 1993; Prins, 1990; Berkowitz, 1990; Duncan & Woods, 1987).

Although the existing literature includes comparative studies, they are limited for the most part to comparisons of benefit and/or service arrangements and organizational structures; operations and outputs usually are ignored. Empirical studies in this area either focus on medical or on vocational and other non-medical interventions, but they tend not to focus equally on both. What is missing, and what the WIR Project seeks to contribute, is a systematic, longitudinal study of the various social security and health care interventions, incentives, and disincentives along the pathway from work incapacity to reintegration. The Project described and monitored work incapacity and reintegration as an on-going process, including both medical and vocational and other non-medical interventions. The data collected allows both comparison and evaluation of output.

The orientation of the Project was thus toward the operational consequences of sickness and disability benefit schemes, and related medical and social measures and services, on return to work. The component parts of the work incapacity-reintegration scenario are well known, at least within a given country. Nonetheless, social security programs are overwhelmed by extraordinarily large numbers of long-term sickness and disability beneficiaries. Little progress has been made to return those beneficiaries to work, and little new has been tried. The important questions are how and when the different component parts of the scenario are in play and, more importantly, whether they work—not only in one country, but in several countries facing similar problems. At the most practical level, the results of the Project will provide national policy makers a base on which to reconsider the repertoire of interventions available and in use in their own countries to help return work incapacitated persons to work.

Notes

1. Day 2-3, 65%; days 4-365, 80%; from day 366, 70%. There are exceptions: recipients on a predetermined rehabilitation plan can receive 95%; recipients in medical treatment or rehabilitation at the end of one year of incapacity may receive 80%.
2. In 1999 this changed for public sector employees; by labor agreement, the right of the public employer to dismiss after 120 days was abolished.

References

Badura, B., Schott, T. & Waltz, M. (1993). *Work incapacity and reintegration, Proposal for a cross-national research study on return to work (RTW) after coronary heart disease in the European Region.* Bielefeld: Universität Bielefeld.

Beljaars, P. L. M. M. & Prins, R. (1996). *Combating a Dutch disease: recent reforms in sickness and disability arrangements in the Netherlands.* Leiden: AS/tri.

Berkowitz, M. (1990). *Forging Linkages: Modifying Disability Benefit Programs to Encourage Employment.* New York, NY: Rehabilitation International.

Bloch, F. S. (1994a). Assessing disability: a six nation study of disability pension claim processing and appeals. *International Social Security Review*, 47(1/1994), 15-35.

Bloch, F. S. (1994b). *Disability Benefit Claim Processing and Appeals in Six Industrialised Countries.* ISSA Occasional Papers on Social Security. Geneva: International Social Security Association.

Bonner, D. (1995). Incapacity for Work: A New Benefit and New Tests. *Journal of Social Security Law*, 1995, 2, 86.

Duncan, B. & Woods, D. (1987). *Social Security Disability Programs: An International Perspective.* New York, NY: Rehabilitation International.

Einerhand, M. G. K., Knol, G., Prins, R. & Veerman, T. J. (1995). *Sickness and invalidity arrangements, Facts and figures from six European countries.* Den Haag: Vuga uitgeverij.

Emanuel, H. (1994). *Controlling admission to and stay in Social Security Benefit Programs*, ISSA Research Meeting on Social Security: A Time for Redefinition? Geneva: International Social Security Association.

Häussler, B. (1991). *Anwendungsmöglichkeiten von Qualitätssicherungsprogrammen und - Massnahmen in den USA für die medizinische Rehabilitation in der Deutschen Rentenversicherung, Reha- Kommission, Abschlussberichte- Band IV.* Frankfurt: Verband Deutscher Rentenversicherungsträger (VDR).

ISSA (1994). *Social Security Benefit Programs*, ISSA Research Meeting on Social Security: A Time for Redefinition? Geneva: International Social Security Association.

Lonsdale, S. (1992). *The growth of disability benefits: an international comparison.* York: Beveridge Conference Papers.

Lonsdale, S. (1993). *Invalidity benefit; an international comparison.* London: Department of Social Security.

Mashaw, J. L., Reno, V., Berkowitz, M. & Burkhauser, R. (eds.) *Disability, Work, and Cash Benefits.* Kalamazoo: W. E. Upjohn Institute for Employment Research.

Ploug, N. (1994). The welfare state in liquidation? In *Recent trends in cash benefits in Europe.* Copenhagen: Danish Institute of Social Research:

Ploug, N. & Kvist, J. (1994). *Recent trends in cash benefits in Europe.* Copenhagen: Danish Institute of Social Research.

Prins, R. (1990). *Sickness absence in Belgium, Germany (FR) and the Netherlands, a comparative study*. Amsterdam: Nederlands Instituut voor Arbeitsomstandigheden (NIA).

Prins, R., Veerman, T. J. & Koster, M. K. (1993). *Work incapacity and invalidity in Belgium, Germany, Sweden and the Netherlands: four monographs on benefit and rehabilitation arrangements*. Zoetermeer: Sociale Verzekeringsraad (Svr).

Raspe, H. H. (1992). Back pain. In A. J. Silman & M. C. Hochberg (eds.), *Epidemiology of the Rheumatic Diseases*. Oxford: Oxford University Press.

Rupp, K., Bell, S. H. & McManus, L. A. (1994). Design of the Project NetWork Return-to-Work Experiment for Persons with Disabilities. *Social Security Bulletin*, 57, 2, 3-20.

Sim, J. (1999). Improving Return-to-Work Strategies in the US Disability Programs, with Analysis of program Practices in Germany and Sweden. *Social Security Bulletin*, 59, 3, 41-50.

Simanis, J. G. (1990). National Expenditures on Social Security and Health in Selected Countries. *Social Security Bulletin*, 53, 1, 12-16.

Soeters, J. & Prins, R. (1985). Health care facilities and work incapacity: a comparison of the situation in the Netherlands with that in six other West European countries. *International Social Security Review*, 38(2/1985), 141-56.

Thornton, P. (1998). *International Research Project on Job Retention and Return to Work Strategies for Disabled Workers*. Geneva: Gladnet/ILO.

U.S. General Accounting Office (1996). *SSA Disability: Program Redesign Necessary to Encourage Return to Work*. Washington, D.C.: Government Printing Office.

Zeitzer, I. R. (1990). *Innovative rehabilitation techniques in the United States for the hard to rehabilitate*. New York, NY: Rehabilitation International.

Zeitzer, I. R. (1994a). *Quality, effectiveness and efficiency of rehabilitation measures*. Geneva: International Social Security Association.

Zeitzer, I. R. (1994b). Recent European Trends in Disability and Related Programs. *Social Security Bulletin*, 57, 2, 21-26.

3

Work Incapacity and Reintegration: A Literature Review

Jan Høgelund

Introduction

The reintegration of work incapacitated persons into the labor market has been the subject of research in several disciplines. The purpose of this chapter is to provide a literature review of relevant research contributions in this area, and to present the theoretical model of return to work used in the WIR Project against the background of the literature review. Consistent with the scope and design of the Project, this literature review concentrates on factors affecting return to work of long-term work incapacitated workers with low-back pain. A selected list of publications relevant to this review is included at the end of the chapter, as Appendix 3.1. There are also short references in the text, in parentheses, for those publications mentioned specifically in this chapter.

Several studies in the literature are quite comparable to this project, regarding, for example, outcome variables and subject populations. Those studies are of obvious interest because their findings may highlight influential factors that could be assumed to influence return to work for the subjects in the national studies. However, most studies in the literature are not directly comparable to this project in one or more significant respects. For example, in certain disciplines the studies include all types of medical diagnoses, not only low-back pain. Despite such differences, many of those studies are included in the review because they address similar factors having a potential influence on work resumption that may, in this project or later studies, turn out to be of importance.

This review includes contributions from four major research disciplines: 1) clinical studies, 2) economics, 3) public policy, and 4) sociological studies. Including research from several different disciplines allows the review to cover a broad range of findings with possible relevance to the present project. The problem with this approach, of course, is that it is impossible to go into the results from each discipline in depth; therefore, there is a risk that literature considered to be important by researchers within a discipline may not be mentioned. However, as will be seen in the following sections, a multidisciplinary research strategy is necessary in order to illuminate the question of which factors affect return to work of long-term work incapacitated workers.

Another difficulty with this review is that the quantity of literature on work incapacity and subsequent labor market attachment is overwhelming. Two strategies were used in order to search for relevant literature. First, the national experts who participated in the present project informed the author about important books and articles that could be included. Second, a literature search was performed in selected databases. Although this review does not cover all available literature about the subject, it does cover the most important and relevant publications.

Clinical Studies

One important aspect of the clinical approach to research on work disability concerns the relationship between pathology, impairment, functional limitations, and work incapacity. Activation of the body's defense and coping mechanisms may be caused by an injury or a disease. This "stage of active pathology" will result in an impairment, that is, a physiological or anatomical loss or other abnormality, which in turn can lead to functional limitations (Nagi, 1965, 1969; Waddell, 1987; Aarts & De Jong, 1992). Functional limitations can be classified at different levels, e.g. at the level of organs and systems or at the level of activities and tasks. Work disability exists when the inability to perform certain activities or tasks interferes with job demands, that is, activities or tasks which have to be carried out in order to perform a certain job.

In the area of low-back pain, this so-called clinical pathology approach has focused on physical as well as psychological dimensions of work disability. On the physical side, severe physical damage in the low back is assumed to cause work disability. On the psychological side, work disability is thought to arise because of clear secondary psychopathological complications, such as depression or a number of psychosomatic disorders often labeled "compensation neurosis" (Frank et al., 1995).

Another important aspect of clinical research on this subject concerns psychosocial and behavioral aspects of low-back pain (see, e.g. Frank et al., 1995). This approach recognizes that the clinical pathology approach, where physical or psychological abnormalities are assumed to cause work disability, is too narrow. Rather, it stresses the interplay between disease, psychological factors, and social conditions that may cause individual differences in perceptions and responses to diseases (Waddell, 1987). This approach overlaps to some extent with the micro sociological approach, discussed below, where emphasis is put on the costs and benefits associated with the role of being disabled versus the role of worker.

Return to Work in Chronic Low-back Pain Patients

A number of clinical studies have investigated how different variables influence work resumption of long-term work incapacitated workers with chronic low-back pain (Hildebrandt et al., 1997; Hazard, Bendix & Fenwick, 1991; Gatchel et al., 1994; Lacroix et al., 1990; Kummel, 1996; Sandström, 1986; Sandström & Esbjörnsson, 1986; Werneke, Harris & Licther, 1993). Consistent with this project, they all concerned long-term work incapacitated workers with low-back pain and they all used return to work as the outcome variable. They differed from this project and from each other, however, in several other dimensions: duration of sick leave at admission to the study, duration of follow-up period, and whether or not the subjects participated in a rehabilitation program.

Each of these studies illuminates the importance to return to work of one or more of the following groups of variables: socio-demographic variables, e.g. sex, age, education, income and marital status; medical variables, e.g. muscle strength, lifting capacity, pain conditions; and psychological variables such as personality disorders, e.g. symptoms of depression or schizophrenia, and coping strategies. Furthermore, a few studies also include job related variables, e.g. occupation, exposure to stress and physical job demands, and life style variables, e.g. smoking habits. The findings of these studies are summarized in Table 3.1.

These studies suggest that psychological conditions may have a significant influence on the probability of returning to work. Thus, in several studies variables related to psychological aspects are found to be significant. For example, the patient's expectation about the possibility for work resumption as well as the patient's understanding of his or her medical condition appears to affect the probability of return to work. It should be stressed, however, that some other studies find psychological variables insignificant. For instance, Lacroix et al., (1990) found that non-organic

TABLE 3.1
Selected Clinical Studies on Socio-Demographic, Medical, Psychological, Job Related, and Lifestyle Variables on Return to Work of Work Incapacitated Employees with Low-Back Pain

Study	Cohort Size	Multi-Variate Analysis	Findings Related to Type of Variables (Direction of Effect)
Hildebrandt et al. (1997)	70	Yes	*Socio-demographic*: Type of occupation (unskilled workers have low RTW rate)
Hazard, Bendix & Fenwick (1991)	258	No	*Medical*: Physical endurance significant at 1 year but not at 2 year follow-up (persons with high physical endurance have high RTW rate) *Psychological*: Schizophrenia index and intelligent index significant at 1 year but not at 2 year follow-up *Life style*: Cigarette smoking significant at 1 year but not at 2 year follow-up (smokers have low RTW rate)
Gatchel et al. (1994)	152	Yes	*Psychological*: No positive findings; diagnosed psychopathology (axis I clinical disorders and axis II personality disorders) had no influence on RTW
Sandström (1986)	52	No	*Medical*: Previous back pain (low RTW rate) and consumption of analgesics (low RTW rate) *Psychological*: Reported fatigue at the end of working day (low RTW rate)
Sandström & Esbjörnsson (1986)	52	Yes	*Psychological*: Patients attitude towards possibility for work resumption (persons not expecting work resumption have low RTW rate)
Lacroix et al. (1990)	100	No	*Psychological*: Patients understanding of their medical condition (persons with a good understanding have high RTW rate)
Kummel (1996)	717	No	*Psychological*: Non-organic signs (persons with non-organic signs have low RTW rate)
Werneke, Harris & Lichter (1993)	183	No	*Psychological*: Non-organic signs (persons with non-organic signs have low RTW rate)

Note: RTW is acronym for return to work.

signs (indicating the persistence of a psychological impairment) do not predict return to work. This finding is contrary to those of Kummel (1996), and Werneke, Harris, and Lichter (1993).

Variables concerning medical, job related, and lifestyle conditions are found to be significant in only a few of the studies. Moreover, the few positive findings related to these variables are, in several cases, not supported by findings from other studies. For example, the importance of cigarette smoking (Hazard, Bendix & Fenwick, 1991) is not supported by the findings of Sandström (1986). Similarly, medical studies do not support the finding that socio-demographic variables influence the probability of returning to work. However, this conclusion is not supported by studies from other research disciplines. Thus, in most of the other studies that have been reviewed, age is found to influence the likelihood of work resumption, with older persons having a below average chance of returning to work (De Jong, 1987; Aarts & De Jong, 1992; Marklund, 1995; Oleinick, Gluck & Guire, 1996; Meyer & Viscusi, 1995; Johnson, Baldwin & Butler, 1998). In general, neither marital status nor gender are found to be of importance. (The influence of income is discussed below in the context of economic studies.)

Effects of Interventions

Apart from research on predictors for work resumption of long-term work incapacitated workers, a considerable number of studies have been published concerning the effectiveness of clinical interventions aimed at return to work.

Weide, Verbeek, and Tulder (1997) made a very comprehensive literature review about vocational outcomes of clinical interventions for low-back pain patients. The review was limited to randomized clinical trial studies with return to work or other vocational status measures as the outcome variable. With regard to chronic low-back pain (work incapacity lasting more than 12 weeks), the authors considered the following interventions: antidepressants, nonsteroidal antiflammatory drugs, spinal manipulation, back school or back exercises, behavioral therapy, and case management methods. A number of interventions were not considered because no positive evidence of efficacy on the functional ability of low-back pain patients was found in the literature; hence, studies about the use of analgetics, muscles relaxants, epidural and intra-articular injections, traction, orthoses, biofeedback, acupuncture, and transcutaneous nerve stimulation were excluded. They found only limited evidence of efficacy for one type of intervention: the use of antidepressants. No randomized clinical trials were found on case management, and no evidence was found for the efficacy of other interventions.

These rather limited findings do not necessarily imply that various types of clinical interventions do not have an effect. The lack of evidence may result from a lack of studies fulfilling the scientific criteria used by the authors. As noted above, no case management studies performed as a randomized clinical trial were found. Furthermore, although one study with positive results concerning the use of nonsteroidal antiflammatory drugs and one study with positive outcomes of spinal manipulation were found, these studies were considered to be of low quality and it was therefore concluded that there was "no evidence." Accordingly, if the scientific criteria are relaxed, it could be concluded that nonsteroidal antiflammatory drugs and spinal manipulation may have a positive effect.

Weide, Verbeek, and Tulder did not consider vocational or other non-medical interventions other than case management. Two other literature reviews, by Battie (1992) and Frank et al. (1996), considered so-called workplace-based interventions, such as modified work, light duties, and changes in working hours. Frank et al. noted that "there are no rigorously controlled studies showing reductions in long-term or recurrent occupational low-back pain disability that can be unequivocally attributed to specific workplace interventions." They do mention several "before-and-after" studies showing positive effects of workplace-based interventions. However, most studies concern early interventions, and only one study about workplace-based interventions for chronic low-back pain patients is mentioned: Crook (1994). The study suggests that modified tasks at the work place have a positive effect on work status (referred from Frank et al., 1996). The positive effect of modified work is generally supported by findings in other studies concerning other target groups, that is, other diagnosis groups and/or back pain diagnoses with shorter duration of work incapacity. (For an overview see, Krause, Dasinger & Neuhauser, 1998.)

In sum, clinical studies suggest that psychological variables may affect the likelihood of work resumption whereas socio-demographic, medical, job related, and lifestyle variables seem to be of no, or only very limited, importance. However, non-clinical studies find socio-demographic variables (i.e. age) to be of importance. Moreover, only modest evidence of the effect of clinical interventions on the rate of return to work for chronic low-back pain patients has been established. Finally, one study concerning workplace-based interventions for chronic low-back pain patients suggests that workplace-based interventions may have a positive effect on return to work.

Economic Studies

The observation of a simultaneous decline in male labor force participation and growth in the number of persons entering disability programs lead economists to enter the area of reintegration of work incapacitated persons (Berkowitz & Johnson, 1974; Parsons, 1980, 1984; Haveman & Wolfe, 1984a, 1984b; Emanuel et al., 1987; Wolfe & Haveman, 1990; Aarts & De Jong, 1992). These studies were closely related to traditional labor supply models, where a micro-economic theoretical framework is applied. This approach has been used in most studies following Berkowitz and Johnson.

The basic assumption of most micro-economic models is that a work incapacitated person can choose between two options: work and transfer income, e.g. disability benefit. Hence, given the health status of persons who are work incapacitated, the outcome will depend on the utility derived from each of the two options. If utility in the work option exceeds utility in the benefit option, the work incapacitated person will resume work, and vice versa. The utility derived from the benefit option may depend on a number of factors, e.g. the disability benefit amount, health status, attitudes, etc., and the utility in the work option may depend on wages, health status, education, age, etc.

In addition to economic incentives, economists have also been interested in economic costs and benefits of various programs. Within this area of research, the effects of various vocational rehabilitation programs have been investigated. Participation in vocational rehabilitation may increase the likelihood of return to work of long-term work incapacitated persons in two different ways. First, it may increase functional ability and work capacity and thereby increase employment opportunities. In economic terms, vocational rehabilitation may be said to increase the human capital of the affected person. This type of vocational rehabilitation may be job training, different types of courses, and general education. Second, certain other types of vocational rehabilitation instruments, such as wage subsidizes, work place adaptations, and job placement, may create job opportunities for persons with reduced work capacity. If these interventions are followed by permanent non-subsidized employment, they can be considered as having a positive effect on return to work.

Economic Incentives and Return to Work

Several economic studies have analyzed return to work of temporarily work incapacitated persons (De Jong, 1987; Aarts & De Jong, 1992; Butler & Worrall, 1985; Meyer & Viscusi, 1995; Oleinick, Gluck & Guire, 1996; Johnson, Baldwin & Butler, 1998). All of these studies applied multivariate statistical techniques, and some of them corrected for unobserved heterogeneity.

The populations in these studies were not directly comparable to the population in the WIR Project. The studies of De Jong (1987) and Aarts and De Jong (1992) concerned long-term work incapacitated workers, but they do not focus especially on low-back pain diagnoses. The other studies concerned work injury compensation beneficiaries, meaning that the populations studied deviated from the population in the present study with regard to the circumstances causing work incapacity and the duration of the sick leave. In those studies, work incapacity was caused by job-related circumstances, and in most cases they included cases of short-term sick leave. In addition to these differences, the studies also differed in other important aspects, such as outcome measure and how economic incentives are measured. Among the workers' compensation studies, the studies of Oleinick, Gluck, and Guire (1996) and Johnson, Baldwin, and Butler (1998) are of particular interest because they consider back pain beneficiaries. The findings of the studies are summarized in Table 3.2.

These studies provide mixed evidence. On one hand, the most relevant studies in terms of study population and outcome variable (De Jong, 1987; Aarts & De Jong, 1992) give no, or only very limited, support for an effect of economic incentives. Hence, they find no effect of variables directly related to different income streams associated with work relative to the disability benefit option. Aarts and De Jong (1992) found, however, that "other household income" affects self-rated work capacity, which in turn affects the probability of a return to work. On the other hand, the work injury compensation studies suggest in general that economic incentives do have an effect. This includes the study of back beneficiaries who were work incapacitated for more than eight weeks (Oleinick, Gluck & Guire, 1996). Krueger (1990), who also studied work injury compensation beneficiaries, also found support for an effect of economic incentives (referred from Loeser & Hernserlite, 1995).

These differences in findings may be associated with institutional differences. Thus, the lack of an incentive effect in the Dutch study may be caused by the fact that almost all beneficiaries are entitled to full wages. It has been estimated that in 1990, 95 percent of all employees were entitled to full wage during sick leave (Aarts & De Jong, 1992). In contrast, replacement rates are in general considerably lower in the United States. In the study by Johnson, Baldwin, and Butler (1998), beneficiaries had on average a replacement rate of 69 percent.

TABLE 3.2
Selected Economic Studies on Economic Incentives for Labor Market Reintegration of Work Incapacitated Employees

Study	Population	Outcome Measure	Incentives Measured as:	Effect of Economic Incentives
De Jong (1987)	2,418 sickness beneficiaries incapacitated for 17 weeks	RTW versus disability benefit award	Disability benefit amount divided by foregone earnings	No[1]
Aarts & De Jong (1992)	2,534 sickness beneficiaries incapacitated for 17 weeks	RTW versus disability benefit award	Three measures: Expected income loss and expected leisure gain of disability benefit award, and other house hold income	No effect of income loss and leisure gain;[1] Other household income reduces RTW[1]
Butler & Worrall (1985)	Temporary total workers' compensation beneficiaries with low-back injuries[2]	Duration of benefit payment	Benefit level and pre-injury wage	No significant effects (but tendency of higher benefit levels and lower wages increases duration of benefit payment)
Meyer & Viscusi (1995)	6,822 temporary total workers' compensation beneficiaries	Duration of benefit payment	Benefit level	Higher benefit levels significantly increase duration of benefit payment
Oleinick, Gluck & Guire (1996)	2,184 workers' compensation beneficiaries, back injuries, incapacitated more than 8 weeks	Time to first return to work	Weekly compensation amount	Results interpreted as relatively low replacement rates promote RTW
Johnson, Baldwin & Butler (1998)	3,731 permanent partial workers' compensation beneficiaries	RTW	Replacement rate	Relatively low replacement rates increase RTW

Note: RTW is acronym for return to work.
[1] Estimated in a structural model where economic incentives may affect self-perceived work incapacity that affects RTW.
[2] No information on size of cohort.

Effects of Vocational Rehabilitation

In the United States, there is a long-standing tradition of applying cost-benefit analysis to public-funded programs, including vocational rehabilitation programs. This tradition is rooted in a need to justify the cost-effectiveness of programs—that generated benefits exceed program costs—and economic analysis was applied as early as the 1920s to evaluate vocational rehabilitation programs (Lewis et al., 1992).

In general, vocational rehabilitation is found to yield positive net future earnings (see e.g. Lewis et al., 1992; Dean & Dolan, 1991; for an overview, see Berkowitz, 1988). Moreover, several of these studies suggest that the effect of vocational rehabilitation is greater for persons with physical disabilities (including persons with back pain diagnoses) than for persons with other disabilities.

It may be problematic, however, to generalize findings in cost-benefit studies to the research problem considered in this project because of differences in the outcome variable and population studied. Hence, positive net benefits in terms of increased earnings for participants may not necessarily reflect that these persons return to work more often than non-participants. Instead, it could be caused by increased earnings among those who resume work.

A few studies have considered the effect of vocational rehabilitation on work resumption or the likelihood of reporting fit for duty (Bergendorff et al., 1997; Heshmati & Engström, 1999; Hennessey & Muller, 1995). These studies provide mixed evidence on the effect of vocational rehabilitation.

The studies by Bergendorff et al. and by Heshmati and Engström are interesting because the study populations consisted of long-term work incapacitated persons. Although Bergendorff et al. does not apply an economic approach, this study is mentioned in this section because of its focus on vocational rehabilitation. The data in Bergendorff et al. consist of information about 60,000 persons who were work incapacitated for 60 days or more. Heshmati and Engström used a nonrepresentative subset of this data. Bergendorff et al., used "reporting fresh for duty" whereas Heshmati and Engström used work resumption. The results of the two studies are, however, identical: vocational rehabilitation has a negative effect. These results were obtained after correction was made for differences in various factors, and, in the study of Heshmati and Engström, also for unobserved differences between vocational rehabilitation participants and nonparticipants.

Bergendorff et al., found that the effect of vocational rehabilitation is significantly above average among work incapacitated persons with a back pain diagnosis. This finding supports the assumption that the effect of vocational rehabilitation on work resumption is relatively large among work incapacitated persons with back pain diagnoses.

The study by Hennessey and Muller (1995) covered 4,400 persons who were entitled to a disability benefit in the United States in 1980-81 and who were re-interviewed in 1992. The study suggests that vocational rehabilitation significantly increases the tendency to return to work.

The contradictory results between the Swedish studies and the study from the United States may be caused by several circumstances: differences in study population (sickness beneficiaries versus disability beneficiaries), unobserved differences between vocational rehabilitation participants and nonparticipants in the United States study, or cross-national differences between the vocational rehabilitation programs.

In sum, the reviewed literature provides no clear answer with regard to the question whether vocational rehabilitation has a positive effect on work resumption among long-term work incapacitated workers with back pain diagnosis. Put more precisely, the studies most comparable to this project in terms of population and outcome suggest no, or even a negative, effect of vocational rehabilitation, whereas less comparable studies suggest a positive effect.

Public Policy Studies

This section considers research related to how social security schemes affect return to work of long-term work incapacitated persons. These studies consider the importance of legal and formal characteristics of relevant schemes, as well as how they are administered.

Different dimensions may affect the attractiveness of social schemes and how they are used, including how schemes are organized, how they are financed, and how the benefits are provided (see Kvist, 1999).

The organizational dimension concerns how schemes are administered. Questions such as who has the overall administrative responsibility and who has the daily responsibility are addressed. From this perspective, the actors involved, their interests, and their power becomes crucial because actors involved in the administrative process are assumed to pursue their own interest through their administration policy.

Benefit schemes may be financed in different ways, including by public (tax) funds, employer contributions, employee contributions, and by private insurance funds. The financial structure will provide different economic incentives for those involved, which in turn may lead to differences in how the schemes are used.

The main issues related to the provision of benefits are eligibility criteria and benefit formulae. Eligibility criteria regulate the group of persons covered by the scheme, e.g. all work incapacitated persons or only work incapacitated employees, and the conditions which must be fulfilled in order to be eligible for the benefit, e.g. a 50 percent reduction of the earnings capacity. The benefit formulae specify how the benefit is calculated, i.e. the benefit amount and duration of benefit payments (see Kvist, 1999). This aspect, which overlaps with the effect of economic incentives, is described above in the context of economic studies. In addition, the administration of eligibility criteria and benefit formulae may have an important influence on access to benefit programs.

These various aspects of organization, financing, and administration may influence whether work incapacitated employees stay out of work, and may thereby affect whether (or when) they return to work. It should be noted, however, that organizational and administrative characteristics of social security schemes in general do not directly affect work incapacitated employees (and their employers) as much as other factors, such as the work incapacitated person's health condition. Rather, these social security characteristics can be said to influence the individual actors through other circumstances, such as how sickness benefit cases are handled within the social security system, which in turn may affect the outcome of the individual sickness benefit case.

The Importance of Benefit Schemes

These social policy dimensions have been studied frequently, and in general it is found that they have a significant influence on how sickness benefit, rehabilitation, and disability benefit schemes are used. Compared to clinical and economic studies, however, those within the public policy sphere are often faced with methodological problems due to the fact that the organizational and financial structures and the benefit provisions often are the same within a country. As a consequence, researchers often have to rely on within-nation time-series or cross-national comparisons, and therefore conclusions are often based on a combination of data and contextual interpretations. There are, however, some studies concerning within-nation differences in the administration of benefit provisions based to some extent on multivariate quantitative analyses. Selected public policy research findings are summarized below in Table 3.3.

Some of the findings may need some additional comments. The study by Hetzler and Eriksson (1981) illustrates the influence that organizational structure may have for the use of disability benefit schemes. In Sweden, the insurance funds, which are part of the public sector, can apply for disability benefit on behalf of their clients. In the 1970s, the number of awarded disability benefits initiated by insurance funds increased, whereas the number of awarded benefits initiated by beneficiaries decreased. Hetzler and Eriksson stress that this development was facilitated by the institutional structure. The fact that the supervisory body for the sickness and disability benefit schemes, *Riksförsäkringsverket*, was also the supervisory body for the insurance funds made it possible for *Riksförsäkringsverket* to use insurance funds applications as a strategy to stop the growth in the level of sickness absenteeism.

Aarts and De Jong (1998) stress that the financial structure of social security schemes may have contributed to the high number of disability beneficiaries in the Netherlands. The fact that the sickness and disability schemes used to be funded by national pay-as-you-go contributions implied that those in charge of the administration—employers and employees—did not bear the economic costs of an increase in the use of the sickness and disability schemes directly. Aarts and De Jong also found the incentive structure and administrative practices to be the reason why public vocational rehabilitation has been almost completely absent in the Netherlands. In 1993, on per-capita basis, Germany spend 42 times more on vocational rehabilitation than the Netherlands (ibid.).

Findings concerning the provision of benefits relate primarily to four issues: disqualification for continued sickness benefits, eligibility for disability benefit, differences in the daily administration of benefit schemes, and different schemes serving the same purpose.

Disqualification for sickness benefit seems to be a rarely studied topic. De Jong (1987) included the number of medical check-ups performed during the first five months of sick leave as a proxy for the rigidity of the work incapacity check. The variable had no significant effect on the likelihood of return to work among long-term work incapacitated persons. Closely related to regulations concerning disqualification for benefits are regulations of "follow-up" procedures. Follow-up procedures include the administrative evaluation of how the case should be treated in order to facilitate a return to work, such as an assessment of the need for various vocational rehabilitation instruments. Palmer (1990) describes an experiment with early follow-up in a large Swedish production company. The results suggest that there may be a positive return-to-work effect of early screening.

The studies of eligibility criteria for disability benefits suggest that these criteria play a crucial role for the number of benefits that are awarded (Jacobs, Kohli & Rein, 1991; Frick & Sadowski, 1996; Aarts & De Jong, 1992).

Several findings support that administrative practices influence the number of awarded benefits. Hence, identical official rules yield different outcomes because of differences in administration. This problem has also been shown to exist when one compares different regions in the same country (Berkowitz & Burkhauser, 1996; Bengtsson, 1987), in comparisons between gate keepers in the same administration (van der Veen, 1990), and

TABLE 3.3
Selected Public Policy Studies on The Organization of Benefit Schemes and Provision of Benefits

Dimension and Study	Type of Analysis	Finding
Organization		
Hetzler & Eriksson (1991)	Time series, contextual	Organizational structure allowed central authorities in Sweden to use the disability benefit scheme to reduce long-term sickness absence
Aarts & De Jong (1996a)	Contextual	Organizational structure with social partners in charge of daily administration allowed Dutch employers to use disability scheme to shed labor
Aarts & De Jong (1996b)	Contextual	
Wadensjö & Palmer (1996)	Contextual	
Financing		
Aarts & De Jong (1998)	Contextual	Pay-as-you-go financing of Dutch sickness and disability benefits gave limited incentives to limit benefit awards at the administrative level
Benefit Provision and Program Administration		
De Jong (1987)	Quantitative, multivariate	Proxy for the harshness in the Dutch assessment of disqualification for continued sickness benefit receipt was insignificant for RTW
Palmer (1990)	Case study	Experiment in large Swedish company suggests that early follow-up in cases of sickness absence may enhance RTW
Jacobs, Kohli & Rein (1991)	Time series, contextual	A significant drop in disability benefit awards followed tightening of German eligibility criteria
Frick & Sadowski (1996)	Time series, contextual	

Dimension and Study	Type of Analysis	Finding
Benefit Provision and Program Administration *(Cont'd)*		
Aarts & De Jong (1992)	Quantitative	Unemployment of disability benefit claimants were taken into consideration in the Dutch disability benefit assessment; estimated that in 1980, 29 to 48% of the new beneficiaries were able to perform a suitable job
Koitz, Kollman & Neisner (1992)[1]	Quantitative	Administration of the US government disability benefit scheme differed across states
Bengtsson (1987)	Quantitative, multivariate	Significant differences in the regional administration of the public disability benefit scheme when various differences between regions were taken into account
Van der Veen (1990)[2]	Qualitative (interview with gate keepers)	Dutch disability benefit claim assessors ("gatekeepers") applied own informal rules reducing the effect of changes in formal rules
Berkowitz & Burkhauser (1996)	Time series, contextual	Significant drop between 1977 and 1980 in the number of disability benefit awards was probably caused by informal political pressure on assessors ("gatekeepers")
Einerhand et al. (1995)	Cross-national, contextual	Suggest that the high disability rate in the Netherlands compared to Belgium and other countries merely reflect differences in the use of different benefit schemes

Note: RTW is acronym for return to work.
[1] Referred from Berkowitz & Burkhauser (1996).
[2] Referred from Aarts & De Jong (1996b).

in over-time comparisons of the same scheme (Berkowitz & Burkhauser, 1996).

Finally, it should be noted that the study by Einerhand et al., (1995) concludes that the high work incapacity rate in the Netherlands compared to Belgium merely reflects differences in the use of exit routes, i.e. disability benefit in the Netherlands and early retirement in Belgium. In relation to the analysis of return to work of long-term work incapacitated persons, this aspect has far-reaching consequences: not only should the functioning of the disability benefit scheme be taken into consideration, but also the effects of different possible exit schemes.

In sum, research suggests that legal-formal characteristics of sickness benefit and disability benefit schemes and how they are administered influence how these schemes are used. This may in turn affect return to work of long-term work incapacitated persons. For some issues, such as benefit level and some aspects of eligibility criteria, evidence seems to be relatively clear: these conditions do have an effect. However, in most other aspects the picture is rather blurred. It seems likely that financial and organizational conditions are very important, but their possible effects are difficult to measure. The same seems to be true when it comes to the impact of other social security schemes and other institutional conditions.

Sociological Studies

Sociological research related to work incapacity and work resumption can be divided between studies based on a micro approach and those based on a macro approach. The micro approach, or the behavioral approach, emphasizes that factors related to the behavior of the individual and the surroundings of the individual, apart from the impairment, will affect whether a sick person will become work incapacitated. The macro perspective looks to societal conditions in terms of push factors, e.g. poor working conditions and unemployment, in order to explain the level of work incapacity.

The Micro Approach

Several behavioral characteristics may influence whether a work incapacitated person with an injury or disease will return to work or end up in the disability benefit system. Thus, persons may perceive symptoms of the same impairment differently and thus act differently. Some persons may find the incapacitating effects of a symptom to be modest, whereas others may find them severe. As a result, the extent of functional limitations may vary considerably from person to person, and thereby also the extent of work incapacity. Similarly, people may have different perceptions of the social, psychological, and economics consequences of being "disabled."

The choice between work and work incapacity can be understood as a choice between two different roles: a worker role; and an illness, or disability, role. These roles are associated with different expectations as to how the "sick" or the "disabled" worker should behave (see, Mechanic, 1962; Nagi, 1965; Lindqvist, 1995). The sick or disabled person is exempted from the normal roles associated with work. However, other expectations are associated with the disabled role: seeking competent help, cooperating with such help, and resuming usual activities as soon as the condition permits (Nagi, 1965, 1969). Whether or not a work incapacitated person will adapt to the disability role depends on, among other things, the severity of the illness, the individual's reaction to and perception of the situation, and the reactions to the individual by others.

A related approach stresses that health status may be affected by an individual's social network, including family members, close friends or colleagues, and social support, e.g. emotional, informative, and practical support systems (Lindqvist, 1995; Höög & Stattin, 1995; Stattin, 1998; Hanson, 1990). Social network and social support can be seen as resources that enable a sicklisted person to cope better with stress and demands, thereby increasing the potential for work resumption.

Four empirical studies applying a micro sociological approach were found. Three of the studies address the importance of the "disability role" relative to long-term work incapacitated workers (but not exclusively low-back pain diagnoses), and they all use return to work as the outcome variable (De Jong, 1987; Aarts & De Jong, 1992; Marklund, 1995). The fourth study, which addresses the importance of social support, is less comparable to the present study with regard to population studied (persons living in the country) and outcome variable (disability benefit award) (Höög & Stattin, 1995). The findings of these studies are summarized in Table 3.4.

The three studies about the "disability role" all support the importance of this role relative to work resumption. In general terms, De Jong (1987) and Aarts and De Jong (1992) found that persons who are relatively strong oriented towards "work" have a high probability of work resumption. Marklund (1995) found in a similar manner some evidence supporting that work incapacitated workers may be socialized into the disabled role through their wives. The study by Höög and Stattin (1995) provides limited support for the importance of social network and social support. They found that a reduction in social networks and social support increases the probability of persons becoming enrolled in the disability benefit scheme. In sum, there is evidence suggesting that return to work may be affected by variables related to the micro sociological approach.

The Macro Approach

The push perspective, or the "exclusion model" (see, e.g. Marklund, 1995; Stattin, 1998), stresses that work related factors and labor market conditions may push people out of the labor market and into work incapacity.

Push factors may be related to working conditions. For example, strenuous work and poor work environment are often assumed to contribute to sickness and work incapacity. In a similar vein, an increasing level of job

TABLE 3.4

Selected Sociological Studies on Social Support and Socialization into the Role as Disabled

Study	Population	Outcome Measure	Measure of 'Role as Disabled' (Social Support)	Findings
De Jong (1987)	2,534 sickness beneficiaries incapacitated for 17 weeks	RTW versus disability benefit award	Psychological inclination to postpone RTW measured as job satisfaction and how easily adaptation to a workless situation has happened	Low job satisfaction and easy adaptation to workless situation reduces RTW[1]
Aarts & De Jong (1992)	2,534 sickness beneficiaries incapacitated for 17 weeks	RTW versus disability benefit award	Job satisfaction and work ethics measured as various aspects of attitudes towards work	Weak work ethics and low job satisfaction reduces RTW[1]
Marklund (1995)	2,030 sickness beneficiaries incapacitated for at least 60 days	RTW[2] versus disability benefit award	Having a spouse who receives disability benefit	Spouse who receives disability benefit reduces the probability of RTW
Höög & Stattin (1995)	52,000 (61,000) persons awarded a disability benefit in 1988 (1993) and a random sample of people living in Sweden (in 1988 and 1993)	Disability benefit award versus no benefit award	Change of family status from cohabiting to single prior to benefit application is assumed to indicate a reduction in social network and social support	Evidence supporting that a reduction in social support increases probability of disability benefit award (in 1988 data but not in 1993 data)

Note: RTW is acronym for return to work.

[1] Estimated in a structural model where measures of 'disabled role' affect self-perceived work incapacity, which affects RTW.

[2] Is an approximation. Marklund calls this group 'rehabilitated', and it consists of 85% who returned to work and 15% with another status, e.g. under education or outside the labor force.

demands (e.g. demand for skills and flexibility) produces more work incapacitated persons because more people are unable to meet the stricter work demands. If these circumstances are relevant to the prediction of return to work, it should be expected that those who were exposed to relatively good working conditions would often return to work. However, this is not necessarily the case in relation to the likelihood of work resumption among long-term work incapacitated persons. For example, working conditions may have its effect early in the course of a sickness spell, so that work incapacitated workers with good working conditions resume work before they become long-term work incapacitated more often than work incapacitated employees with poor working conditions. As a result, employees with good working conditions who become long-term work incapacitated may have rather poor prospects for returning to work.

Labor market conditions are also assumed to affect the level of work incapacity. It is often assumed that the level of unemployment affects the level of exit from the labor market and, correspondingly, the number of disability benefit recipients (see, e.g. Kohli & Rein, 1991; Marklund, 1995; Höög & Stattin, 1995; Stattin, 1998). In relation to the return to work of long-term work incapacitated persons, a high level of unemployment is assumed to reduce employment opportunities of persons with a reduced work capacity, and thereby to reduce the rate of return to work.

Most studies applying a macro sociological approach have investigated the influence of push factors on the work incapacity incidence rate among persons in the work force (see, e.g. Kolberg, 1991; Piachaud, 1986; Bengtsson, 1987; Disney & Webb, 1990; Frick & Sadowski, 1996; Höög & Stattin, 1995). However, the importance of push factors in relation to work incapacitated workers has been investigated in some studies with a micro economic approach (Aarts & De Jong, 1992; Johnson, Baldwin & Butler, 1998; Johnson & Ondrich, 1990). These studies use multivariate analyses and use return to work or the duration of work absence as the outcome variable. The findings of these studies concerning working conditions and labor market conditions are summarized in Table 3.5.

Based on these few studies, there seems to be some evidence that working conditions have a significant effect on the rate of return to work among work incapacitated workers. Surprisingly, whether unemployment conditions are of any importance seems more uncertain.

TABLE 3.5
Selected Studies on Working Conditions and Labor Market Conditions for Return to Work of Long-Term Work Incapacitated Employees

Study	Population	Outcome Measure	Measure Working Conditions / Labor Market Conditions	Findings
Working Conditions				
Aarts & De Jong (1992)	2,534 sickness beneficiaries incapacitated for 17 weeks	RTW versus disability benefit award	Firm specific disability benefit incidence rate	Employees from companies with a high disability benefit incidence rate have a relatively low probability of RTW
Johnson, Baldwin & Butler (1998)	3,731 permanent partial workers' compensation beneficiaries with back pain diagnosis	RTW	Occupational sector is a proxy for physically demanding jobs	Males employed in sector with physically demanding jobs have a relatively low probability of RTW
Johnson & Ondrich (1990)	1,040 permanent partial workers' compensation beneficiaries	Duration of work absence	Occupational sector is a proxy for physically demanding jobs	Weak evidence suggesting that physically demanding jobs increase duration of work absences
Labor Market Conditions				
Aarts & De Jong (1992)	Cf. above	Cf. above	Individual estimates of the probability of becoming unemployed relative to the probability of reemployment	No effect
Johnson, Baldwin & Butler (1998)	Cf. above	Cf. above	Geographic region is proxy for unemployment level	No effect[1]

Note: RTW is acronym for return to work.

[1] The study compares workers' compensation beneficiaries with back pain diagnoses with beneficiaries without back pain diagnoses and find that the proxy for unemployment level is significant for non-back cases.

A Theoretical Model of Work Incapacity and Work Resumption

Against the background of this literature review, it seems evident that many factors may contribute to explain why some long-term work incapacitated workers return to work while others do not. The present project used the model shown in Figure 3.1 as a framework for understanding of the problem under study (Bloch & Prins, 1997).

The model, which was developed during the course of the WIR Project by researchers from the six participating countries, is informed by the findings and observations from national studies and a literature search that were carried out as part of the feasibility study phase of the Project. As such, the model reflects the aim and design of the project, so that certain types of variables have been given a prominent place, e.g. social security variables, whereas other variables play a more limited role, e.g. social support. The model is also informed by the present literature survey in the sense that it includes variables from the four research disciplines, with a few significant exceptions (e.g. unemployment rate).

Figure 3.1
Theoretical Model of Work Incapacity and Reintegration

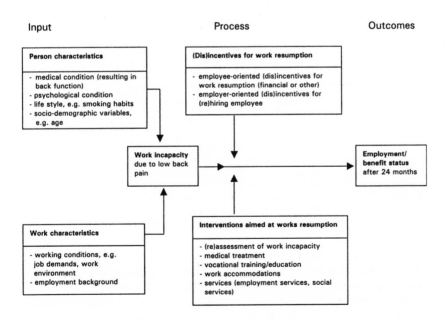

The aim of the model is to capture various return to work factors, and to illustrate in a simplified way how they may affect whether or not a work incapacitated workers will resume work (or alternatively whether or not the individual will end up as a beneficiary of disability benefits). The model may be characterized as a simple input-process-output model. The characteristics of the individual at the time of work incapacity correspond to the input; incentives and interventions that may affect work resumption correspond to process; employment status at the end of the study period correspond to output.

As the figure shows, the characteristics of the work incapacitated person are divided into personal characteristics and work-related characteristics at the onset of work incapacity. Personal characteristics include the work incapacitated worker's medical and psychological condition, life style characteristics, and socio-demographic characteristics (cf. discussion of clinical studies). Personal characteristics may also include the individual's resources in terms of social support received from family, other relatives, and friends (cf. discussion of sociological studies). Work characteristics include working conditions and job-related factors such as occupation, psychological and physical job demands, and job support from superiors and colleagues (cf. discussion of clinical and sociological studies). In a wider context, work characteristics may also include conditions such as previous job demands, previous employment, and unemployment record. These variables are intended to be proxies for the individual's chance of re-employment (cf. discussion of sociological studies).

These characteristics of a work incapacitated individual may, to a certain extent, predict the occupational outcome. In addition, incentives and interventions during sick leave may influence the work incapacitated employee, the former employer, and potential new employers, and thereby enhance or diminish the likelihood of work resumption. The incentives and interventions shown in the figure are related to the health care system (cf. discussion of clinical studies) and the social security system (cf. discussion of economic and public policy studies). In principle, incentives may also comprise other societal "circumstances" which may influence work resumption.

Incentives that may directly affect a work incapacitated employee include, for example, the benefit level, which, in comparison to a return-to-work wage, may make return to work more or less attractive. Direct incentives could also be psychological or social in character. Thus, work absence may be felt as an individual cost because participation in work, social relations on the job, etc., may be highly valued.

Incentives also operate on former and potential new employers. Various types of subsidies may create incentives to re-employ work incapacitated workers, such as wage subsidies. Moreover, job protection legislation that forbids or makes dismissal of work incapacitated workers costly may also give former employers incentives to facilitate work resumption.

Interventions may affect work resumption directly or indirectly. Work place accommodations and job placements are examples of direct interventions, which in themselves may enhance work resumption. Indirect interventions, such as medical treatment, job training, and education aimed at improving skills and work ability, may affect work incapacitated persons, which in turn may affect their chance of re-employment.

Incentives and interventions may affect people differently, as their effect is conditioned by personal and work characteristics. The effect of vocational rehabilitation, for example, may depend on personal characteristics, such as age and educational background. Thus, the model operates with two different types of explanations: conditions that influence work resumption directly, such as personal characteristics, and conditions that may affect return work through their interaction with background characteristics, such as incentives and interventions.

Summary and Conclusions

Literature from four major research disciplines—clinical studies, economics, public policy, and sociological studies—have been reviewed in this chapter in order to provide an overview of how various factors affect return to work among long-term work incapacitated persons with a low-back pain diagnosis.

It is striking that the review does not offer clear answers to the question under study. Taken alone, none of the research disciplines seems able to offer a convincing explanation of why some work incapacitated workers return to work whereas others do not. Neither has the review revealed a handful of variables that beyond doubt are important factors. Each of the four described theoretical disciplines seems to contribute to an explanation of the phenomenon, and several variables may be of importance; however, the review does not allow one to draw firm conclusions about the relative importance of various variables. Moreover, in many cases variables that are found to be important in some studies are found to be insignificant in other studies.

There are a number of reasons why this current state of affairs is not as surprising as it might seem. First, studies concerning factors related to one research approach seldom involve factors related to other approaches. This may imply that the effect of some or all of the factors found to be significant in one study would be altered if variables from other disciplines had been included. Second, most of the reviewed studies have been designed differently, making a comparison of findings doubtful or impossible. The major differences are the population under study, the length of the observation period, and the definition of the outcome variable. Third, different research approaches can demand to some extent different research strategies. Thus, as institutional characteristics, such as the organizational structure of social security schemes, normally are the same within a nation, a cross national or over-time study design would be needed. Finally, different methodological research strategies yield different types of evidence. National studies using survey data and/or register data with relatively high number of cases are able to produce "firm" scientific evidence in the sense that the data can be analyzed with multivariate techniques. Several independent competing variables might be tested against each other. Often this is not possible, or at least not possible to the same extent, in cross-national studies where "nations" or "social security systems" are treated as observations. As a consequence, research findings tend to be less conclusive.

While this analysis may suggest that it is impossible to be certain about significant effects of specific variables, it may be instead that certain groups of variables seem to have an effect and that the different theoretical approaches should be considered as complementary rather than competing.

Appendix 3.1: Selected Literature from the Review

Aarts, L. J. M. & De Jong, P. R. (1992). Economic Aspects of Disability Behavior. Elsevier Science Publishers B.V. Amsterdam, Holland.

Aarts, L. J. M. & De Jong, P. R. (1996a). The Dutch disability program and how it grew in: Aarts, L.J.M., De Jong, P.H., Burkhauser, R.V. (eds.): Curing the Dutch Disease. An International Perspective on Disability Policy Reform. Avebury Aldershot. England.

Aarts, L. J. M. & De Jong, P. R. (1996b). Evaluating the 1987 and 1993 social welfare reforms: From disappointment to potential success in: Aarts, L.J.M., De Jong, P.H., Burkhauser, R.V. (eds.):Curing the Dutch Disease. An International Perspective on Disability Policy Reform. Avebury Aldershot. England.

Aarts, L. J. M. & De Jong, P. R. (1998). Privatization of Social Insurance and Welfare State Efficiency. Evidence from the Netherlands & United States. Paper prepared for the 2nd International Research Conference on Social Security, Session Public versus Private Provision, Jerusalem, 25-28 January, 1998.

Battie, M. C. (1992). Minimizing the impact of back pain: Work place strategies. Semin Spine Surg 1992;4:20-28.

Bengtsson, S. (1987). En lov - femten nævn. Regionale forskelle i ansøgning, tilkendelse og afslag på førtidspension, Socialforskningsinstituttet. Publikation no. 167. København.

Bergendorff, S. et al. (1997). Resultat av arbetslivsinriktad rehabilitering och köb av tjänst in: Marklund, S. (eds.): Risk- & Frisk faktorer - sjukskrivning och rehabilitering i Sverige. Riksförsäkringsverket Redovisar 1997:6.

Berkowitz, E. D. & Burkhauser, R. V. (1996). A United States perspective on disability programs in: Aarts, L.J.M., De Jong, P.H., Burkhauser, R.V. (eds.):Curing the Dutch Disease. An International Perspective on Disability Policy Reform. Avebury Aldershot. England.

Berkowitz, M. (ed.) (1988). Measuring the Efficiency of Public Programs. Costs and Benefits in Rehabilitation. Philadelphia: Temple University Press.

Berkowitz, M. (ed.) (1990). Forging Linkages: Modifying Disability Benefit Programs to Encourage Employment. New York: Rehabilitation International.

Berkowitz, M. & Johnson, W. G. (1974). Health and Labor Force Participation. The Journal of Human Resources, Vol. IX, No. 1. Winter.

Bloch, F. S. & Prins, R. (1997). Work incapacity and reintegration: Theory and design of a cross-national study. International Social Security Review, Vol. 50, No. 2.

Butler, R. J. & Worrall, J. D. (1985). Work Injury Compensation and the Duration of Nonwork Spells. The Economic Journal, 95 (379).

Crook, J. M. (1994). A longitudinal epidemiological study of injured workers: Prognostic indicators of work disability. PhD Thesis, University of Toronto, Toronto, Ontario, Canada.

Dean, D. H. & Dolan, R. C. (1991). Assessing the Role of Vocational Rehabilitation in Disability Policy. Journal of Policy Analysis and Management, Vol. 10, No. 4:568-587.

De Jong, P. (1987). Work capacity and the probability of entry into the Dutch disability insurance program in: Emanuel, H., De Gier, E. H. & Konijn, P. A. B. K. (eds.): Disability benefits: Factors determining application and awards. JAI Press Inc. New York.

52   Who Returns to Work and Why?

Disney, R. & Webb, S. (1990). Why Social Security Expenditure in the 1980s has Risen Faster than Expected: the Role of Unemployment. Fiscal Studies, Vol. 11, p. 1-20.

Einerhand, M. G. K., Knol, G. Prins, R. & Veerman, T. J. (1995). Sickness and invalidity arrangements. Fact and figures from six European countries. Ministerie van Sociale Zaken en Werkgelegenheid. The Hague.

Emanuel, H., De Gier, E. H. & Konijn, P. A. B. K. (eds.) (1987). Disability benefits: Factors determining application and awards. JAI Press Inc. New York.

Frank, J. W. et al. (1995). Occupational Back Pain: An unhelpful polemic. Scandinavian Journal of Work, Environment & Health, 21, p. 3-14.

Frank, J. W. et al. (1996). Disability Resulting from Occupational Low Back Pain. Part II: What Do We Know About Secondary Prevention? A Review of Scientific Evidence on Prevention After Disability Begins. Spine, Vol 21, No. 24, p. 2918-2929.

Frick, B. & Sadowski, D. (1996). A German perspective on disability policy in: Aarts, L.J.M., De Jong, P.H., Burkhauser, R.V. (eds.):Curing the Dutch Disease. An International Perspective on Disability Policy Reform. Avebury Aldershot. England.

Gatchel, R. J., Polatin, P. B. & Mayer, P. D. (1994). Psychopathology and the rehabilitation of patients with chronic low back pain disability. Archives of Physical Medicine & Rehabilitation, Vol. 75: 666.

Hanson, B. S. (1990). Hur kan en individs sociala nätverk och sociala stöd påverka hälsan? Socialmedicinsk tidsskrift. 1990, 67:e årg. häfte 1-2. p. 32.

Haveman, R. H. & Wolfe, B. L. (1984a). Disability transfers and early retirement: A causal relationship? in: Journal of Public Economics, Vol. 24, No. 1, June 1984.

Haveman, R. H. & Wolfe, B. L. (1984b). The decline in male labor force participation: A comment. Journal of Political Economy, 92, June, p. 532-541

Hazard, R. G., Bendix, A. & Fenwick, J. W. (1991). Disability exaggeration as a predictor of functional restoration outcomes for patients with chronic low back pain. Spine 16, 1062.

Hennessey, J. C. & Muller, S. L. M. (1995). The Effect of Vocational Rehabilitation and Work Incentives on Helping Disabled-Worker Beneficiary Back to Work. Social Security Bulletin. Vol. 58, no. 1, 1995.

Heshmati, A. & Engström, L. G. (1999). Estimating Effects of Vocational Rehabilitation Programs in Sweden. SEE/EFI Working Paper Series in Economics and Finance No. 293. Sweden.

Hetzler, A. & Eriksson, K. (1981). Ökad förtidspensionering - en rättssociologisk analys, Lund: Rättssociologiska Institutionen.

Hildebrandt J., Pfingsten, M., Saur, P. & Jansen, J. (1997). Prediction of success from a multidisciplinary treatment program for chronic low back pain. Spine 22, 990.

Höög, J. & Stattin, M. (1995). Orsaker till förtidspensionering in: Marklund, S. (eds.) Rehabilitering i ett samhällsperspektiv. Second edition, Studentlitteratur, Lund.

Jacobs, K., Kohli, M. & Rein, M. (1991). Germany: The diversity of pathways in: Kohli, M, Rein, M., Guillemard & van Gunsteren (eds.): Time for Retirement - Comparative studies of early exit from the labor force. Cambridge University Press. New York.

Johnson, W. G., Baldwin, M. L. & Butler, R. J. (1998). Back Pain and Work Disability: The Need for a New Paradigm. Industrial Relations, Vol 37 no. 1. January 1998.

Johnson, W. G. & Ondrich, J. (1990). The Duration of Post-injury Absences from Work. Review of economics and statistics. Vol. 72.

Kohli, M. & Rein, M. (1991). The evolution of early exit: A comparative analysis of labor force participation patterns in: Kohli, M, Rein, M., Guillemard & van Gunsteren (eds.): Time for Retirement - Comparative studies of early exit from the labor force. Cambridge University Press. New York.

Koitz, D., Kollman, G. & Neisner, J. (1992). Status of the Disability Programs of the Social Security Administration. Congressional Research Service. Washington, DC.

Kolberg, J. E. (1991). En empirisk prøvning av utstøtningsmodellen in: Hatland, A. (1991): Trygd som fortjent? Oslo: Ad Notam.

Krause, N., Dasinger, L. K. & Neuhauser, F. (1998). Modified Work and Return to Work: A Review of the Literature. Journal of Occupational Rehabilitation, Vol. 8, No. 2:113-139.

Krueger, A. B. (1990). Workers' Compensation Insurance and the Duration of Workplace Injuries. NBER Working Paper no. 3523, National Bureau of Economic Research.

Kummel, B. M. (1996). Nonorganic signs of significance in low back pain. Spine 21, 1077.

Kvist, J. (1999). New Perspectives in Comparative Social Policy. PhD Thesis. The National Institute of Social Research.

Lacroix, J. M. et al. (1990). Low-back pain. Factors of value in predicting outcome. Spine 15, 495.

Lewis, D. R., Johnson, D. R., Chen, T. & Erickson, R. N. (1992). The Use and Reporting of Benefit-Cost Analysis by State Vocational Rehabilitation Agencies. Evaluation Review, Vol. 16, No. 3: p. 266-287.

Lindqvist, R. (1995). Arbete, sjukdom och rehabilitering in: Marklund, S. (eds.), Rehabilitering i ett samhällsperspektiv. Studentlitteratur. Lund.

Loeser, J. D. & Hernserlite, S. E. (1995). Incentive effects of workers' compensation benefits: A synthesis. Medical Care Research & Review, Vol. 52, no 1.

Marklund, S. (1995). Indledning in: Marklund, S. (eds.): Rehabilitering i ett samhällsperspektiv. Second edition, Studentlitteratur, Lund.

Mechanic, D. (1962). The Concept of Illness Behavior. Journal of Chronic Diseases. February 1962. p. 189-194.

Meyer, B. D. & Viscusi, K. W. (1995). Workers' Compensation and Injury Duration: Evidence from a Natural Experiment. American Economic Review. Vol. 85. No. 3.

Nagi, S. Z. (1965). Some Conceptual Issues in Disability and Rehabilitation in: M. B. Sussman (eds.): Sociology and rehabilitation. American Sociological Association.

Nagi, S. Z. (1969). Disability and Rehabilitation. Columbus, OH: Ohio State University.

Oleinick, A., Gluck, J. V. & Guire, K. E. (1996). Factors Affecting First Return to Work Following a Compensable Occupational Back Injury. American Journal of Industrial Medicine, Vol. 30.

Palmer, E. (1990). Potential Gains from Early Intervention in Sickness Absenteeism at the Workplace: An Overview of the Current State of Knowledge and Trends in Sweden. In: Berkowitz, M. (ed.): Forging Linkages: Modifying Disability Benefit Programs to Encourage Employment. Rehabilitation International: New York.

Parsons, D. O. (1980). The Decline in Male Labor Force Participation. Journal of Political Economy, 88, February, p. 87-93

Parsons, D. O. (1984). Disability Insurance and Male Labor Force Participation: A Response to Haveman and Wolfe. Journal of Political Economy, Vol. 92, no. 3, p. 542-549.

Piachaud, D. (1986). Disability, Retirement and Unemployment of Older Men. Journal of Social Policy, Vol. 15, part 2, p. 145-162.

Sandström, J. (1986). Clinical and social factors in rehabilitation of patients with chronic low back pain. Scandinavian Journal of Rehabilitation Medicine, 18: 35-43.

Sandström, J. & Esbjornsson, E. (1986). Return to work after rehabilitation. The significance of patient's own prediction. Scandinavian Journal of Rehabilitation Medicine 18:29.

Stattin, M. (1998). Yrke, yrkesförändring och utslagning från arbetmarknaden - en studie av relationen mellan förtidspension och arbetsmarknadsförändring. Umeå University.

van der Veen, R.J. (1990). De sociale grenzen van beleid. Stenfert Kroese, Leiden.

Waddell, G. (1987). 1987 Volvo award in clinical sciences. A new clinical model for the treatment of low-back pain. Spine 12, No. 7:632-44.

Wadensjö, E. & Palmer, E. E. (1996). Curing the Dutch disease from a Swedish perspective in: Aarts, L.J.M., De Jong, P.H., Burkhauser, R.V. (eds.): Curing the Dutch Disease. An International Perspective on Disability Policy Reform. Avebury Aldershot. England.

Weide, W. E. van der, Verbeek, J. H. A. M. & Tulder, M. W. v (1997). Vocational outcome of intervention for low-back pain. Scandinavian Journal of Work, Environment & Health, Vol. 23:165-178.

Werneke, M. W., Harris, D. E. & Lichter, R. L. (1993). Clinical effectiveness of behavioral signs for screening chronic low-back pain patients in a work-oriented physical rehabilitation program. Spine 18.

Wolfe, B. L. & Haveman, R. (1990). Trends in the Prevalence of Work Disability from 1962 to 1984, and Their Correlates. The Milbank Quarterly, Vol. 68, no. 1.

4

Research Design and Methodology

Jockel Wolf

This chapter concerns the research design of the WIR Project, including the construction of cohorts, cohort creation outcomes, the methods used for data collection, and the Project's international database. After explaining the unique cross-national design of the Project and how it was implemented in the participating countries, the chapter addresses cohort inclusion criteria, measured cohort characteristics, the observation period and measurement points, and the use of standardized measurements. Following that, cohort creation outcomes are presented for each national study, including a short overview on initial non-response and the number of subjects at the different measurement points. Methods of data collection across national studies are shown and methods used in data analyses are described briefly. Finally, the construction and structure of the Project's international database are described.

Background and Aim of Research Design

The WIR Project was designed to follow a well-described category of subjects at repeated measurements in order to study the timing and effects of measures applied to regain health and work capacity. From the outset, the intent was to measure both medical and vocational and other non-medical interventions in a cross-national study. There were two main purposes in setting up the Project as a cross-national study. First, it was felt that running a set of national studies with a common core design would produce greater insight into the problems of work incapacity and reintegration than the sum of six independent studies. Second, it was hoped that the experience gained from running this unique research design would assist others interested in cross-national social security research, and would stimulate future collaborative studies.

Feasibility studies were carried out, which indicated that there was a substantial basis for comparison among different national schemes in terms of which medical, vocational, and other non-medical interventions are applied to a work incapacitated person with a low back disorder. As mentioned in Chapter 2, a conceptual classification of the domestic repertoire of interventions used in each participating country was prepared based on information gathered from the national teams. Twenty-six vocational and other non-medical interventions, incentives, and disincentives were identified and classified into five categories: 1) training and education (general, vocational); 2) work accommodations (e.g. adaptations in work place, transportation, working hours); 3) motivators (e.g. wage subsidies, negative sanctions); 4) assessment of work capacity/incapacity (including rehabilitation inquiry); and 5) services (e.g. job search, day care for children). These interventions are discussed in detail in Chapter 8.

Project guidelines specified that participating national sponsors would commission studies that would follow a common core design for the Project, with the possibility for each national research team to address additional goals, issues, and measurements relevant to national research aims. The thrust of the core design was to support a coordinated program of national studies covering a minimum set of common issues in a comparable way.

As the main goal of the Project was to learn how to improve the process for returning people with work incapacity to the workforce, several basic features for a common design were identified. First, each study had to be prospective. Second, the cohort of subjects had to be homogeneous regarding the basic medical condition; the condition chosen was low back disorders. Third, the cohorts had to be composed of persons who were employed, or were employed immediately before work incapacity, and who had been work incapacitated for three consecutive months upon entering the cohort. Fourth, the studies had to cover a full range of interventions and incentives, in order to broaden the study from the more limited focus on medical treatments and rehabilitation to actions aimed at recovery and work resumption. Fifth, these interventions were to be evaluated in light of critical social security indicators. Finally, the observation period would last two years from the onset of work incapacity, with at least three measurements.

The above features constituted a minimum package; however, national teams were free to add goals and issues that were of interest from their own national research perspective. This flexibility in the national adaptation of the common research design was essential; without this flexibility, it is unlikely that any of the national studies would have taken place.

During the study, internal expert groups distributed specific questionnaires to all national research teams to gain insight into differences and similarities among the participating countries with respect to the medical and vocational treatments applied within each system. Owing to these efforts and to a lively communication among researchers from all teams, it was possible to integrate the results into a homogeneous set of international data, even though national circumstances in the conduct of the study were heterogeneous as far as sponsors, composition of research teams, and methods of data collection were concerned.

Operationalizing the Research Design

Inclusion Criteria and Cohort Creation

To qualify for inclusion in a national cohort, subjects had to meet four sets of entry criteria relating to medical diagnosis, employment conditions, work incapacity, and demographics.

The central diagnostic criterion was that work incapacity had to be caused primarily by low-back pain, i.e. pain between the lower edge of the 12th rib and the gluteal folds. Persons with spinal fractures or any type of surgery within the previous 12 months were excluded. Moreover, there had to be no information indicating an infectious or malignant cause of the subject's back pain. In terms of the World Health Organization's International Classification of Diseases, Revision 9 (ICD-9), the cases included are found within codes 721, 722, and 724.

With respect to employment, subjects had to be employed—either full-time or part-time—at the onset of the work incapacity. They also had to be covered, through employment, by the relevant social insurance scheme for sickness or disability benefits.

Two work incapacity criteria were applied, both of which addressed the severity of the subject's condition at the time the subject entered the study. First, they had to have stopped working due to back pain three months before the date of entry in the cohort, i.e. be in the fourth month of work incapacity at the moment of inclusion in the cohort. Second, they had to have stopped work completely (not only for a part of working hours) and had to be fully incapacitated for their former jobs. The decision to choose a time span of three months for inclusion in the cohort was driven mainly by administrative reasons; the earliest common point where all countries were able to identify subjects was three months after reporting sick.

Demographically, the subjects had to be between 18 and 59 years of age at the moment of inclusion in the cohort.

According to the original design, the cohort from each country was supposed to include enough subjects so that at least 300 could be followed through the entire observation period of 21 months. Also, the various national cohorts were to be filled at approximately the same time. However, as a result of delays in decision making and/or logistical problems in some countries, the cohort creation period—and the start of the national studies—varied from country to country.

The Danish subjects were recruited from the 24 local municipalities with the most inhabitants (out of 275), selecting according to the inclusion criteria based on data from a central municipality register. Selection took place over a 15-week period, with the exception of one municipality where the selection took place over 10 weeks.

The German team recruited its subjects from two statutory health schemes in large industrial cities in Northern and Southern Germany, which have a high percentage of "blue-collar" workers. Data concerning inclusion criteria were obtained from the agencies and checked by the national research team.

Due to the lack of a centralized database of sickness benefit claimants, the cohort from Israel consisted of work injury benefit claimants from all over the country. All claimants who met the inclusion criteria within a period of 15 months according to a national database were approached to determine whether they met additional inclusion criteria.

The Dutch team drew its cohort from employees from all over the country, who were insured under the Sickness Benefit Plan for the private sector and who were also covered by an occupational health service. After an initial selection by social security offices, additional cohort inclusion criteria were checked through questionnaires that each subject was asked to complete. The selection process took seven months.

The Swedish subjects were selected by social insurance offices in five regions of the country. Since not all cohort inclusion criteria were available through those offices, subjects had to be excluded as additional information became available later in the data collection process.

Subjects were selected in the United States on a voluntary basis from two out of five states with temporary disability programs, namely New Jersey and California. Initial selection for inclusion in the cohort was based on data available for persons in these programs; further selection was made after additional information became available.

The recruited cohorts cannot be assumed to be representative samples of the countries' labor forces. Moreover, as the approaches to recruiting a cohort were so different from country to country, they should be regarded as six different cohorts that are comparable with respect to major variables known to affect work incapacity.

Cohort Characteristics, Interventions, and Outcomes

Following the theoretical model described in Chapter 3, cohort characteristics measured in this study can be organized along an input-process-output structure continuum. Input was measured by characteristics of the subjects at the time of the onset of work incapacity. The sociodemographic characteristics measured included age, gender, educational level, mother language, household composition, income, and occupation. Also included were work characteristics, such as employment history and working conditions; health status indicators, such as life style, risky habits, exact medical condition, and perceived health status; socio-psychological aspects, such as work motivation, attitudes on work and health, coping behavior, and social support; and opinions on incentives and disincentives offered by social security relative to work resumption. Health care characteristics covered the type of health care suppliers, timing, and referrals, as well as waiting periods, e.g. before hospitalization or during referral. Employment characteristics sampled the local labor market situation, the company size and branch, the economic prospects of the company, absence strategies, reintegration policy, working conditions, and the employer's opinions on interventions, incentives and disincentives, and re-employment of the subject.

The process component was measured by a set of medical, vocational, and other non-medical interventions. A clear set of medical interventions aimed at recovery were developed with additional information from medical sources and experts within the research group. It covered treatment by various kinds of doctors, physiotherapy, x-ray, hospitalization, operation, a number of passive treatments (heat or cold, electric therapy, acupuncture, pain relieving injections or medicines, bed rest, massage, manipulation, traction or zone therapy, mud packing or medicinal baths), as well as active treatments (training of muscles, range of motion or other physical activities, back/pain school) and some other treatments (use of walking aids, use of a brace, corset or other external support). As noted earlier, inventory of 26 vocational and other non-medical interventions based on information gathered from the national teams was developed, classified into five categories: training and education, work accommodations, motivators, assessment of work capacity/incapacity, and services.

Finally, because the Project was intended to examine return-to-work initiatives for persons receiving social security benefits, the output measured included the subjects' benefit status, in addition to the obvious measures of full or partial work resumption. Consequently, the outcomes covered—both during the observation period and at the end of the project—included doing paid work, receipt of benefit, participation in a rehabilitation program, and other (e.g. deceased). Changes in health conditions and functional limitations were also observed.

Observation Period and Measurement Points

An observation period of 24 months following the first day of work incapacity was chosen to monitor inventions and their outcomes for each subject. As arrangements for temporary work incapacity in most countries cover a duration from less than one year up to 18 months, the interventions and outcomes related to those schemes were fully covered. Furthermore, this period allowed an insight into rehabilitation and evaluation measures and outcomes which are carried out in relation to the operation of disability benefit programs; the cohorts were defined by three months of work incapacity, which, in several countries, marks the point for social security agency intervention.

Three measurement points were used to allow adequate assessment of actions and outcomes in the cohort:

T1 was measured as soon as possible after three months of work incapacity. T1 measurements covered a range of issues and variables, including relevant retrospective data on employment, health, and work incapacity in the first three months. The measurement was set to coincide with the creation of the cohort. Usually, the period of time for inclusion (and for measuring T1) was between 90 and 120 days after the date of work incapacity, but in some countries subjects had to be included into the cohort far later due to administrative reasons. In those countries, efforts were undertaken to make clear to the subject that some questions, such as those regarding health status, referred to the situation at 90 days after the date of work incapacity. Analyses on the effects of late date of testing T1 gave an amorphous picture with very few significant deviations.

T2 was measured approximately one year after the first day of work incapacity. This measurement focused retrospectively on interventions carried out and the subjects' opinions concerning incentives and disincentives between T1 and T2, as well as outcomes at T2.

T3 was measured about two years after the start of work incapacity. T3 measurements addressed the interventions in the second year and the outcomes of those and earlier interventions, as well as certain other data relative to the relevant social security context. The second year thus focused on the consequences of interventions during the first year, as well as further actions taken that year.

Standardized Measurements

The measured cohort characteristics mentioned above included a number of standardized measurements. The Hannover ADL scale (calculated from a total of 12 variables measuring the client's functional limitations), the von Korff Pain scale, and other scales on general health, vitality, mental health, and social functioning (calculated from a total of 15 variables measuring the health status and outcomes from the client's point of view) were used at T1, T2, and T3. Additional scales on decision latitude, job demands, social support, smoking habits, client's attitudes on work, and client's coping behavior were used at T1. The scales used in the Project are discussed in more detail in the technical guide accompanying the Project data base. The outcomes for selected scales are discussed in Chapter 5.

The National Cohorts

At the outset of the Project, subjects were approached in different ways in each country. The six national cohorts followed in the national studies are compared in some detail in Chapter 5.

Non-Response at T1

Table 4.1 shows the percentages of persons that qualified for cohort inclusion, but either could not be reached/located or did not respond at T1, and the resulting cohort size. An analysis of non-response/dropout at T2 and T3 is presented in Chapter 5.

TABLE 4.1
Non-Response (%) and Cohort Size at T1

	Denmark	Germany	Israel	N'lands	Sweden	US
Non-response	Approx. 15,4	≤ 22,9	≤ 10,6	≤ 21,9	≤ 20,8	≤ 23,6
Cohort size	565	410	327	427	539	484

Cohort Sizes

The number of subjects participating in each country at T1, T2, and T3 is given in Figure 4.1.

Data Collection Methods

As noted earlier, a special feature of the Project's organization allowed different approaches to carrying out the national studies. As a result, various methods of data collection were used to create the cohorts in the different countries. Table 4.2 gives an overview of these methods and their usage throughout the study.

FIGURE 4.1
Number of Subjects (T1, T2, T3)

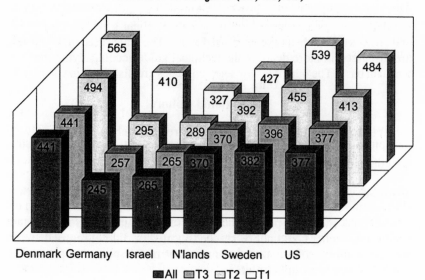

TABLE 4.2
Methods of Data Collection Applied

	Denmark	Germany	Israel	N'lands	Sweden	US
Face-to-Face interview	Yes (if the client had no phone)		Yes (T1)			
Telephone interview	Yes		Yes (T2,T3)	Yes		Yes
Postal questionnaire		Yes		Yes	Yes	
Files from social security or health care administration	Yes (only for a few variables)	Yes (for some special variables)	Yes	Yes (only a few, such as age and gender)	Yes (for some special variables)	

At the same time, all data were gathered and compiled in accordance with guidelines agreed to by the national research teams. Throughout the data sampling and cleaning process, successful efforts were undertaken to ensure that the data collected that would be used for analyses was as reliable as possible, even if it was compiled from different sources for different cohorts.

Data Analysis Methods

A number of statistical methods were used to analyze the data from the national studies. A cluster analysis was used in Chapter 5 to comment on the comparability of the cohorts in relation to certain work characteristics and subjective health status. The discussion of main outcomes in Chapter 6 made use of correlations with significance checked with chi-square tests to identify possible associations between work status at T3 and selected variables sampled at T1. Bivariate tests were performed in Chapter 7 in an effort to reveal possible dependencies between work resumption and certain health indicators. Chapter 8 identified significant relationships between work resumption and vocational and other non-medical interventions. The evaluative analysis of the results in Chapter 10 took a three-step approach: after eliminating baseline characteristics variables with a number of missings exceeding 15 percent and converting missing values for the remaining variables in order to avoid cumulating missing values, these baseline variables were checked for significant bivariate correlation and then a stepwise regression procedure was applied to the remaining variables.

International Database

To ensure that the participating countries' data would be of high quality and that all researchers would use an identical database for analyses, the Project contracted with an independent third party—the IEA Data Processing Center (DPC) in Hamburg, Germany—for data cleaning and the creation of an international database.

The first step toward standardized data was the creation of codebooks for all three measurements. These codebooks give detailed definitions for all variables, including a standardized international name, format, type, label, valid values or valid range, and a description of full content. A full description of the codebook format and a codebook for each of the three measurements are included in the technical guide accompanying the Project data base. All countries delivered their data according to the international format.

For all three measurements—T1, T2, and T3—the DPC supplied the national research teams with reports on their data and the teams sent back information needed to improve the data. All national datasets that were sent to the DPC were checked against the international format; all missing or additional variables and all deviations from the valid values/ranges and inconsistencies were recorded and reported to the concerned national team. After all team-submitted changes had been implemented, the participating research teams received national cleaning documentation with a list of all the changes made and univarite statistics. Research teams were asked to check these carefully; if problematic data were identified by a national team, it sent in further corrections to their data which were then implemented by DPC staff.

The project includes a number of standardized index variables/scales, such as the Hannover ADL, that needed to be calculated from existing variables. After the data sets were edited, the indexes were computed and appended to the existing data.

Finally, all country data sets were merged into a single international database, adding country identification variables. An international database was created/updated after all three measurements. After the last measurement's data were edited, the international database including all data from all measurements was created. It consists of all variables in the international codebooks for T1, T2, and T3; all index variables/scales, additional country identification variables, and participation indicators for T1, T2, and T3; and the unemployment rates from 1994 to 1997, as supplied by the national teams.

With this international database, it can be assured that all countries' data meet the international format, that all index variables are calculated in exactly the same way, that the same cleaning process has been applied to all data, and that the ID system is consistent. The international database is accompanied by a technical guide. It is available for research purposes in digital format as well. Thus, the ISSA WIR International Database comprises of one CD-ROM, including both SAS™ export and SPSS™ portable format data sets and the programs that help users in accessing them, along with a digital codebook in ASCII, RTF™, MS Word™ and dBASE™ formats.

5

Cohorts Compared: Cross-national Similarities and Differences

Andreas Weber

Introduction

The previous chapters demonstrated that a great deal of attention was paid to ensure comparability of cohorts and measurements. This chapter examines how far the Project's guidelines for selecting subjects produced comparable cohorts for the various national studies. This analysis will include comparisons among the cohorts as to some of the main characteristics of the subjects.

From the beginning of the Project, it was clear that full comparability of cohorts would not be feasible. As the subjects for the national studies had to be found and selected by making use of social security or health care files, it was obvious that this would affect the composition of the cohorts. Also, no effort was made to achieve a regionally representative distribution; such an effort would have required finding too large a number of social security agencies willing to provide subjects that met the cohort selection criteria. It was not expected that the persons surveyed in the participating countries would have identical socio-demographic characteristics, as in some regions and for some social insurance bodies certain subject characteristics may be over-represented.

An attempt is made in this chapter to describe accurately the persons surveyed in the various countries. In order to obtain an impression of the uniqueness of the cohorts, they have been compared with the labor force data in the relevant countries. For this purpose, certain selected socio-demographic variables were taken from the Labour Force Survey 1997 and the Key Indicators of the Labour Market (KILM) 1999. It is also of interest, both for the comparability of the cohorts and relative to the presented outcome results, whether the respondents in the various national studies are distinguishable from the non-respondents at the time-points T2 (one year after the onset of work incapacity) or T3 (after two years), so that selective drop-outs are detectable.

The cohorts will be compared at the baseline measurement T1 as to selected variables from the fields of "demographic characteristics," "work characteristics," "subjective health status," and "subjective work prognosis." These comparisons will be used to show which cohorts have rather unique features, and the degree of similarity among the cohorts.

Even though the results and outcomes from the Project will be of great interest, a warning must be expressed not to be too hasty in interpreting them as assessment criteria for the functional and performance characteristics of the particular social security systems.

Demographic Characteristics

This section compares the six cohorts with regard to certain socio-demographic features: age, gender, native language, education and household unit.

As seen in Table 5.1, the mean values for age distribution in the six cohorts cover a relatively wide range. For example, for the Israeli cohort, the mean was 39.2 years of age, while for the Germany cohort, it was 49.3. For the Swedish cohort, the mean age was roughly between those two, at 44 years of age. The standard deviations for the various cohorts were quite close together.

TABLE 5.1
Mean Age at T1

	Denmark	Germany	Israel	N'lands	Sweden	US
Mean (yrs)	40.5	49.3	39.2	39.9	44.2	42.0
Std. Dev.	10.6	8.8	10.2	9.4	10.0	9.0
% Omit	0	0.2	0.3	0	0	0

It becomes even clearer that the age structures of the six cohorts were really quite different if the overall age distribution is divided into five age categories, as shown in Table 5.2. The relatively large number of German participants aged 55-59 (approximately 38%) is then particularly notable.

TABLE 5.2
Age Distribution at T1 (%)

	Denmark	Germany	Israel	N'lands	Sweden	US
up to 24 years	7.8	1.0	7.4	4.9	2.4	3.7
25-34 years	23.4	7.8	28.8	28.1	16.9	19.2
35-44 years	28.7	17.1	32.8	34.2	18.6	35.3
45-54 years	28.3	35.7	20.6	26.7	33.8	32.2
55-59 years	11.9	38.4	10.4	6.1	18.4	9.5
Total	100	100	100	100	100	100
% Omit	0	0.2	0.3	0	0	0

Table 5.3 shows the gender distribution of the cohorts. The most gender-balanced cohort was the cohort from Denmark, where the percentage of women was 53 percent and that of men was 46 percent. The least balanced cohort was the one from Israel, where the percentage of women was 26 percent and that of men was 74 percent. In the German and Dutch cohorts, the percentage of men was also higher than that of women, at 64 percent and 61 percent, respectively. On the other hand, the female participants were predominant in the Swedish and American cohorts, at 62 percent and 56 percent, respectively.

TABLE 5.3
Gender Distribution at T1 (%)

	Denmark	Germany	Israel	N'lands	Sweden	US
Male	46.4	64.1	74.0	61.4	38.6	44.4
Female	53.6	35.9	26.0	38.6	61.4	55.6
Total	100	100	100	100	100	100
% Omit	0	0	0	1.2	0	0

The results for the question whether the national language was the subject's native language is shown in Table 5.4. It is noticeable, but not surprising, that in Israel a third of the subjects identified some language other than Hebrew as their native language. In the German and Dutch cohorts, the national language was the native language of almost all subjects; in Denmark, the percentage of native Danish speakers was also high, at 92 percent. In the cohorts from Sweden and the United States, which are both immigrant countries, about 82 percent of the subjects responded that the national language was their native language.

TABLE 5.4
National Language as Mother Tongue at T1 (%)

	Denmark	Germany	Israel	N'lands	Sweden	US
Yes	91.7	97.3	65.7	97.9	82.1	82.6
No	8.3	2.7	34.3	2.1	17.9	17.4
Total	100	100	100	100	100	100
% Omit	0	0.7	0.9	0.2	1.3	0.2

Table 5.5 shows that the members of the German cohort had, by far, the lowest level of education; for 87 percent of those subjects, their qualifications were no higher than primary level. In the cohorts from the other countries, most of the subjects had completed school at either the lower or the upper secondary level. The American cohort had the largest proportion of subjects with tertiary level qualifications, at 45 percent.

TABLE 5.5
Educational Level at T1 (%)

	Denmark	Germany	Israel	N'lands	Sweden	US
Pre-primary	0.2	16.1	0.9	0.0	0.7	0.0
Primary	6.9	71.0	5.2	14.4	25.0	5.2
Lower secondary	38.1	8.0	52.3	53.5	16.5	6.0
Upper secondary	36.8	1.7	31.2	26.2	36.3	42.1
Tertiary #1 stage	10.1	2.0	3.1	0.0	13.0	28.3
Tertiary #2 stage	6.7	0.0	5.2	5.2	7.2	13.2
Tertiary #3 stage	1.1	0.0	2.1	0.7	0.4	3.7
Not definable	0.2	1.2	0.0	0.0	0.9	1.4
Total	100	100	100	100	100	100
% Omit	0	0	0	0.7	14.7	0

The distribution of household types for the six cohorts is shown in Table 5.6. Subjects were asked whether they lived alone, with a partner, with a partner and children, only with children, with no other person, or with "others." The largest share of subjects who lived alone (19.6%) was found in the Danish cohort, followed by those in the cohorts from Sweden, Germany, the United States, and the Netherlands; the smallest share was in the cohort from Israel, at only 2.2 percent. The largest proportion of subjects living only with a partner was found in the German cohort (45%). In the cohorts from Denmark, Israel, the Netherlands, Sweden, and the United States, most subjects lived with a partner and children. The largest proportion of those who lived only with children were found in the cohorts from Sweden and the United States, at approximately seven percent.

TABLE 5.6
Household Composition at T1 (%)

	Denmark	Germany	Israel	N'lands	Sweden	US
Living alone	19.7	14.7	2.2	8.2	15.9	12.8
Living with partner only	34.8	45.0	8.9	27.9	34.5	17.6
Living with partner and children	36.5	34.1	66.1	55.4	41.6	40.3
Living with children only	5.7	2.7	2.5	1.4	7.1	7.4
Other	3.4	3.5	20.3	7.0	0.9	21.9
Total	100	100	100	100	100	100
% Omit	0.2	2.0	3.4	0.2	0.9	0.0

Work Characteristics

This section describes the cohorts on the basis of selected work characteristics. Table 5.7 shows how many hours per week the members of the various cohorts worked. The proportion of subjects who worked up to 19 hours per week was the highest, by far, in the cohort from the Netherlands, at 14 percent. The proportion of subjects who had a full-time job (35 or more working hours per week) was highest in the cohort from Israel, at 92 percent, followed by the cohorts from the United States (87%) and Germany (86%).

Table 5.8 shows the results for the Physical Job Demands Scale. That scale has a range of values from 1 (high demands) to 4 (low demands), and is based on three questions: working in a twisted position, working in the same position for a long time, and lifting heavy objects. Since the mean for all countries was 2.0 or less, it may be assumed that the subjects overall had relatively high physical demands in the workplace.

TABLE 5.7
Working Hours per Week at T1 (%)

	Denmark	Germany	Israel	N'lands	Sweden	US
Up to 19 hrs	1.4	2.0	1.2	13.9	3.6	1.1
20-34 hrs	18.4	11.6	6.5	14.8	21.5	12.0
35 hrs and more	80.2	86.4	92.2	71.3	74.9	86.9
Total	100	100	100	100	100	100
% Omit	0.9	2.9	1.8	3.7	2.6	1.9

TABLE 5.8
Physical Job Demands at T1

	Denmark	Germany	Israel	N'lands	Sweden	US
Mean	1.9	1.7	1.9	1.7	1.7	2.0
Std. Dev.	0.7	0.5	0.5	0.6	0.6	0.7
% Omit	0.5	2.0	0.9	2.8	2.8	1.4

Note: Range 1 to 4 (1: high demands; 4: low demands)

Subjective Health Status

The condition of the subjects' health was assessed by means of subjective self-examinations. These included a dorsopathy-based ADL to measure back function (Hannover ADL), a numerical ratings scale to measure the intensity of pain, and scales for measuring quality of life.

The results for the mental health scale, which has a range of values from 0 (greatest possible limitation) to 100 (no limitation) are presented in Table 5.9. With a mean score of 69 and 68, the subjects in the Dutch and Danish cohorts had the fewest limitations with regard to mental health. The subjects in the Swedish cohort also gave quite positive responses, with a mean score of 61. On the other hand, the German subjects, with a mean score of 48, and the subjects from Israel, with a mean score of 32, reported considerable limitations.

TABLE 5.9
Mental Health at T1

	Denmark	Germany	Israel	N'lands	Sweden	US
Mean	67.6	48.1	32.0	69.1	61.3	*
Std. Dev.	22.7	19.6	17.5	17.6	23.6	*
% Omit	0.5	6.6	0.9	1.4	0.9	*

Note: Range 0 to 100; a higher score means better mental health
* data missing

Table 5.10 shows the pain intensity results for the six cohorts, which were collected on a scale from 1 ("hardly any pain") to 10 ("unbearable pain"). With a mean value of 6.5, the German subjects reported the highest intensity of pain, followed by those from Israel, with a mean score of 6.3. In the cohorts from the Netherlands, Sweden, and the United States, the means were approximately the same at 5.8 or 5.9; with a mean score of 5.6, the Danish subjects reported the lowest intensity of pain among those questioned.

TABLE 5.10
Pain Intensity at T1

	Denmark	Germany	Israel	N'lands	Sweden	US
Mean	5.6	6.5	6.3	5.8	5.9	5.9
Std. Dev.	2.3	2.0	2.2	2.2	2.2	2.8
% Omit	0.5	1.0	0.3	0.9	3.7	0.6

Note: The Von Korff pain intensity scale ranges from 0 to 10. 0: no pain; 10: "pain as bad as it could be." In the WIR Project a scale from 1 to 10 was used.

The values for the Hannover ADL Scale are brought together in Table 5.11. This scale collects current limitations of functions on the basis of back pain using 12 items of daily use. The range of values on the scale is 0 (the greatest possible limitation) to 100 (no limitations). A score of 70 points is deemed to be clinically relevant. If one views the mean values of the six cohorts, it turns out that all of them were considerably less than 70; therefore, it appears that virtually all of the subjects in the study had functional limitations which were both considerable and deserving of treatment. Those in the Israeli cohort were especially affected, with a mean value of 34.

TABLE 5.11
Back Function (Hannover ADL) at T1

	Denmark	Germany	Israel	N'lands	Sweden	US
Mean	48.4	47.1	34.0	47.8	53.1	51.6
Std. Dev.	24.4	20.1	21.6	22.2	20.5	25.8
% Omit	12.6	1.5	2.8	0.2	2.2	0.4

Note: Range 0 to 100; a higher score means a better back function

Subjective Work Prognosis

The subjective self-assessment of future employment is of particular interest as a predictor for returning to work because an individual's ideas concerning his or her future life plans play an important part in these assessments. For this reason, the subjects were asked how their situation would develop in the long term and what ideas they had about their future work situation.

As can be seen in Table 5.12, there were considerable differences among the six cohorts. Most notable in a positive sense was the Dutch cohort. Thus, approximately 75 percent of the subjects from the Netherlands

TABLE 5.12
Work Prognosis, Long-Term at T1 (%)

	Denmark	Germany	Israel	N'lands	Sweden	US
Able to work w/in usual sphere	25.1	37.5	27.9	74.8	60.5	56.7
Able to work, not w/in usual sphere	56.2	30.6	58.4	23.5	23.2	29.8
Not able to work again	18.7	31.9	13.8	1.7	16.2	13.5
Total	100	100	100	100	100	100
% Omit	18.8	7.6	17.7	15.5	23.4	8.5

were of the opinion that they would be able to return to their old workplaces within the foreseeable future; 24 percent counted on returning to work in some other workplace situation, and only two percent believed that they would not be able to work again. The subjects from Sweden and the United States had a similar predominantly positive attitude. The least favorable prognosis was among the German subjects, where approximately one-third were of the opinion that they would not be able to work again.

Non-response Analysis

This section analyzes the drop-out rate for the subjects from the various countries involved in the Project. Table 5.13 shows the cohort sizes for the individual countries at the times the data were collected. The proportions of responders are also given in relation to T1 and T2. The numbers and percentages of participants who responded on all three occasions when data were collected are given in the last lines of the table.

TABLE 5.13
Cohort Size and Non-Response Rates at T1, T2, T3

	Denmark	Germany	Israel	N'lands	Sweden	US
T1 Cohort size	565	410	327	427	539	484
T2 Responders: cohort size	494	295	289	392	455	413
in %, basis T1	87.4	72.0	88.4	91.8	84.4	85.3
T3 Responders: cohort size	441	257	265	370	396	377
in %, basis T2	89.3	87.1	91.7	94.4	87.0	91.3
in %, basis T1	78.1	62.6	81.0	86.7	73.5	77.9
Responders at all three time points: cohort size	441	245	265	370	382	377
in %, basis T1	78.1	59.7	81.0	86.7	84.0	77.9

The percentage of original cohort members who were no longer taking part at the end of the study varied from 13.3 percent in the Netherlands to 37.4 percent in Germany. The greatest loss in the cohorts for all countries occurred between T1 and T2. At both T2 and T3, the difference in the rates of participation are highly significant (χ^2 - tests, $p < .0001$) and may be due in part to the different survey techniques used. For example, in Germany, surveys were conducted only by mail, while in the Netherlands, telephone interviews were also conducted as well (cf. Chapter 4).

In order to analyze the drop-out mechanism and compare the responders with the non-responders in each country at T2 and T3, multiple logistic regressions with a significance level of 0.05 were carried out, using the variables age, gender, education, pain, back function (Hannover ADL), and working status at T2. The goodness of fit for the regressions is high, varying from 72 percent to 95 percent. The results of this analysis are presented in Table 5.14.

Gender had an influence on willingness to participate at T2 for the Danish and Swedish cohorts, with more women responding in both countries. A higher age of the subjects had a positive influence on response behavior only in the Swedish cohort. It is possible to trace a connection between a higher level of education and more willingness to participate for the Israeli cohort. In the American cohort, responders had less pain than non-responders. At T3, older persons responded significantly more often in both the German and the Swedish cohorts. In the Danish and the American cohorts, more women took part than men; in the Israeli cohort, less women participated than men.

Comparison with Working Population

This section compares the data from the national studies with the results of the Labour Force Survey 1997 and analogous data from Israel, with regard to age, gender, education, and household type (ILO, 1999).

The concepts and definitions used in the Labour Force Survey are those contained in the Recommendation of the 13th International Conference of Labour Statisticians, convened in 1982 by the International Labour Organization (ILO guidelines). The definitions given below are applied in accordance with the ILO guidelines. All these definitions apply to persons aged 15 years and over, living in private households.

Persons in employment are those who did any work for pay or profit during the reference week, or were not working but had jobs from which they were temporarily absent. Family workers are also included. Unemployed persons are those who, during the reference week, had no employment, were available to start work within the next two weeks, and had actively sought employment at some time during the previous four weeks. Unemployed persons also include those who had no employment and had already found a job to start later. Duration of unemployment is defined as follows: the duration of searching for a job, or the length of the period since the last job was held (if this period is shorter than the duration of

TABLE 5.14
Results of Drop-out Analysis at T2 and T3

	Denmark	Germany	Israel	N'lands	Sweden	US
Respondent at analysis T2						
Age					Older persons	
Gender	More women					
Educational level			Higher education			
Pain intensity (T1)						Less pain
Back function (T1)						
Respondent at analysis T3						
Age		Older persons			Older persons	
Gender	More women		Less women			More women
Educational level						
Pain intensity (T2)						
Back function (T2)						
Work status (T2)						

searching for a job). The labor force is defined as the sum of persons in employment and unemployed persons. Inactive persons are those who are not classified as persons in employment or as unemployed persons. Activity rates represent the labor force as a percentage of the working age population.

If the age structure of the cohorts in this project is compared with the Labour Force reference values (Table 5.15), the cohorts from all six countries show a greater proportion in the older-age groups. This effect is especially noticeable in the German cohort.

With respect to gender (Table 5.16), the cohorts from Germany, Israel, and the Netherlands have a higher proportion of men than in the Labour Force, while in the cohorts from Denmark and Sweden the gender proportions are reversed relative to Labour Force, with more women than men.

Comparing the distribution of educational levels for the cohorts in this project to the results from the Labour Force Survey (Table 5.17), a definite tendency toward the lowest educational level is apparent—most noticeably in the Dutch cohort and, especially, in the German cohort.

With regard to household types (Table 5.18), it is clear that the type "2 adults & kids" is represented much more frequently in the cohorts in this project than in the Labour Force data, while the proportion of singles households is clearly lower than in that survey.

Table 5.19 shows the comparison of working hours for the subjects in this project with the ILO reference data (KILM). The composition of the working population in this project is not out of range compared to the data sets the ILO has for the respective national composition of the working population.

In summary, the cohorts in this project often differ considerably in their structure from the Labour Force in the various countries. The reason for this is most likely the work incapacity of the subjects due to the design of the Project.

Comparability of Cohorts

A so-called cluster analysis was carried out for particular variables in order to make it possible to comment on the comparability of the cohorts in relation to work characteristics and subjective health status. This is a statistical procedure designed to bring together into one group or cluster the cohorts which are similar with regard to variables of interest. For this purpose, degrees of difference between the median values of the variables were calculated and cohorts with similar values were agglomerated.

TABLE 5.15

Age Distribution in Cohorts at T1 and in Labour Force (1997) (%)

	Denmark		Germany		Israel		Netherlands		Sweden	
	ISSA Cohort	Labour force	ISSA Cohort	Labour force	ISSA Cohort	Labour force	ISSA Cohort	Labour force	ISSA Cohort	Labour force
15-19 years	0.4	8.4	0.2	3.6	0.0	6.0	0.0	6.0	0.0	2.1
20-29 years	18.9	23.7	3.2	20.3	21.2	23.8	15.2	25.3	8.7	20.8
30-39 years	27.3	28.4	13.4	29.5	32.8	27.6	32.8	29.0	27.1	26.6
40-49 years	29.9	25.6	21.8	25.7	28.5	27.2	34.2	25.2	27.9	27.0
50-59 years	23.5	13.9	61.4	20.9	17.5	15.4	17.8	14.5	36.3	23.5
Total	100	100	100	100	100	100	100	100	100	100

TABLE 5.16

Gender Distribution in Cohorts at T1 and in Labour Force (1997) (%)

	Denmark		Germany		Israel		Netherlands		Sweden	
	ISSA Cohort	Labour force	ISSA Cohort	Labour force	ISSA Cohort	Labour force	ISSA Cohort	Labour force	ISSA Cohort	Labour force
Male	46.4	54.0	64.1	56.7	74.0	56.6	61.4	57.9	41.5	52.6
Female	53.6	46.0	35.9	43.3	26.0	43.4	38.6	42.1	58.5	47.4
Total	100	100	100	100	100	100	100	100	100	100

TABLE 5.17

Educational Level in Cohorts at T1 and in Labour Force (1997) (%)

| | Denmark | | Germany | | Netherlands | | Sweden | |
	ISSA Cohort	Labour force	ISSA Cohort	Labour force	ISSA Cohort	Labour force	ISSA Cohort	Labour force
Third level education	17.9	28.7	2.0	25.3	5.9	27.3	18.0	28.5
Upper secondary level	36.8	54.0	1.7	56.8	26.0	44.3	31.4	49.7
< Upper secondary	45.1	17.3	95.1	14.0	67.4	28.1	35.8	21.4
No answer	0.2	0.0	1.2	3.8	0.7	0.3	14.9	0.4
Total	100	100	100	100	100	100	100	100

TABLE 5.18

Household Types in Cohorts at T1 and in Labour Force (1997) (%)

	Germany		Israel		Netherlands	
	ISSA Cohort	Labour force	ISSA Cohort	Labour force	ISSA Cohort	Labour force
Living alone	14.7	34.8	2.2	17.1	8.2	31.7
Living with partner only	45.0	43.2	8.9	31.9	27.9	44.3
Living with partner and children	34.1	15.0	66.1	32.4	55.4	17.9
Living with children only	2.7	2.3	2.5	2.9	1.4	1.8
Other	3.5	4.7	20.3	15.7	7.0	4.3
Total	100	100	100	100	100	100

TABLE 5.19

Working Hours per Week in Cohorts at T1 and in Labour Force (1997) (%)

	Denmark		Germany		N'lands		Sweden		US	
	ISSA	KILM	ISSA	KILM	ISSA	KILM	ISSA	KILM	ISSA	KILM
% Part-time	19.8	17.1	13.6	14.9	28.7	29.1	25.1	14.2	13.1	13.2
% Full-time	80.2	82.9	86.4	85.1	71.3	70.9	74.9	85.8	86.9	86.8
Total	100	100	100	100	100	100	100	100	100	100

The results of the cluster analysis are summarized in Table 5.20. For example, for the "age" variable, subjects from Denmark, the Netherlands, and Israel form cluster 1; cluster 2 covers subjects from Sweden and the United States; and cluster 3 consists of subjects from Germany alone.

TABLE 5.20
Outcomes of Cluster Analysis

Variable	Denmark	Germany	Israel	N'lands	Sweden	US
Age	I	III	I	I	II	II
Physical job demands	II	I	II	I	I	III
Mental health	I	III	IV	I	II	I
Pain intensity	I	II	II	I	I	I
Back function	II	II	III	II	I	I

To obtain an overview of how often the country cohorts are similar with respect to the variables shown above, Table 5.21 presents the number of times allocations were made to the same cluster.

TABLE 5.21
Similarities of Cohorts, T1

	Denmark	Germany	Israel	N'lands	Sweden	US
Denmark		1	2	4	1	2
Germany	1		1	2	1	0
Israel	2	1		1	0	0
N'lands	4	2	1		2	2
Sweden	1	1	0	2		3
US	2	0	0	2	3	

Of the five possible identical allocations, the country-couples of Denmark-Netherlands and Sweden-United States have the highest number of matches, at four and three, respectively. Least similar according to this analysis were Germany-United States, Israel-Sweden, and Israel-United States, with no matches.

Summary and Conclusions

If one examines the results for the socio-demographic variables, the German cohort is particularly notable for its age span and low educational level. The reason for this is that the target population in Germany was made up of members of two statutory health insurance schemes which are focused on an older age group, and especially on a distinctively working class group ("blue collar workers"). The American cohort had by far the highest educational level in comparison to the other countries, which is probably also due to certain selection effects. Also notable was the sometimes very different gender distribution in the six countries.

Looking at the results of the cluster analysis, it can be concluded further that some countries show quite some similarities in the characteristics of their cohorts. The best examples of these cohort similarities are those from the Netherlands and Denmark, and from Sweden and the United States. Some other cohort pairs had no similarities at all.

Considering these differences among the cohorts, it is sensible for further analyses to take account of some baseline variables, such as age, gender, education, working hours, back function, and subjective work prognosis, in order to be able to manage the various baseline conditions. Furthermore, in comparing the results of the cohorts one has to be aware of smaller and larger differences among the cohorts.

Reference

ILO (1999). *Key Indicators of the Labour Market.* Geneva: International Labour Office.

6

Work Status and Benefit Status

Theo J. Veerman

One of the main questions sought to be addressed in the WIR Project was what happens in the long run to workers who receive sickness and disability benefits after a period of work incapacity of three months—that is, two years after the onset of sickness or injury. Do they go back to work? Are they off or on the benefit rolls? This chapter describes the national cohorts in terms of outcomes—work status and benefit status—two years after the onset of work incapacity and receipt of benefits. It also relates these outcomes to some basic demographic and health characteristics, as well as to some characteristics of the subjects' former job. These outcomes, especially work status, are related to medical interventions in Chapter 7 and to vocational and other non-medical interventions in Chapter 8. In Chapter 9, the outcomes from the studies are described in more detail in terms of work status.

The first section of this chapter describes work and benefit status after two years, as well as work resumption and benefit patterns in the preceding period. The second section is devoted to work status after two years in relation to some demographic, health, and work characteristics. As this chapter covers the whole two-year observation period, from T1 to T3, the data described are from those respondents who participated in all three measurements.

Work Status and Benefit Status after One and Two Years

Work Status

There were considerable differences among the cohorts in terms of work status, both after one year and after two years. Table 6.1 gives the percentages of "resumers" at these two points in time. Resumers are those subjects who were working at the time of the second (T2) and third (T3) measurement (one and two years after work incapacity), irrespective of the moment of work resumption; subjects who may have resumed work during this period, but stopped working again for whatever reason, are not counted as "resumers."

Work resumption at T3 (two years after work incapacity) ranged from 35 percent in the German cohort to 72 percent in the Dutch cohort. In some cohorts, the full percentage of resumers was reached after one year. Thus, there was no net gain of resumers during the second year, and even some loss, for the cohorts from Germany, the Netherlands, and the United States. There was, however, a net increase in work resumption rates during the second year for the cohorts from Denmark, Israel, and Sweden.

The resumption rates as reported in Table 6.1, as well as the differences in these rates among the six cohorts, should be interpreted with care. As explained in Chapter 5, the cohorts differed in several important respects, such as demographic composition, which may influence resumption rates; indeed, as shown in the next section of this chapter, they seem to do so.

TABLE 6.1
Work Status at T2 and T3 (% of cohort working)

	Denmark	Germany	Israel	N'lands	Sweden	US
Working at T2 (1 year after onset of work incapacity)	32	41	49	73	53	63
Working at T3 (2 years after onset of work incapacity)	40	35	60	72	63	62
Correlation between work status at T2 and T3	.60	.69	.47	.57	.50	.64

As shown also in Table 6.1, there was considerable correlation between work status at T2 and T3, meaning that work resumption after two years was predicted well by resumption after one year. In other words, work resumption (or lack of it) is a rather static process; resumers after one year have a good chance of still working after two years, and non-resumers after one year tend not to work after two years either. The implication is that whatever happens toward resumption or non-resumption happens largely in the first year, with the second year adding only marginal improvement. This can be shown also by discerning four patterns of work resumption: continuous working, those who worked at T2 and still worked at T3; late resumers, those who did not work yet at T2, but who worked at T3; relapse, those working at T2 but not working at T3; and non-resumers, those neither working at T2 nor at T3. Note that these patterns are based on work status at two distinct points in time. Therefore, subjects not working at T2 or T3 may have worked for some time during the first or second year, but may then have relapsed to a non-working status by T2 or T3.

The distribution of these work resumption patterns for all cohorts is shown in Table 6.2. The vast majority of subjects followed either the pattern of continuous resumption or the pattern of continuous non-resumption.

TABLE 6.2
Work Resumption Patterns (% of cohort)

	Denmark	Germany	Israel	N'lands	Sweden	US
Continuous resumers: Working T2 and T3	26	31	41	64	50	54
Late resumers: Not working T2, working T3	14	5	19	8	14	8
Relapse: Working T2, not working T3	5	10	8	9	9	9
Non-resumers: Not working T2 and T3	55	54	32	19	27	29
Total	100	100	100	100	100	100

Benefit Status

Seen from an economic perspective, benefit status is a relevant outcome quite apart from work status. The cohorts were selected from workers covered by sickness benefit schemes who were receiving benefits three months after the onset of work incapacity. What was their benefit status one and two years after work incapacity? Due to differences between national insurance schemes, benefit status may or may not be independent of work status. In some countries, employees who resume work may continue to receive additional sickness, disability, or work injury benefits; on the other hand, non-resumers may no longer be on the benefit rolls. Unfortunately, no data on benefit status was obtained for the German cohort. For the other cohorts, benefit status is described in Tables 6.3 through 6.5.

Table 6.3 presents the benefit status (percentage of cohort members receiving benefit) for all cohorts.

TABLE 6.3
Benefit Status: Subjects Receiving Sickness, Disability, or Work Injury Benefit at T2 and T3 (%)

	Denmark	Germany	Israel	N'lands	Sweden	US
Receiving benefit at T2	54	*	16	29	39	10
Receiving benefit at T3	51	*	14	32	37	10

* data missing

Receipt of sickness-related benefits varied widely among the cohorts, ranging from 10 percent in the American cohort to over 50 percent in the Danish cohort (both at one and two years after work incapacity). Already from these figures, compared to the work resumption figures from Table 6.1, it can be seen that work and receipt of benefits are not mutually exclusive. In some cohorts, the percentages of persons working and receiving benefits add up to over 100 percent, meaning that work and benefits must coincide in some cases; in others, they add up to under 100 percent, meaning that not all non-resumers still are on the benefit rolls. This is reflected in Tables 6.4 and 6.5, respectively.

TABLE 6.4

Combination of Work and Benefits: Working Respondents Receiving (Additional) Sickness, Disability, or Work Injury Benefits (%)

	Denmark	Germany	Israel	N'lands	Sweden	US
Working with benefit, T2	19	*	6	14	23	3
Working with benefit, T3	15	*	6	19	26	4

* data missing

In the European cohorts, receipt of benefits in combination with work was quite common. This is in line with the benefit schemes in those countries, which allow for several types and degrees of partial benefits. In the Israeli and the American cohorts, a combination of work and receipt of benefits was rare, which reflects the "all or nothing" character of the benefit schemes in those countries.

Non-resumers may receive various types of benefits. If still sick, they may receive sickness, disability, or work injury benefits. Otherwise, possibly they are unemployed and therefore may receive unemployment benefits or social assistance. In some countries, several benefits may be provided at the same time. Table 6.5 describes the benefit status at T3 of the non-working respondents in each cohort.

There were huge differences among the cohorts in benefit status for non-workers at T3. In the United States and Israel, the majority of these subjects received none of the benefits mentioned. In Denmark, Sweden, and the Netherlands, those not working at T3 usually received sickness or disability benefits. In the Netherlands, a substantial number of non-resumers received either unemployment benefits or a combination of benefits, usually a combination of partial disability and partial unemployment benefits.

TABLE 6.5
Non-Resumers at T3: Benefit Status (%)

	Denmark	Germany	Israel	N'lands	Sweden	US
Sickness, disability, injury benefit only	74	*	25	52	71	18
Unemployment benefit only	12	*	11	19	9	4
Social assistance only	3	*	12	0	0	3
Various combinations of benefits	0	*	1	17	4	1
No benefit receipt	11	*	51	13	17	73
Total	100		100	100	100	100

* data missing

The differences in coverage of benefit schemes is also reflected in the reported income development of non-resumers at T3, as set out in Table 6.6.

TABLE 6.6
Development of Total Personal Net Income from T0 to T3,
in Non-Workers at T3 (%)

	Denmark	Germany	Israel	N'lands	Sweden	US
Increase	17	2	10	21	24	11
No change	13	50	7	12	15	6
Up to 30% decrease	42	12	27	47	32	19
>30% decrease	28	36	56	20	29	64
Total	100	100	100	100	100	100

In the American and Israeli cohorts, more than half of the non-working respondents at T3 reported a drop in personal income of over 30 percent, compared to their income before work incapacity. In the European cohorts, the income loss was generally much smaller—drops of over 30 percent were reported by only one-fifth to one-third of the non-workers—and an increase in income was quite common, especially in the Swedish and Dutch cohorts.

Work Status at T3 and Demographic, Health, and Job Characteristics

This section focuses on some background factors related to work status at two years after the onset of work incapacity. Are there marked differences in work resumption relative to demographic, health, and (former) job characteristics? A first overview of these results is presented in Table 6.7, which reports the significance of associations between work status at T3 and selected variables as measured at T1.

TABLE 6.7

Significance of Associations between Work Status at T3 (Working/Not Working) and Selected Demographic, Health, and (Former) Job Characteristics as Measured at T1

	Denmark	Germany	Israel	N'lands	Sweden	US
Demographic characteristics						
Age	xx	xxx	—	xxx	xxx	x
Gender	xxx	—	—	xxx	—	—
Educational level	xx	—	xxx	xxx	xx	—
Household composition	x	x	—	x	xx	—
Mother language (native/other)	x	—	—	—	—	—
Nationality (native/foreign)	x	—	—	—	—	—
Health indicators						
Pain intensity	xxx	xxx	xxx	xxx	xxx	xxx
Back function	xxx	—	x	xxx	xx	xxx

TABLE 6.7 *(Cont'd)*

	Denmark	Germany	Israel	N'lands	Sweden	US
Job characteristics						
Working hours per week	—	—	—	xx	—	—
Physical job demands	—	—	—	xx	xxx	xxx
Job strain	xxx	—	—	xxx	xx	—

Legend: xxx : p ≤ .001   xx : p ≤ .01   x : p ≤ .05   — : not significant

Most of the characteristics included in Table 6.7 show some association with work status at T3, at least in some countries. The only characteristic having a highly significant association in all cohorts is pain intensity (as expressed in the T1 interviews). In a majority of the six cohorts, back function capacity (ADL score), age, educational level, and household composition were also related to final work status. Language, nationality, and weekly working hours were each related to work status in only one of the cohorts.

The directions of these associations—excluding language, nationality, and working hours, which hardly show any relationship with work status—are shown in Tables 6.8 through 6.10.

Table 6.8 gives the work resumption rates at T3 by selected demographic characteristics. Some patterns in the association between demographics and work status can be seen in all, or most, of the cohorts. These are:

Age: in all cohorts, the oldest group (aged 55 and over) had less chance of working at T3; in several cohorts, this was also the case for the next-oldest group (ages 45-54). Generally, the highest resumption rates were found not in the youngest, but in the next-youngest groups (ages 25-44).

Gender: in most cohorts, females had a lower resumption rate than males.

Educational level: a low educational level (lower secondary level or below) was associated regularly with lower resumption rates.

Household composition: those living alone had a consistently lower-than-average resumption rate. For other types of household composition, the association with work status was less consistent over the cohorts.

It should be noted that these associations are not mutually independent. For example, age, lower educational level, and household composition often will be interconnected.

TABLE 6.8
Demographic Characteristics and Respondents Working at T3 (%)

	Denmark	Germany	Israel	N'lands	Sweden	US
All respondents	40	35	60	72	63	63
Age (at onset of work incapacity)						
≤24 years	52	.	63	58	.	64
25-34 years	47	23	69	82	72	68
35-44 years	44	55	60	77	72	67
45-54 years	36	48	58	57	62	61
≥55 years	18	17	35	68	47	38
Gender						
Male	49	33	61	79	62	65
Female	33	38	57	60	63	60
Educational level completed						
≤ lower secondary (levels 0-2)	31	34	51	68	54	51
Upper secondary (level 3)	45	.	75	84	69	60
≥ Tertiary (levels 4-6)	49	.	64	79	73	67
Household composition						
Living alone	31	13	.	50	55	53
Living with partner only	35	35	58	78	54	66
Living with partner and children	44	41	57	72	73	66
Living with children only	54	.	.	.	61	67
Other	57	.	74	60	.	55

. less than 10 observations

All associations between health indicators (again, as at T1) and work status at T3 were consistently linear in all cohorts: the less pain and the better the functional capacity, the higher the resumption rates. Nevertheless, there were marked differences among the cohorts as to the resumption rates within equal levels of pain intensity and functional capacity. In some countries, the resumption rate of subjects with severe pain and low functional capacity at onset (T1) was twice that of those in other countries.

TABLE 6.9
Health Indicators (at T1) and Respondents Working at T3 (%)

	Denmark	Germany	Israel	N'lands	Sweden	US
All respondents	40	35	60	72	63	63
Pain intensity						
None (1)	79	.	.	88	.	92
Mild (2-4)	63	70	86	84	80	79
Moderate (5-7)	29	33	58	74	60	55
Severe (8-10)	27	25	51	54	45	47
Back function (Hannover ADL)						
Low (0-40)	28	31	56	59	56	42
Moderate (41-70)	36	39	67	76	61	64
Good (71-100)	59	39	87	90	76	84

. less than 10 observations

In all cohorts, the relationship between two job characteristics (job demands and job strain) and work resumption at T3 was consistent in its direction—although not always statistically significant. (See Table 6.7.) As to physical job demands, the lower these demands were, the higher were the resumption rates. As to job strain (defined as imbalance between socio-psychological demands and control) the association was also consistent: the lowest job strain was related to the highest resumption rates in all cohorts, and high job strain was related to the lowest resumption rates.

TABLE 6.10
Job Characteristics and Respondents Working at T3 (%)

	Denmark	Germany	Israel	N'lands	Sweden	US
All respondents	40	35	60	72	63	63
Physical job demands						
Low (≥7)	46	38	68	82	78	73
Moderate (4-6)	40	35	60	74	66	60
High (≤4)	33	34	53	65	51	50
Job strain						
Low (<1)	48	39	64	82	72	66
Moderate (1 - 1.3)	33	34	57	65	58	60
High (>1.3)	29	32	57	39	52	51

Conclusions

This chapter covers the main outcomes of the Project in terms of work resumption and benefit status, as well as associations between work status and some basic demographic, health, and (former) job characteristics. Conclusions on benefit status do not include the German cohort, for which no data on benefit status are available.

In terms of work resumption, there were considerable differences among the six cohorts. At T2 (one year after onset of the work incapacity), work resumption rates varied from 32 percent in the Danish cohort to 73 percent in the Dutch cohort. At T3 (two years after onset), they varied from 35 percent in the German cohort to 72 percent in the Dutch cohort. In all cohorts, the pattern of resumption or non-resumption turned out to be rather stable; the vast majority (ranging from 73% to 85%) was either working both at T2 or T3, or was not working at T2 or at T3. Obviously, the "final" T3 outcome in terms of work resumption usually was reached already within the first year of observation, with the second year yielding little, if any, increase in work resumption. This is paralleled by a finding in Chapter 8 that the increase of back function capacities (ADL score) within the cohorts, if any, was reached usually also within the first year, with hardly any further net improvement in the second year.

In terms of benefit status, the percentage of cohort members receiving sickness, work injury, or disability benefits ranged from 10 percent

(United States, at both T2 and T3) to 54 percent and 51 percent (Denmark, at T2 and at T3).

Work resumption and receipt of benefits are often independent situations. On the one hand, in some cohorts—especially the Northwest-European ones (Sweden, Denmark, the Netherlands)—work resumption combined with receipt of benefits was quite common; in those cohorts, a combination of both was observed in one-quarter to one-fifth of work resumers. On the other hand, non-resumption does not imply that cohort members still are on the benefit rolls. For the Israeli and the American cohorts, a majority of non-resumers at T3 reported no income from any benefit. This finding was paralleled by findings on income development. A majority in the Israeli and American cohorts reported a drop in income of at least 30 percent (as compared to income before work incapacity); in the other cohorts, this was reported by between one-fifth and one-third of respondents.

Work resumption at T3 showed associations with a number of "baseline characteristics" as measured at T1, with several of these associations found in all, or nearly all, of the cohorts. Thus, the oldest age group (55 years and older), and, in several cohorts, the next-oldest (45-54 years), showed lower-than-average resumption rates, whereas higher-than-average rates were found usually not in the youngest, but in the "intermediate" ages (usually between 25 and 44 years). Subjects with the lowest educational levels consistently had the lowest work resumption rates, and those living alone consistently had lower-than-average work resumption rates. With respect to pain intensity and functional limitations measured at T1, those subjects with less pain and better back function consistently had the higher resumption rates. And with respect to physical job demands and the socio-psychological job strain of the subject's (former) job, the lower the job demands and job strain were, the higher were the resumption rates.

Despite the seemingly universal direction of these associations, there were some highly significant cross-national differences in work resumption rates within subgroups. Thus, even between the subgroups which had the lowest resumption rates within each of the cohorts, resumption rates varied widely: in the oldest age group (55 years and older), resumption rates varied from 17 percent in the German cohort to 68 percent in the Dutch cohort; within the lowest educated group, resumption rates varied from 31 percent (Denmark) to 68 percent (the Netherlands); among those living alone, resumption rates ranged from 13 percent (Germany) to 55 percent (Sweden); for respondents reporting severe back pain (at T1), resumption rates varied from 27 percent (Denmark) to 54 percent (the Netherlands), and in those reporting low functional abilities from 28 percent (Denmark) to 59 percent (the Netherlands).

Apart from these universalities, there were also some particularities, that is, associations which obviously were specific for one or a few cohorts. Thus, gender, nationality/mother language, and weekly working hours were associated with resumption rates in only one, or a few, of the cohorts. Similarly, household composition types other than living alone showed diverging patterns of resumption rates.

In summary, outcomes in terms of work resumption varied widely among the six cohorts. Even though some baseline variables were consistently related to resumption rates in all of the cohorts, those universalities do not account for the cross-national differences. Moreover, resumption rates varied considerably among cohorts within socio-demographic subgroups.

The interesting question now is whether cross-cohort differences in resumption rates can be ascribed to differences in the repertoire of interventions undertaken in the six cohorts. The next two chapters will consider this question relative to medical and to vocational and other non-medical interventions, respectively.

7

The Role of Medical Interventions

Tommy Hansson & Elisabeth Hansson

Introduction

As noted in Chapter 4, the WIR Project core research design required that all subjects included in a national cohort meet four sets of entry criteria relating to medical diagnosis, employment conditions, work incapacity, and demographics. The central medical diagnostic criterion was that work incapacity had to be caused primarily by low back pain, defined as pain between the lower edge of the 12th rib and the gluteal folds. Before discussing the role of medical interventions in the context of the national studies and return to work, a brief medical introduction to back problems is in order.

Back problems are among the most expensive health problems in the industrialized world (Spengler et al., 1986; Snook, 1988; Waddell, 1991; Frank et al., 1996; Nachemson & Jonsson, 2000). Back problems have been assessed repeatedly as the most expensive industrial injury, as well as the most expensive of all musculo-skeletal problems (Spengler et al., 1986; Abenhaim & Suissa, 1987; Shekelle et al., 1995). The reason back problems are so expensive is that they are the most common reason for work incapacity (Oleinick et al., 1998). The lifetime incidence of back problems has been found in numerous studies from many countries to be up to more than 80 percent (Frank et al., 1996). In most societies, back problems are the most common reason for physician appointments after the common cold (Linton et al., 1998; Rossignol et al., 1988; Nachemson, 1992).

In the majority of cases, back problems have a very good prognosis. Recovery from all symptoms occurs before 10-15 days in more than 50 percent of all cases, and for 80-90 percent within six weeks (Spitzer et al., 1987; Turner et al., 1998). In a minority of cases, the problem remains for an extended period of time and becomes chronic. Back problems are considered acute within the first few weeks, subacute between 6-12 weeks, and chronic when they last for longer than three months. Generally, the prognosis for the recovery of back problems is strongly time dependent. In contrast to many other health problems, the prognosis for back problems tends to deteriorate with time; that is, the longer the duration of the problem, the less likely is the chance for a complete recovery.

Another frequently used characteristic for recovery prognosis is whether a back problem is specific or non-specific. Back problems are called specific when their patho-physiology (the reason for the problem) is known, e.g. a symptomatic disc herniation in the lumbar spine. They are called non-specific when the cause of the pain is unknown. In acute back problems, a distinct patho-anatomic diagnosis can be found in less than 10 percent of all patients. In case of chronic problems—those with a duration of more than three months—specific diagnoses explaining the problem can be expected in around 30 percent of patients.

Returning to the question of costs, an almost exponential relation has been found between the duration of back problems and their costs. For example, in one comprehensive back study which included more than 10,000 subjects from a large industrial setting, 10 percent of the back problem cases accounted for almost 80 percent of the total costs for the entire group (Spengler et al., 1986). The longevity of the problem was the strongest predictor for high costs.

As a result of intensive worldwide research aimed at understanding the genesis of, as well as the most effective treatment for, back problems, there is a well accepted, and, to a great extent, evidence-based rationale for the treatment of back problem patients (Nachemson & Jonsson, 2000). However, the obvious shortcomings in being able to identify a specific patho-anatomical diagnoses in the majority of back sufferers have stimulated, and will continue to stimulate, numerous scientific trials of new diagnostic methods and new concepts for the treatment of these problems.

Since the early 1980s, more and more evidence has been gathered which indicates that work incapacity because of a back problem often has only a very loose relationship to its strict medical aspects, such as pain, dysfunction, etc. (Bergenudd & Nilsson, 1988; Bigos et al., 1991; Frymoyer, 1992; Greenough, 1993). The often questionable results of back treatment efforts might be explained to a considerable extent by the fact that the outcome of medical treatments usually has been judged through the non-medical measure of work incapacity.

This chapter begins by presenting the typical career of a back patient through the medical systems in the six countries that participated in the Project. It then explains the medical interventions followed in the study and describes health characteristics, such as back function, social function, vitality, mental and general health, pain intensity, and the history of the then-present back problems of the cohort members. It also presents the frequencies of all medical interventions received by the subjects in the different cohorts within 90 days (T1), one year (T2), and two years (T3). The effect of the separate medical interventions on the outcome measures working/not working are evaluated, as well as the effect of the medical interventions on health measures of back function, pain, and aspects of quality of life. Finally, this chapter analyzes the effect of the separate medical interventions on health measures and outcome measures simultaneously.

National Health Care Systems and the Back Patient

Differences in the health care systems can work as incentives or disincentives for the utilization of different medical interventions aimed at returning work incapacitated persons to work. Therefore, each national team in the Project was asked to describe a typical career of a work incapacitated back patient through their medical system. These typical back patient careers in the six different countries are presented below.

Denmark

In Denmark, a general practitioner (GP) usually certifies back patients for work incapacity. A certification by a GP or some other physician is needed on the fourth day. After two weeks of work incapacity, the certificate has to include the diagnosis. Patients receive either a full salary or compensation amounting to 100 percent of his or her full salary. Typically, a GP will treat a back patient within the first two weeks of the back pain episode. If there is no improvement, the GP may refer the patient for treatment to a specialist, usually a rheumatologist, or to a physiotherapist, back school, etc. Referrals to private specialists are rare. All examinations and treatments are free of charge, except for treatments by physiotherapists or chiropractors, where the patient has to pay part of the cost. All referrals for examinations or treatments have to be made by a physician. During the period of the national study, there were waiting lists; for example, the waiting time for a specialist and for back schools varied from three to eight weeks. Medication is covered only partially by the general health insurance. The patient's share varies between 25 to 50 percent of the costs of medication.

Germany

In Germany, the medical reason for work incapacity is certified only by specially contracted physicians. There is no deferred period; patients receive 100 percent reimbursement of their full salary from the first day of reported work incapacity. After six weeks, the reimbursement is reduced to 80 percent. Health insurance covers the majority of the costs for examinations and treatments. A smaller share, including a portion of the costs of medication, is paid by the patient. Back pain patients can be referred to a special back rehabilitation program. The cost for rehabilitation programs are covered either by health insurance or by special pension funds.

Israel

In Israel, all physicians are eligible to certify illness. Typically, the attending physician refers the patient to a specialist, who in turn is responsible for hospital referrals, rehabilitation programs, etc. There is a deferred period of one day before benefits are paid. The national health insurance covers the cost of most types of examinations, treatments, etc. The costs of medications are, to some extent, shared by the patient.

The Netherlands

In the Netherlands, the employee reports directly to the employer when back pain causes work incapacity. This report substitutes for certification by a physician. One to two weeks after the initial report, there is a required visit to an occupational physician who approves or disapproves the work incapacity. Wage compensation is 100 percent from the first day of reported back problems. The compensation period lasts for a maximum of one year. The general practitioner can refer the patient to a specialist, who in turn refers the patient to a hospital, if needed. Special back rehabilitation programs are relatively uncommon; however, a GP or a specialist can refer the patient to such a program if it is covered by the patient's health insurance or if authorized by the policy of the social security agency. In general, the cost of examinations and treatments are covered fully by public health insurance. The same is the case for medication. Referrals are needed from a physician for the different treatments. In general, health care providers are reimbursed according to the number of visits, treatments, examinations, etc.

Sweden

In Sweden, a medical certification is needed after seven days of work incapacity. All licensed physicians are entitled to certify the medical cause of work incapacity. There is a deferred period of one day for payment of benefits. The general health insurance reimburses the patient with 80 percent of his or her salary; labor agreements might cover additional income loss, up to 90 percent. The majority of back pain patients are treated by a GP. Referrals are made to specialists within hospitals, physiotherapists, etc. Private specialists provide primary care for only a minority of the patients. The general health insurance covers most of the costs for visits, examinations, treatments, etc. There is a high cost protection, meaning that health insurance covers all costs when the patient's share reaches a certain amount. There are waiting lists (a few weeks to several months) for certain planned examinations, e.g. MRI, visits to orthopedic specialists at hospitals, and back surgery. Most general practitioners, physiotherapists, and private specialists are paid per examination, up to a certain contracted level. Specialists within hospitals have a fixed monthly salary.

The United States

The medical system in the United States varies considerably among the different states. The states represented in the national study, California and New Jersey, are among the few with temporary work incapacity programs. Benefits from these programs vary to some extent between California and New Jersey. Benefits are paid in both programs after one week of work incapacity. A certification of the back problem is needed from the patient's physician for coverage. The compensation is 55 percent of the recipient's wage in California; 70 percent in New Jersey. In California, it is payable for a maximum of one year; in New Jersey, it is payable for six months. There are numerous different health insurances available, many of which are offered through the employer. It is the patient's responsibility to arrange his or her insurance plan. Financing of health care providers is based primarily on private health insurances for visits, examinations, treatments, etc.

Medical Interventions and their Providers

Before comparing the treatments and providers across the cohorts followed in the Project, a brief description of the main features of the treatments and therapies that may have been applied to the cohort members may be useful.

Caregivers

The majority of patients with low back pain turn primarily to general practitioners in case of work incapacity. In the United States, specialists are involved to a significant extent in the primary care of low back patients.

In the Netherlands, occupational physicians have a special role in the early primary care of back patients since they have to approve or disapprove the medical basis for otherwise self-reported work incapacity.

Individual physicians, irrespective of their specialties, are involved differently in the treatment of low back pain patients. Some emphasize special examination techniques while others practice manipulative techniques, injections, blockades, etc. Others restrict their involvement with back pain patients to an examination at every appointment, and add to those examinations various referrals when indicated, e.g. for X-ray, physiotherapy, etc. If surgery is required, orthopedic surgeons and, to some extent, neurosurgeons, are chiefly responsible.

Physiotherapists are involved in the treatment of the majority of patients with back problems in all the represented countries. Physiotherapy aims at prevention, examination, and treatment of pain and/or function disturbances. Physiotherapists have developed or adopted numerous treatment methods, techniques, or strategies. Examples include massage, traction, relaxation, aerobics, body awareness, heat/cool treatment, Mackenzie technique, and acupuncture.

The main objectives for chiropractors are examination, treatment, and prevention of pain and functional restrictions of the musculo-skeletal system. Chiropractors typically use special maneuvers when manipulating the spine. In several of the participating countries, the chiropractors practice outside coverage of the public health insurances. In the United States, chiropractors are a large professional group treating a considerable fraction of all back pain patients. In Sweden, chiropractors may apply for a license that enables them to work within the public health insurance system.

Other caregivers for patients with low back problems include osteopaths, homeopaths, naprapaths, etc. Most of them work outside the coverage of public health insurances.

Imaging Techniques

Three techniques are commonly used to image the painful back: X-ray, CT-scan (Computerized Tomography) and MRI-scan (Magnetic Resonance Imaging).

An X-ray examination reveals primarily the mineralized skeletal structures of the spine. Certain degenerative or age-related changes can be seen. Indirectly, an X-ray examination may reflect the status of some soft tissues, such as the intervertebral discs. However, it cannot make a disc herniation, for example, visible.

CT combines the use of X-rays and advanced computer technology. This technique allows, for example, a visualization of "slices" of the spine in pre-selected planes. Conflicts between the nerve roots in the spinal canal and surrounding structures, such as a disc herniation, can be detected with high precision.

With MRI, the human body, or part of the body, is placed in a strong magnetic field. The echoing properties of the examined structure are then turned into a detailed picture. In contrast to plain X-ray and CT, MRI does not involve the use of ionized radiation. In comparison to CT, MRI allows an even more detailed examination of the soft tissues, e.g. in the spinal canal.

Hospitalization, Surgery, and Bed Rest

After imaging the painful back, often one of the three following therapies is used: hospitalization, surgery and bed rest.

In case of acute intolerable pain, some patients with back problems might be hospitalized. Other reasons for hospitalization are special examinations or surgery. Within the studied age group, 18 to 59 years of age, the most common reason for back surgery is a disc herniation. Other reasons for back surgery in that age group are for conditions such as spinal stenosis, spondylolisthesis, and degenerative disc disorders.

Disc herniation of the lumbar spine is one of the most common specific causes of back pain, as well as one of the most frequent reasons for surgery of the spine. The natural course of the symptoms caused by a disc herniation of the lumbar spine is relatively well established. Typical symptoms associated with a disc herniation of the lumbar spine are pain localized to the lower part of the spine and the buttocks, and, in addition, sciatic pain radiating down one or sometimes both legs. Sciatic pain, or sciatica, is pain located, or radiating, along the sciatic nerve of the leg. A disc herniation of the lumbar spine is the most common cause of sciatic pain.

A considerable number of patients with acute sciatic pain improve from their problems within the first two to three months. Improvement is usually measured as a relief of pain. Others, however, do not improve. The pain, predominantly leg pain and sometimes other neurological problems, may warrant surgery. It is generally agreed that severe pain is the main indication for surgery. Nevertheless, there are reasons to believe that the indications for surgery vary somewhat among different countries. In Sweden, for example, conservative treatment of patients with disc herniation is the treatment of choice during the initial two to three months. Surgery is considered only when no, or only a slight, improvement occurs during this observation period. In other countries, a more aggressive surgical approach prevails. That usually means that surgery is undertaken much earlier and already in the course of the acute phase of symptoms. In the long run, after four to five years, it has been shown that the results are essentially the same irrespective of whether the patient had surgery or conservative treatments (Weber, 1994).

The surgical technique used for a lumbar disc herniation has become more and more non-traumatic. That means more or less immediate activation and rehabilitation of the patient is prescribed after surgery.

Bed rest has for many years been one of the most frequently suggested treatments for patients with back problems. The effect of bed rest has been questioned, however, more and more (Deyo et al., 1986). Today, recommendations to resume as normal activities as possible have replaced those of bed rest.

Treatments

There are numerous different techniques and treatments for diagnosing, treating, and rehabilitating patients with low back problems. The questionnaires used in the WIR Project aimed at including those most commonly used in the participating countries. An overview of ten therapies used regularly in the different countries is presented below.

Heat and cool: Heat-therapy is used frequently for patients with functional limitations because of pain and/or stiffness. It is usually combined with motion practices. Cooling of a tissue is used in the treatment of pain and inflammation.

TENS (Transcutaneous Electrical Nerve Stimulation): TENS is used for treatment of pain, and especially pain of a longer duration. Electrodes placed on the skin illicit stimulation of the underlying tissues through waves of different frequencies and intensities.

Ultrasonic technique: Ultrasonography uses high frequency electrical signals conveyed into a mechanical stimulation, which heats the tissue.

Acupuncture: Acupuncture has been practiced in China for centuries. The most common technique is to use thin needles inserted into the muscles and deeper located structures at special locations or points. These points are believed to be located along special regions of the body. Acupuncture is usually performed by physiotherapists, nurses, or specially educated therapists.

Massage: Massage is used for the treatment of pain and ache caused by sore or contracted muscles around the spine. Massage is practiced by physiotherapists, but other types of therapists might use it as well.

Manipulation and traction: Manipulation and traction are therapies usually practiced by chiropractors, physiotherapists, and other therapists. Manipulation involves the use of special maneuvers in order to resume a normal pattern of motion. Traction involves a distraction of the spine aimed at producing a load on the spine, but also to correct assumed minor dislocations of back structures.

Zone therapy: Zone therapy involves pressure or motions of the body part under treatment.

Medical baths: This type of treatment of back pain has a long tradition, especially in Germany. It is used also in other countries as one way of improving motion and fitness.

Physical therapy (strength, fitness, aerobics, etc): Physical therapy usually consists of programs performed individually, or as a group therapy, together with or under the supervision of a physiotherapist. The objective of the therapy is to improve the function of the entire locomotion apparatus, or parts of it. When treating a back patient, an important aspect of this type of therapy might be to make the patient understand that some of the motions and practices are important even if they are not completely pain-free. Different types of muscle-strengthening and motion-improving exercises are used. Experimental studies have demonstrated clearly a relation between the performance of motions and the relevant tissue's healing ability.

Special rehabilitation programs and/or school programs: Specially designed programs are used in many countries, not only to improve physical capacities but also to address psychosocial and psychological aspects of low back pain. The programs started initially in the United States and were aimed at a functional restoration of patients with long-lasting back problems. The first back school was introduced in Sweden during the 1970s. The school programs usually aim at improving the patient's knowledge and understanding of the spine's anatomy, function, and pain generating mechanisms.

Medication and Injections

Pain relieving substances, or analgetics, are prescribed frequently for all types of back pain. Anti-inflammatory drugs—NSAID—are used frequently for different types of back pain. Apart from their direct pain-reducing effect, these types of pharmaceuticals might, in addition, affect the inflammatory reaction believed to contribute to the pain caused by a disc herniation. Several types of injections and blocks are in use in the treatment of low back pain. The injected substances might vary from sterile water to different types of anesthetics and strong pain relievers.

Braces and Supports

A wide variety of braces are used for the treatment of back problems. Some braces aim at immobilizing the lumbar spine, while others are meant only to heat the tissues surrounding the spine or to protect the spine from overloading during, for example, heavy lifting. Back pain patients might use supports, such as crutches, sticks, or other walking aids, to facilitate walking and standing.

Back-related Health within the National Cohorts

This section compares the six cohorts as to several health indicators: back function, general health, social function, vitality, mental health, and pain intensity. The development in health is given throughout the study period, from T1 to T2 to T3. It must be emphasized that the analysis, in relation to the studied outcome measures of working/not working and pain, function, and other health measures, is focused primarily only on one or two dependent variables. The analyses have been performed solely on a group level within the six national cohorts.[1]

The participants in the studies were asked to describe their back function through the Hannover ADL back function instrument. As can be seen in Table 7.1, the function of the back improved considerably between T1 and T2 in four of the cohorts. The German and American cohorts were exceptions in this respect, showing no, or just slight, improvement. During the second year (T2 to T3), there were only marginal changes of the back functions in all of the cohorts.

TABLE 7.1
Back Function (Hannover ADL) (Mean) at T1, T2, and T3

	Denmark	Germany	Israel	N'lands	Sweden	US
T1	48	47	34	48	53	52
T2	56	48	42	65	59	52
T3	56	47	43	65	59	55

Note: Range: 0-100, a higher score means a better back function.

Changes of general health within the cohorts, as reflected by the General Health scale (range 0-100), were minimal in all of the cohorts. This indicated that the General Health Scale was either inappropriate or insensitive in reflecting any of the health changes caught by most other scales used in this study.

As shown in Table 7.2, the Social Function Scale reflected a substantial improvement in all the national cohorts between T1 and T2. For this scale, as for most other instruments, the changes found during the second year were, with few exceptions, just slightly positive or even negative.

TABLE 7.2
Social Function (Mean) at T1, T2, and T3

	Denmark	Germany	Israel	N'lands	Sweden	US
T1	81	57	36	61	59	47
T2	86	61	43	81	63	57
T3	85	57	37	82	63	63

Note: Range 0-100, a higher score means a better social function.

The pattern of the most significant improvement occurring during the first year held true for the Vitality Scale as well. The results are shown in Table 7.3. Denmark was an exception for which there is no apparent explanation. Data were missing from the United States.

TABLE 7.3
Vitality (Mean) at T1, T2, and T3

	Denmark	Germany	Israel	N'lands	Sweden	US
T1	46	31	29	57	39	*
T2	48	34	35	66	44	*
T3	55	34	35	65	45	*

Note: Range 0-100, a higher score means a better vitality.
* data missing

The changes recorded through the Mental Health Scale were consistent with the main trend, i.e. the significant improvement occurred between T1 and T2. These results are shown in Table 7.4.

TABLE 7.4
Mental Health (Mean) at T1, T2, and T3

	Denmark	Germany	Israel	N'lands	Sweden	US
T1	68	48	32	69	61	*
T2	73	52	38	77	64	*
T3	77	52	37	76	64	*

Note: Range 0-100, a higher score means better mental health.
* data missing

The von Korff instrument reflects pain intensity of back problems. As shown in Table 7.5, the Danish, Swedish, and Dutch cohorts reported a decrease in pain between T1 and T2. The German and American cohorts reported increased pain intensity, while it was constant in the Israeli cohort.

TABLE 7.5
Pain Intensity (Mean) at T1, T2, and T3

	Denmark	Germany	Israel	N'lands	Sweden	US
T1	5.6	6.5	6.3	5.8	5.9	5.9
T2	4.7	6.6	6.3	4.0	5.1	6.2
T3	4.7	6.1	5.9	4.0	5.1	5.1

Note: The von Korff pain intensity scale ranges from 0 to 10. 0: no pain, 10: "pain as bad as it could be." In this study a 1 to 10 scale was used.

Table 7.6 shows large differences among the cohorts in the reporting of the start of current back problems. The Israeli cohort included exceptionally large numbers of subjects with predominantly acute problems, i.e. with a duration of less than one week. This most probably reflected the fact that the Israeli cohort consisted of subjects having a work related injury.

TABLE 7.6
Response to the Question: When Did the Health Complaints Start? (%)

	Denmark	Germany	Israel	N'lands	Sweden	US
< 1 week before reporting sick	16	7	85	21	13	30
1 week – 1 year before reporting sick	31	23	9	47	32	36
> 1 year before reporting sick	53	70	6	31	55	34

Medical Interventions

A common finding in the six countries was that the great majority of all the different medical interventions measured in the study occurred predominantly within the first year. Visits, examinations, referrals, admittance, surgery, etc. tended, with few exceptions, to occur during the early phases of the studies. The analysis in this chapter concentrates, therefore, on the results obtained from the second questionnaire, at T2, which covered the time from the first day of the reported back problem causing work incapacity until one year later. Results from T3, which covered the time between one and two years, are not commented on, with a few exceptions.

The percentage of subjects who reported that they had seen a physician about their present back problem already during the year preceding the actual report of work incapacity ranged from 79 percent to 22 percent: 79 percent in Germany, 52 percent in Sweden, 50 percent in the United States, 45 percent in Denmark and the Netherlands, and 22 percent in Israel. Numerous studies have found that a history of earlier back problems predicts new episodes (Nachemson & Jonsson, 2000). The close relation between previous and new back problems seemed obvious, if not even extra convincing, in this project. The current results apparently indicate that back problems causing long-lasting (more than three months) work incapacity are likely in almost every second case to be preceded by recent back problems of a magnitude sufficiently severe that a visit to a physician was considered necessary.

Consultation with Physician

As can be seen in Table 7.7, a great majority of subjects in all the countries, except the United States, visited a general practitioner (GP) within the first 90 days of work incapacity due to their present back problems. The median number of visits to a GP within 90 days was six for the American subjects, five for those from Israel, four for those from Denmark and Sweden, and three for those from Germany and the Netherlands. Within the first year, more than 75 percent of the subjects in all of the countries had visited a GP. These findings indicate that in all countries involved in the Project, the GP is the primary contact with the health care system for back patients.

When visits/no visits to the GP during the first year was tested versus working/not working at one year, the only statistically significant dependency noted was in the Danish cohort. For that cohort, those who had not visited a GP within one year had, not surprisingly, a higher tendency to be working again within a year.

Since almost all subjects visited a general practitioner at least once during the study, the discrimination from a statistical standpoint between those who did and those who did not was difficult. A consistent finding was that at T2, back function (Hannover ADL), social functioning, vitality, mental health, and pain intensity (von Korff) did not differ between these two groups, except in Germany. For the German cohort, consistent negative dependencies were found. This suggests that those in the German cohort who did not visit a GP and who also had better results, were healthier than those who did visit a GP.

TABLE 7.7
Visit to Physicians (%) at T1, T2, and T3

	Denmark	Germany	Israel	N'lands	Sweden	US
General practitioner						
T1: 0 to 90 days	95	72	74	97	74	34
T2: 0 to 365 days	98	85	96	97	86	77
T3: 365 to 720 days	60	63	60	35	72	46
Company doctor						
T1: 0 to 90 days	3	4	8	86	22	1
T2: 0 to 365 days	4	15	17	97	27	15
T3: 365 to 720 days	2	20	2	30	20	8
Specialist						
T1: 0 to 90 days	64	80	96	81	53	65
T2: 0 to 365 days	83	87	99	88	73	84
T3: 365 to 720 days	33	79	72	27	59	32

In the Netherlands, 86 percent of all the subjects had visited a company doctor (Occupational Safety and Health) within the first year. In the five other countries, a minority (less than 27%) had seen a company doctor. The exceptionally high rate in the Netherlands reflected the special position the company doctor has in that country in cases of health-related work incapacity.

The presence or absence of visits by subjects to a company doctor within the first year following work incapacity showed no statistically significant dependency versus working/not working in any of the countries.

Negative dependencies were found in the Dutch study between visit/no visit to a company doctor and better mental health and less pain. The number of subjects not visiting a company physician in that country was very low (n=8), however, making the validity of the results questionable.

In all of the countries, more than 50 percent of the cohort members visited a specialist within the first 90 days of their current back problem episode. The highest attendance rate was found in Israel, at 96 percent. This might reflect the fact that the Israeli cohort consisted of subjects with a work related back injury. The median number of visits by subjects to a specialist during the same period was two in Sweden, three in the Netherlands, four in Denmark and Germany, five in Israel, and eight in the United States. After the first year, the great majority in all cohorts (73 to 99%) had paid at least one visit to a specialist.

The only statistically significant finding in relation to specialist visits and working status at one year was for the German cohort. For that cohort, a higher proportion than expected of those not visiting a specialist had resumed work within one year. It seems reasonable to assume that visit to a specialist would indicate the presence of a back problem complicated at least to some extent by whatever motivated the visit to the specialist. The opposite might be true in the German case, suggesting a group of subjects with problems of a less serious magnitude and consequently a better prognosis.

Those not visiting a specialist in Denmark (n=85) and Germany (n=34) had better back function than those who did visit a specialist. Especially in Denmark, referrals to specialists (rheumatologists) are part of the typical career of a back patient with long-lasting problems. The German group of subjects who did not visit a specialist had better social function and mental health and less pain than those who visited a specialist. This held true also in the American cohort, but only for mental health.

Consultation with a Physiotherapist or Other Caregivers

As can be seen in Table 7.8, the number of subjects from the different national cohorts who had visited a physiotherapist within the first 90 days of work incapacity ranged from 52 percent in the United States to 75 percent in Netherlands. The median number of visits within these 90 days was: eight for the German subjects, 10 for those from Israel and Sweden, 11 for those from Denmark, 20 for those from the Netherlands, and 18 for those from the United States. The first appointment with a physiotherapist (median) occurred on day 11 in the Netherlands, day 16 in Sweden, day 17 in Denmark, day 23 in the United States, and day 33 in Israel (German data missing). During the first year, the number of subjects who had visited and/or been treated by a physiotherapist at least once ranged from 74 percent in Germany to 95 percent in the Netherlands.

TABLE 7.8
Visit to Physiotherapist and/or Other Caregivers (Chiropractor, Homeopath) (%) at T1, T2, and T3

	Denmark	Germany	Israel	N'lands	Sweden	US
Physiotherapist						
T1: 0 to 90 days	61	68	70	75	63	52
T2: 0 to 365 days	79	74	88	95	90	77
T3: 365 to 720 days	28	55	42	36	86	16
Other caregivers						
T1: 0 to 90 days	29	11	15	36	23	34
T2: 0 to 365 days	37	21	25	54	34	46
T3: 365 to 720 days	16	20	13	25	32	27

When visiting or not visiting a physiotherapist during the first year was cross-tabulated against working/not working, the only statistically significant dependency was in the cohort from Sweden. For the Swedish cohort, the 10.5 percent who had not visited a physiotherapist included a higher proportion than expected of subjects who had returned to work within the first year. A reasonable explanation for this could be, as suggested earlier, that the sample of the cohort that asked for or needed fewer interventions had less problems and/or a better prognosis. Another possible interpretation of the same finding, likely or not, could be that visits to a physiotherapist delayed, or even prevented, work resumption.

The number of visits to a physiotherapist during the first year (around 10 for the subjects from Denmark, Germany, Israel, and Sweden, and around 20 for the subjects from the Netherlands and the United States) did not relate to working status in a statistically significant way. A considerable number of visits to physiotherapists occurred during the second year as well. This was especially true in the cohort from Sweden (86%). As was the case in the first year, however, no statistically significant relationships were found between visits/no visits to physiotherapists during the second year and the subject's working status at the end of the two-year period. Moreover, it is unclear whether visits to physiotherapists during the second year were motivated by the original back problem episode or recurrences.

The only positive dependency relative to health measures was found in the cohort from Sweden. Swedish subjects who had visited a physiotherapist had less pain than those who did not. Negative dependencies were found in the American cohort, where subjects who did not visit a physiotherapist (n=96) had better back function measured with the Hannover ADL instrument and better social functioning than those who visited a physiotherapist.

The frequency of visits during the first year to the different therapists covered under the heading "other caregivers" ranged from 21 percent in the cohort from Germany to 54 percent in the cohort from the Netherlands. The average number of visits to these professionals during the first 90 days was four for the subjects from Germany, seven for those from Sweden, eight for those from Israel, 11 for those from Denmark and the Netherlands, and 37 for those from the United States.

No statistically significant dependencies were found in any of the countries between visits/no visits to chiropractor, homeopath, or others, and working status after one year. This held true also for number of visits and working status. Neither positive nor negative dependencies were found between any of the health measures and visits to "other caregivers."

Imaging the Lumbar Spine

As shown in Table 7.9, the frequency of a radiographic (X-ray) examination of the lumbar spine within the first 90 days varied widely, between 35 percent in the German cohort and 92 percent in the Israeli cohort. After one year, the frequency of having had an X-ray, CT (Computerized Tomography), or MRI (Magnetic Resonance Imaging) examination varied between 72 percent for the subjects from Germany and 99 percent for those from Israel. X-ray examination took place, on average and counted from the first day of the reported work incapacity, at day 25 in Sweden, day 27 in Denmark, day 32 in Israel, day 48 in Netherlands, and day 67 in the United States. No data for the German cohort was available on this point.

Although there is no general agreement among back pain specialists, there are at least tendencies towards a consensus as to the appropriate indications for imaging a troublesome spine. For an otherwise healthy subject between 20 and 50 years of age, there seems to be no indication for an X-ray examination of the lumbar spine during the first six weeks of non-specific back problems. For subjects younger than 20 and above 50 years of age, indications for a much earlier X-ray examination are considerably stronger. In case of specific back problems, there might be indications for an earlier examination. This project could not distinguish between specific or non-specific back problems. Therefore, the difference in time before the first X-ray examination in the different countries cannot be evaluated in a meaningful way.

TABLE 7.9
Examinations by X-ray, CT and/or MRI (%) at T1, T2, and T3

	Denmark	Germany	Israel	N'lands	Sweden	US
X–ray						
T1: 0 to 90 days	64	35	92	74	58	75
X–ray, CT, MRI						
T2: 0 to 365 days	86	72	99	86	81	94
X–ray						
T3: 365 to 720 days	21	65	23	17	19	29
CT						
T3: 365 to 720 days	11	44	25	12	6	*
MRI						
T3: 365 to 720 days	6	15	12	11	10	*

* data missing

The only statistically significant dependencies between having had an X-ray, CT, and/or MRI examination or not and working/not working at one year, was an overrepresentation of subjects not having had an imaging examination of their spine among those who had returned to work within one year.

In Germany and the United States, subjects who had had an imaging examination reported worse back function. Similar negative dependencies among those having had an examination were found between social functioning in the cohorts from Germany, Netherlands, and the United States, and relative to vitality and mental health in the cohort from Germany.

Treatments

Table 7.10 presents data on treatment with hospitalization, surgery, and/or bed rest. The frequency of hospitalization for back pain problems during the first 90 days varied from 11 percent for the subjects from Sweden to 32 percent for those from the Netherlands, with the frequency for the subjects from the other countries falling in between. After one year, frequencies varied between 24 percent for the subjects from Sweden to 49 percent for those from the Netherlands. As noted in the following section, the frequency of inpatient treatment correlated to the frequency of back surgery during the corresponding time periods.

TABLE 7.10
Treatment with Hospitalization, Surgery, and/or Bed Rest (%)
at T1, T2, and T3

	Denmark	Germany	Israel	N'lands	Sweden	US
Hospitalization						
T1: 0 to 90 days	21	19	25	32	11	31
T2: 0 to 365 days	31	29	38	49	24	45
T3: 365 to 720 days	6	15	10	8	9	7
Surgery						
T1: 0 to 90 days	11	9	10	18	6	32
T2: 0 to 365 days	15	15	18	31	17	41
T3: 365 to 720 days	3	12	5	5	6	6
Bed rest						
T1: 0 to 90 days	23	0	84	51	7	48

The lowest rate of back surgery in any of the cohorts was found in Sweden. Six percent of the subjects in the Swedish cohort had back surgery within the first 90 days of the study period. A fivefold higher surgical rate was found for the subjects from the United States than for those from Sweden during the same time period. Although not asked for in the studies, it is reasonable to assume that the most prevalent indication for treating subjects between 18 and 59 years surgically was a herniated lumbar disc. The indication for surgery in case of a disc herniation is pain typically radiating down one, sometimes both, legs and along the sciatic nerve. It is known that in a substantial fraction of patients with acute symptoms of a disc herniation, the prognosis for a relatively fast alleviation of the symptoms is good. In some countries, for example, Sweden, acute surgery is considered usually only in the few cases where the pain is intolerable or when it is combined with serious neurological impairments.

The low surgical rates for the subjects from Sweden, Germany, and Denmark could be an effect of a systematic tendency to wait and see whether the symptoms will decrease spontaneously or remain at a level indicating surgery. The upper time limit for such a wait-and-see approach is usually thought to be less than three months. There are some indications in the literature that the outcome of surgery becomes less favorable when performed after more than around three months. Another explanation for the low surgery rates in some of the cohorts could be that in certain countries more severe symptoms are regarded as acceptable. At least hypothetically, there could be several explanations for the high surgical rates in the United States and the Netherlands. One explanation could be that the indications for surgery differ between the countries. Another explanation could be that the cohorts represented different populations, and that for a larger number of subjects in those countries surgery, as opposed to waiting for surgery, was the reason for work incapacity in the first place. A third explanation could be different economic incentives of the different health care systems.

The frequency of surgery during the second year was lower than during the first year for all the cohorts, and especially so for the cohorts from Denmark, Israel, the Netherlands, Sweden, and the United States.

A statistically significant dependency was noted for the Swedish and Danish cohorts between having had surgery during the first year and return to work. The finding of a dependency between surgery and return to work during the first year for subjects from Sweden and Denmark might indicate that a so-called non-radical and apparently more selective approach to surgery improves the chances of a positive outcome, at least when measured against work resumption.

Subjects operated on in Sweden (n=53) reported better back function (Hannover ADL), higher vitality, better mental health, and less pain than those not undergoing surgery. Less pain was also reported by subjects who had had surgery in the Netherlands (n=100) and the United States (n=127).

As seen in Table 7.11, heat or cold treatment was a relatively common type of therapy for subjects in all six participating countries. No statistically significant dependencies could be detected, however, in any of the cohorts between this type of treatment and an increased frequency of return to work.

No positive dependencies were found between these types of treatment and an improvement of any of the health measures. Negative dependencies, on the other hand, were found between this type of intervention and worse back and social functioning, lower vitality, mental health, and more pain in the cohort from Germany, and worse back function in the cohort from the United States.

TENS, ultrasound, and short wave were other types of frequently tried therapies against low back problems. As with heat or cold treatment, no statistically significant dependencies were detected in any of the cohorts between these types of treatment and an increased frequency of return to

TABLE 7.11

Treatment with Heat or Cold; TENS, Ultrasound, and/or Short-Wave; Acupuncture; Massage; Manipulation, Traction, and/or Zone Therapy; Mud-Packing and/or Medicinal Baths (%) at T1, T2, and T3

	Denmark	Germany	Israel	N'lands	Sweden	US
Heat or Cold						
T1: 0 to 90 days	42	27	43	23	28	60
T2: 0 to 365 days	56	45	75	36	43	84
T3: 365 to 720 days	18	36	27	12	34	42
TENS, Ultrasound, Short Wave						
T1: 0 to 90 days	42	31	37	55	46	40
T2: 0 to 365 days	53	53	68	70	62	71
T3: 365 to 720 days	19	54	22	17	46	23

TABLE 7.11 *(Cont'd)*

	Denmark	Germany	Israel	N'lands	Sweden	US
Acupuncture						
T1: 0 to 90 days	9	6	6	3	26	8
T2: 0 to 365 days	14	15	16	5	34	13
T3: 365 to 720 days	8	13	5	4	26	5
Massage						
T1: 0 to 90 days	50	42	24	67	30	44
T2: 0 to 365 days	69	69	53	81	55	65
T3: 365 to 720 days	29	55	22	26	43	23
Manipulation, Traction, Zone Therapy						
T1: 0 to 90 days	46	18	26	18	29	50
T2: 0 to 365 days	59	34	54	29	44	66
T3: 365 to 720 days	23	30	20	9	28	23
Medicinal Baths, Mud Packing						
T1: 0 to 90 days	1	41	3	3	3	3
T2: 0 to 365 days	2	65	7	10	8	9
T3: 365 to 720 days	1	49	10	1	6	3

work. Subjects in the German and American cohorts who had not received any of these treatments consistently reported better results on all health measures.

Acupuncture treatment of back problems was especially common for the subjects from Sweden. Between 26 and 34 percent had received this type of treatment within 90 days and one year, respectively. In the other cohorts, this treatment was applied less, or, in the case of the Dutch cohort, almost not at all. No influences of acupuncture treatment could be detected on the return-to-work rate after one or two years. Negative dependencies were found between treatment with acupuncture and back and social functioning in the cohort from Germany, and relative to vitality and pain intensity in the cohort from Sweden.

Massage was one of the most frequently tried therapies in each of the cohorts. After one year, use of massage ranged between 53 percent for the subjects in Israel and 81 percent for those from the Netherlands. No statistically significant dependencies were found between massage and return to work in any of the national cohorts, neither after one nor after two years.

Although frequently used, there was no positive correlation between massage and health status. Subjects who had not received massage in the German cohort scored higher in back function, mental health, and pain, while subjects not treated with massage in the United States had higher scores for back and social functioning.

Manipulation, traction, and zone therapy were the most frequently used therapies in all of the countries. In all cohorts, between one-third and two-thirds of the subjects experienced one of these types of therapy. There is scientific evidence from several studies that treatment with manipulation might have a positive effect on pain in chronic low back problems (Koes et al., 1992). However, no statistically significant dependencies were detected between any of the three therapies and an increased return-to-work rate. A few correlations between these therapies and health measures were found. A positive dependency was found between these treatments and the report of less pain in the Swedish cohort. Negative dependencies were found in the German and American cohorts.

Medical baths and mud packing were used rarely in all cohorts, except the cohort from Germany. Forty-one percent of the German subjects received these types of treatments within 90 days, and 65 percent after one year. No effects on the return-to-work rate could be detected. Only negative dependencies were reported for these treatments, also in the German cohort.

As can be seen in Table 7.12, physical activities, such as muscle strengthening, aerobics, etc., were used frequently in all of the cohorts. Only for the Israeli cohort was the frequency relatively low, at 34 percent during the first year. For the cohorts from the other countries, the percentages of subjects who used these treatments ranged from 63 percent to 86 percent.

Interestingly, the only statistically significant dependency detected was in the Israeli cohort, where a higher proportion of those who had received this type of therapy had a higher return-to-work rate within one year. Thus, the only dependency was found in the country with the lowest use. A negative dependency was found in the German cohort, where subjects who had not participated in this type of treatment had better back function.

Back school programs were used regularly during the first 90 days, and even more so during the first year. Participating in a back school program had a positive effect on return to work after one year in the Danish cohort. The only dependency found relative to health measures was in the American cohort, where subjects who had not participated in a special program had better back function.

TABLE 7.12

Treatment with "Active Treatment": Physical Activities and/or Back School/Pain School (%) at T1, T2, and T3

	Denmark	Germany	Israel	N'lands	Sweden	US
Physical Activities						
T1: 0 to 90 days	47	54	14	61	42	55
T2: 0 to 365 days	66	75	34	84	63	86
T3: 365 to 720 days	35	54	15	40	49	44
Back School/Pain School						
T1: 0 to 90 days	18	19	1	7	11	7
T2: 0 to 365 days	33	49	4	16	38	17
T3: 365 to 720 days	13	38	0	9	10	6

Not surprisingly, Table 7.13 shows that pain medication and pain-relieving injections were the most common intervention practiced in all the cohorts. Almost all cohort members received this type of medication, especially in the first year. In the second year, the usage dropped in most countries to very different levels; in the Netherlands, for example, only 33 percent of the subjects had medication in the second year. By contrast, for the German subjects use was still at 83 percent. It could not be shown, however, that the pain relievers used had any positive effect on the return-to-work rate, neither during the first year nor during the second year.

TABLE 7.13

Treatment with Pain Relieving Injections or Medications (Analgetics, Tranquilizers, Sleeping Pills, etc.), Walking Aids (Crutches), and/or Brace (%) at T1, T2, and T3

	Denmark	Germany	Israel	N'lands	Sweden	US
Pain Relieving Injections or Medications						
T1: 0 to 90 days	80	66	95	73	77	71
T2: 0 to 365 days	90	83	99	86	87	85
T3: 365 to 720 days	68	83	81	33	67	56
Walking Aids						
T1: 0 to 90 days	10	9	13	4	18	26
T2: 0 to 365 days	16	13	24	7	30	37
T3: 365 to 720 days	6	*	6	4	13	11
Brace						
T1: 0 to 90 days	19	20	51	13	29	51
T2: 0 to 365 days	32	32	77	19	45	66
T3: 365 to 720 days	19	*	63	14	36	32

* data missing

Several negative dependencies were noted between the use of medication and health measures in most of the cohorts; the Israeli and Dutch cohorts were exceptions. Those dependencies showed that the subjects who were not medicated scored better or higher.

The use of walking aids during the first year varied in frequency from seven percent for the subjects from the Netherlands to 37 percent for those from the United States. The use of walking aids showed no statistically significant positive dependencies with an increased return-to-work rate, neither after one nor after two years.

No positive dependencies were found between wearing a brace and return to work in any of the countries. In the cohort from the Netherlands, the use of a brace was more common among subjects not returning to work within both one and two years.

Health Indicators and Return to Work

Bivariate testing was performed to reveal possible dependencies between work resumption and the recorded health indicators of back function, social functioning, vitality, mental health, and pain intensity. It must be emphasized that statistically significant results obtained through this type of testing do not necessarily have the same significance in a final multiple variate analysis. The treatments and interventions tested were those occurring with the highest frequencies: surgery, massage, manipulation/traction and zone therapy, physical activities, acupuncture, TENS, school programs, and analgetics. The testing was performed on the results after one year (T2).

Back Function

Table 7.14 shows that in all six cohorts, subjects who had resumed work within one year had a statistically significant better back function than those who had not. The Hannover ADL score, in which higher is better, ranged between 52 in the Israeli cohort and 72 in the Danish cohort, among those who were working at one year, and between 32 in the Israeli cohort and 50 in the Swedish cohort among those who did not work at one year. The only distinct positive dependency among those who were working and had improved their back function was found among those who had undergone back surgery in Sweden and resumed work, as shown in Table 7.15.

TABLE 7.14
Back Function (Mean) and Work Status at T2

	Working	Not Working
Denmark	72	49
Germany	57	42
Israel	52	32
Netherlands	73	45
Sweden	66	50
US	62	36

TABLE 7.15
Surgery, Work Status, and Back Function within the
Swedish Cohort at T2

Surgery	Work Status	Mean	95% CI
Yes	Working	78	73 – 84
	Not Working	43	31 – 56
No	Working	63	58 – 67
	Not Working	52	47 – 56

General Health

In Sweden, Germany, and the United States, general health was higher (better) among subjects who had resumed work within one year than among those who had not. No positive dependencies were found for any of the interventions between the general health score and working status.

Social Functioning

Table 7.16 shows that social function, measured through the social function scale, was higher in all of the national cohorts for subjects who had resumed work within one year than among those who had not. For those subjects who were working, the average value in the different countries varied between 52 in the Israeli cohort and 93 in the Danish cohort. The 95 percent confidence interval for this scale in the general Swedish population varied between 83 and 85 percent. For those subjects who were not working at one year, the social function score varied between 34 in the Israeli cohort and 83 in the Danish cohort. The only intervention with a statistically significant dependency for the social function scale was found in the Swedish cohort. Table 7.17 shows that Swedish subjects who had surgery and returned to work had a better social function than those who were operated on but were still not working, and those who were treated without surgery irrespective of working status.

TABLE 7.16
Social Function (Mean) and Work Status at T2

	Working	Not Working
Denmark	93	83
Germany	70	55
Israel	52	34
Netherlands	87	64
Sweden	72	51
US	69	35

TABLE 7.17
Surgery, Work Status, and Social Function for the Swedish Cohort at T2

Surgery	Work Status	Mean	95% CI
Yes	Working	86	79 – 93
	Not Working	35	21 – 48
No	Working	71	66 – 75
	Not Working	54	49 - 60

Vitality

Table 7.18 shows that in all of the cohorts, the vitality score was higher, where higher indicates more vitality, among those who had resumed work at one year than among those who had not. The mean values from the different countries varied between 40 in the German cohort and 70 in the

Dutch cohort (United States data were missing). Among subjects who had not resumed work after one year, the values varied between 29 in the Israeli cohort and 55 in the Dutch cohort (again, United States data were missing). When the effect of the medical interventions was tested separately against vitality, a couple of statistically significant dependencies were revealed. In both the Swedish and German cohorts, vitality was highest among those who had undergone surgery and then resumed work (Tables 7.19 and 7.20, respectively). No positive relations in this respect were found after treatment with massage, manipulation/traction, physical activities, acupuncture, TENS, school programs, or treatment with analgetics.

TABLE 7.18
Vitality (Mean) and Work Status at T2

	Working	Not Working
Denmark	59	42
Germany	40	30
Israel	41	29
Netherlands	70	55
Sweden	51	36
US	*	*

* data missing

TABLE 7.19
Surgery, Work Status, and Vitality for the Swedish Cohort at T2

Surgery	Work Status	Mean	95% CI
Yes	Working	66	60 – 71
	Not Working	33	21 – 46
No	Working	46	43 – 52
	Not Working	36	32 – 40

TABLE 7.20
Surgery, Work Status, and Vitality for the German Cohort at T2

Surgery	Work Status	Mean	95% CI
Yes	Working	54	47 – 60
	Not Working	32	23 – 40
No	Working	37	35 – 41
	Not Working	30	27 – 33

Mental Health

As was the case with vitality, mental health was higher in a statistically significant way among those who had resumed work within one year than among those who had not in all of the cohorts. The data presented in Table 7.21 show that mental health values varied among subjects who were working from 45 in the Israeli cohort to 81 in the Danish and Dutch cohorts (United States data were missing). The 95 percent confidence interval for mental health in a normal Swedish population of corresponding age was 75 to 77. Among those not resuming work, the value for mental health in the different cohorts ranged from 31 in the Israeli cohort to 70 in the Danish cohort.

TABLE 7.21
Mental Health (Mean) and Work Status at T2

	Working	Not Working
Denmark	81	70
Germany	58	47
Israel	45	31
Netherlands	81	66
Sweden	70	58
US	*	*

* data missing

As with vitality, the only positive dependency was found for surgery in the cohort from Sweden (Table 7.22) and the cohort from Germany (Table 7.23). Subjects in Sweden and Germany who had back surgery and had resumed work had better mental health than those who had surgery and did not work, and they also scored better than those who had not had surgery, irrespective of whether they were working or not.

TABLE 7.22
Surgery, Work Status, and Mental Health for the Swedish Cohort at T2

Surgery	Work Status	Mean	95% CI
Yes	Working	79	73 – 85
	Not Working	61	50 – 73
No	Working	69	66 – 74
	Not Working	59	55 - 62

TABLE 7.23
Surgery, Work Status, and Mental Health for the German Cohort at T2

Surgery	Work Status	Mean	95% CI
Yes	Working	72	64 – 81
	Not Working	47	37 – 57
No	Working	46	43 - 51
	Not Working	56	51 - 60

Pain Intensity

Table 7.24 shows that, as was the case with back function, the level of pain intensity recorded through the von Korff pain instrument was lower (less pain) in a statistically significant way among subjects who had resumed work after one year than among those who had not. Subjects who had back surgery in the Swedish, German, and American cohorts had statistically significant less pain if working than if not working, and they also had less pain than those who had not had surgery, irrespective of working or not (Tables 7.25, 7.26, and 7.27, respectively).

TABLE 7.24
Pain Intensity (Mean) and Work Status at T2

	Working	Not Working
Denmark	3.3	5.3
Germany	6.1	7.1
Israel	5.5	7.1
Netherlands	3.4	5.8
Sweden	4.2	6.3
US	5.4	7.4

TABLE 7.25
Surgery, Work Status, and Pain Intensity for the Swedish Cohort at T2

Surgery	Work Status	Mean	95% CI
Yes	Working	2.2	1.7 – 3.0
	Not Working	6.6	5.2 – 8.0
No	Working	4.6	4.2 – 5.0
	Not Working	6.2	5.8 – 6.6

TABLE 7.26
Surgery, Work Status, and Pain Intensity for the German Cohort at T2

Surgery	Work Status	Mean	95% CI
Yes	Working	4.6	3.5 – 5.7
	Not Working	7.4	6.8 – 8.1
No	Working	6.1	5.8 – 6.6
	Not Working	7.0	6.7 – 7.2

TABLE 7.27
Surgery, Work Status, and Pain Intensity for the US Cohort at T2

Surgery	Work Status	Mean	95% CI
Yes	Working	4.5	4.0 – 5.1
	Not Working	6.8	6.2 – 7.5
No	Working	5.9	5.4 – 6.3
	Not Working	7.6	7.2 – 8.1

Summary and Conclusions

A strikingly similar spectrum of medical interventions was used for the treatment of low back pain for the subjects in all of the participating countries. Most of the interventions were practiced during the first year. General practitioners were, not surprisingly, the physicians most frequently consulted by these subjects. Physiotherapists were responsible for most of the specific interventions.

Great variations were noted in the frequencies of practiced therapies. The frequency with which surgery was performed in the six countries differed profoundly. It was evident that return to work of the subjects in all six countries was dependent on improvements of the health measures recorded, i.e. pain, back function, and quality of life. Consequently, those not resuming work within one year reported less favorable scores in all of these measures.

It was just as evident that among those not resuming work, more than expected received different kinds of treatments. Several negative dependencies were noted. The most plausible interpretation of the negative dependencies is that the subjects who reported milder problems received fewer and less frequent treatments, while those with more pronounced problems received a greater number and higher frequencies of different treatments.

Tested separately, none of the medical interventions, with one apparent exception, had any positive effects on resumption of work or on the health measures. The exceptional intervention was back surgery, and especially so in Sweden. The Swedish subjects who were operated on had a consistently higher return-to-work rate, less pain, better vitality, mental health, social function, general health, and better back function.

The positive effects found for surgery, manipulation, and, to some extent, physical exercises, are supported by the scientific evidence reported in the literature.

Note

1.   Chi square tests and Fisher's exact test were used for comparing qualitative variables. The level of statistical significance was calculated through the Chi square distribution. T-test for equality of means and Mann-Whitney test was used for quantitative variables. P-values < 0.05 were regarded as statistically significant.

References

Abenhaim, L. & Suissa, S. (1987). Importance and economic burden of occupational back pain: A study of 2,500 cases representative of Quebec. *Journal of Occupational Medicine*, 29, 670-674.

Bergenudd, H. & Nilsson, B. (1988). Back pain in middle age: Occupational workload and psychologic factors. An epidemiologic survey. *Spine*, 13, 58-60.

Bigos, S. J., Battie, M. C., Spengler, D. M., Fisher, L. D., Fordyce, W., Hansson, T., Nachemson, A. L. & Wortley, M. (1991). A prospective study of work perceptions and psychosocial factors affecting the report of back injury. *Spine*, 16, 1-6.

Deyo, R. A., Diehl, A. K. & Rosenthal, M. (1986). How many days of bed rest for acute low-back pain? A randomized clinical trial. *New England Journal of Medicine*, 315, 1064-1070.

Frank, J. W., Kerr, M. S., Brooker, A. S., DeMaio, S. E., Maetzel, A., Shannon, H. S., Sullivan, T. J., Norman, R. W. & Wells, R. P. (1996). Disability resulting from occupational low back pain. *Spine*, 21, 2908-2917.

Frymoyer, J. W. (1992). Predicting disability from low back pain. *Clinical Orthopaedics*, 279, 101-109.

Greenough, C. G. (1993). Recovery from low back pain. 105 year follow-up of 287 injury-related cases. *Acta Orthopaedics Scandinavian Supplement*, 254, 1-34.

Koes, B. W., Bouter, L. M. & Mameron, H. et al. (1992) A randomized clinical trial of manual therapy and physiotherapy for persistent back and neck complaints. Results of one year follow-up. *British Medical Journal*, 304, 601-605.

Linton, S. J., Hellsing, A. L. & Halldén, K. (1998). A population-based study of spinal pain among 35-45-year-old individuals. *Spine*, 23, 13, 1457-1463.

Nachemson, A. L. (1992). Newest knowledge of low back pain: A critical look. *Clinical Orthopaedics*, 279, 8-20.

Nachemson, A. L. & Jonsson, E. (2000). *Neck and back pain. The scientific evidence of causes, diagnosis and treatment*. Philadelphia, PA: Lippincott, Williams & Wilkins.

Oleinick, A., Gluck, J. V. & Guire, K. E. (1998). Diagnostic and management procedures for compensable back injuries without serious associated injuries. *Spine*, 23, 1, 93-110.

Rossignol, M., Suissa, S. & Abenhaim, L. (1988). Working disability due to occupational back pain: Three year follow-up of 2300 compensated workers in Quebec. *Journal of Occupational Medicine*, 30, 502-505.

Shekelle, P. G., Markovich, M. & Louie, R. (1995). Comparing the costs between provider types of episodes of back pain care. *Spine*, 20, 221-227.

Snook, S. H. (1988). The costs of low back pain in industry. *Occupational Medicine*, 3, 1-5.

Spengler, D., Bigos, S., Martin, N., Zeh, J., Fisher, L. & Nachemson, A. L. (1986). Back injuries in industry: A retrospective study. *Spine*, 11, 241-245.

Spitzer, W. O., LeBlanc, F. E. & Dupuis, M. et al. (1987). Scientific approach to the assessment and management of activity-related spinal disorders. *Spine*, 12, (Suppl),1-59.

Turner, J. A., LeResche, L., von Korff, M. & Ehrlich, K. (1998). Back pain in primary care. *Spine*, 23, 4, 463-469.

Waddell, G. (1991). Low back disability: A syndrome of Western civilization. Neurosurgery Clinics of North America, 2, 719-738.

Weber, H. (1994). The natural history of disc herniation and the influence of intervention. *Spine*, 19, 2234-2238.

8

Vocational and Other Non-medical Interventions

Sisko Bergendorff & Dalia Gordon

This chapter has three main objectives. First, it will describe the vocational and other non-medical interventions available to promote work resumption in the six countries involved in the WIR Project. Second, it will describe the major incentives and disincentives in the six countries that may affect an individual's behavior and decision making relative to work resumption. Finally, it will describe the interventions actually used in the cohorts of the six national studies.

Although the theoretical model presented in Chapter 3 drew a distinction between interventions and incentives and disincentives, return-to-work interventions as well as incentives and disincentives are addressed in this chapter. Major incentives and disincentives, or employer and employee motivators, were included in the national studies. They are all described in detail in Appendix 8.1 at the end of this chapter. Together with Chapter 7 on medical interventions, this chapter provides a basis for the analysis of effects of interventions, incentives, and disincentives presented in Chapter 10.

The most important part of this chapter is the group of sections which include descriptions of interventions, incentives, and disincentives in several aspects based on empirical data for the cohorts. However, the interventions available at the time the national studies were run, as well as major existing incentives and disincentives, are presented first. Thus, the next section describes the content of the interventions and the

135

responsibilities of the various actors involved in the process aimed at work resumption. These descriptions can be used as a frame of reference for interpreting the results presented in the following sections, which discuss the main findings of the national studies and describe the frequency and the timing of the different categories of interventions. Those sections deal with, respectively, training and education, work accommodations and employer motivators, so-called employee motivators, benefit assessment and rehabilitation procedures, and job services. Conclusions are presented in the last section of the chapter.

Scope and Provision of Interventions

Repertoire of Vocational and Other Non-medical Interventions

As might be expected, the repertoire of vocational and other non-medical interventions in the different participating countries is enormous, especially if one takes into consideration differences in context, actors, responsibility, finance, and rigidity of "gate keepers." It was impossible to include the full variety of these interventions in this project. Inspection and classification of the main kinds of interventions in use led to five categories:

Training and education: interventions involving acquisition of new vocational skills, including vocational education, on-the-job training, courses, general education, etc.

Work accommodations and employer motivators: interventions involving changes in the work environment in order to enable the worker to overcome incapacity.

Employee motivators/Disciplinary actions and labor relationships: warning and actual dismissal, contacts with employer/colleagues during the period of work incapacity.

Work incapacity assessment/Benefit withdrawal and rehabilitation procedures: procedures, timing, and context of wage replacement and of work capacity assessments for purposes of planning rehabilitation or wage replacement.

Job services and other services: employment and social services connected with work integration, such as job search, job offer, counseling, etc.

The "core list" of vocational and other non-medical interventions to be followed in the national studies focused on the content of the interventions, in order to allow each participating country to formulate its questions in the most appropriate way to suit its own structure and terminology relative to the interventions. The formulations could be adapted, but substantial effort was made to ensure functional equivalence. Each national team could add topics and questions beyond the core list in order to meet domestic goals of its study.

The research design included the subject of interventions in the second and third questionnaires. For each intervention, subjects were asked at the second questionnaire (T2): Was it implemented? What was the date of implementation? At the third and last questionnaire (T3), the question on the date of implementation was deleted in order to shorten the questionnaire.

Table 8.1 presents the 26 vocational and other non-medical interventions included in the Project, stating which of them existed as a public service in the respective participating countries. Detailed information on the contents of each of the interventions and its context in the different countries is presented in Appendix 8.1.

This overview makes it clear that on the level of arrangements and measures in each country that participated in the Project, a wide range of measures was available. With the exception of the United States, regulations or provisions were available for 10 to 16 of the measures listed, or the measure legally could be taken (e.g. dismissal during work incapacity). Each country had the social security related tests (vocational capacity, benefit eligibility assessments) and arrangements as to work place adaptations. Furthermore, education and training measures were available in most countries, whereas interventions related to employer-employee relationship seemed to be applied less frequently.

Actors, Timing and Procedures in the Work Incapacity Process

This subsection presents a short description of a typical work incapacitated person's career in the participating countries, at the moment of cohort creation. (For Israel, the process described here is the one relevant to work-related injury.) The main legal and administrative features of the various sickness and disability schemes are described in Chapter 2. Here, the differences in timing and responsibilities of the main actors involved are accentuated, namely, the work incapacitated employee, the employer, doctor(s), and social security agencies. Schematic charts of these procedures are presented in Appendix 8.2 at the end of this chapter.

In all participating countries, employees had to notify their employer of work absence due to work incapacity close to its onset. This notice should have been accompanied by a doctor's certificate in Germany (on the third day after onset of work incapacity), Israel, the United States, and Sweden (on the eighth day). In Denmark, a certificate was required only at a later date, but the employer could ask for it earlier; however, if an employer asked for a certificate, the employer had to pay for it. In the Netherlands, a doctor's certificate was not required.

TABLE 8.1

Vocational and other Non-Medical Interventions in Participating Countries

Intervention	Denmark	Germany	Israel	N'lands	Sweden	US	Notes
Training and education							
Vocational education and job training	+	+	+	+	+	+	In Sweden and the Netherlands, may be employer's obligation
General education	+	+	+		+		Only for completion of education
Work accommodations and employer motivators							
Adaptation of workplace	+	+	+	+	+	+	In Sweden, it is the employer's obligation
Special transport to workplace	+	+			+		
Change of workplace/Job redesign				+			
Change in working hours	+	+		+	+		Also called "partial work resumption"
Sheltered workshop			+	+	+		Usually confined to mental handicapped

Job training with compensation from social security	+	+	+	+	+	+	Also called "therapeutical work resumption"
Wage subsidy	+	+	+	+	+		
Client-employer relations							
Warning and realization of dismissal – protection against dismissal	+	+	+	+			
Contacts with employer/colleague			+				
Work incapacity assessments							
Threat and actual withdrawal of sickness benefit	+	+	+	+			
Test of vocational incapacity	+	+	+	+	+	+	Special technique for this assessment
Medical examinations for assessment for sickness benefit	+	+	+	+	+	+	
Rehabilitation inquiry and plan	+	+	+	+			
Assessments of eligibility for disability benefit	+	+	+	+	+		

TABLE 8.1 (Cont'd)

Intervention	Denmark	Germany	Israel	N'lands	Sweden	US	Notes
Job services and other services							
Job and benefit counseling	+	+	+		+		This service is different in the different countries. See appendix.
Job search							Job search by client
Job offer							Job offer by labor exchange or social security authorities
Activation group/Job club							This service is operated occasionally by public authority
Change in daycare for children							
Psychotherapy/Counseling	+		+		+		
Reduction in waiting periods in health care							

In Israel, social security authorities had to be notified by a potential claimant right away; this was done by claiming a work injury benefit. In the Netherlands, the claimant completed a social security form, also close to the onset of work incapacity. In Sweden, the employer had to notify social security authorities after 14 days of wage payment. In Denmark, claimants notified social security by the end of the second week after onset of work incapacity; in Germany, by the end of third week; and in the United States, after eight days.

Rehabilitation measures started quite close to onset of work incapacity in Sweden, the Netherlands, Denmark, and Germany. In those countries, claimants had to cooperate with the appropriate rehabilitation services agency.

Claimants could request disability benefits at the end of the sickness benefit period in Germany and the United States. In Sweden and in Israel, they could do it any time. In Denmark, timing was flexible; usually, claims were presented after medical and vocational rehabilitation was completed. In the Netherlands, claimants were invited by social security in the seventh month after work incapacity in order to assess eligibility for a disability benefit.

Attending doctors gave sickness certificates in all countries, except the Netherlands. They also provided assessments of work ability and rehabilitation potential in Sweden.

Social security or occupational doctors assessed work ability and rehabilitation potential in all of the countries by actually examining the claimant or by consulting the benefit authority and using attending doctors' assessments. This was done in Israel upon the request for benefits. In the Netherlands, work ability was assessed during the second or third week after onset of sickness in order to determine eligibility for sickness benefit and rehabilitation potential. In Germany, doctors assessed work ability for these purposes at the end of the third week, and in Sweden, they did this a week later. In Denmark, this assessment was made by the end of third month.

The employer paid sickness benefits for two weeks in Denmark, for 42 days in Germany, for two weeks in Sweden, and for one year in the Netherlands. In Israel, the employer paid sickness pay for three months if work injury benefits were denied.

The employer was responsible for a rehabilitation inquiry in Sweden starting at the end of the fourth week, and for a rehabilitation inquiry and plan in the Netherlands after two to three weeks. Rehabilitation plans were made in Sweden at the social insurance offices.

Dismissal on grounds of work incapacity was forbidden in the Netherlands for two years after onset. In Sweden, dismissal was possible only after all reintegration measures were taken and had proved to be unsuccessful. In Denmark, many employees could be dismissed 120 days after onset of work incapacity. Germany also had some job protection for work incapacitated workers; the United States and Israel had none.

Sickness benefits were paid by social security authorities in Denmark, Germany, the Netherlands, Sweden, and by some states in the United States. In Israel, the social security authority paid work injury benefits.

Social security paid sickness benefits from the second week for a period of one year in Denmark and from day 43 until 78 weeks in Germany. Sickness benefits were paid from the first week to the 26th week in New Jersey and until the 52nd week in California. In Sweden, social security paid sickness or rehabilitation benefits from the third week until all possibilities of rehabilitation had been exhausted; after that, usually around one year, claims for disability benefits were initiated. In the Netherlands, the employer paid sickness benefits for a year. In Israel, work injury benefits were paid by social security for six months.

In Denmark, rehabilitation potential was assessed, planned and financed by social security three months after the onset of work incapacity. In the Netherlands, social security supervised rehabilitation efforts made by employer from the 13th week. Social security coordinated and planned rehabilitation in Sweden starting at the eighth week, in collaboration with the employer and others. In Germany, social security initiated rehabilitation at the onset of social security payments. In Israel, public financed rehabilitation started only after disability benefits were granted. In the United States, social security had no responsibility for rehabilitation.

Partial work resumption or job training with compensation from social security was quite common in Sweden, the Netherlands, and Denmark.

Disability benefit payments started after one year in the Netherlands. This was usually the case in Sweden, as well. In Denmark, these payments could start earlier. In New Jersey and California, benefits started after two weeks, and in Germany after 72 days. In Israel, work injury benefits could start any time. If connection of sickness or injury to work was not established, sickness pay was paid by the employer for 90 days, after which a general disability benefit could be claimed from social security.

In the Netherlands, social security was responsible for the initiation of disability benefit assessments, and it invited the client to pursue these procedures during the second half of the first year after the onset of work incapacity. In Denmark, social security referred claimants to apply for a disability benefit.

In Sweden, social security usually initiated a claim for disability benefits after one year of work incapacity, if the claimant had not done so already. In Israel and the United States, requesting disability benefits was entirely the claimant's responsibility.

Conclusions

The above description shows wide differences among the participating countries as to the repertoire of interventions and actions that follow onset of work incapacity, leading to work resumption or an exit from the labor force and receipt of benefit. Even where similar interventions were found in different countries, their contexts, the actors responsible for their execution, and their timing in the benefit administration process created great differences in their practical content and implications.

In Denmark, the Netherlands, and Sweden, rehabilitation assessment and planning started very close to the onset of work incapacity. In Germany, it also started relatively early; in Israel and the United States, it came much later. The employer had no responsibility for rehabilitation in Denmark, Germany, Israel, and the United States. In Sweden and the Netherlands, on the other hand, there was strong protection against dismissal on grounds of work incapacity for a long period of time, combined with involvement of employers for rehabilitation. As a result, employees cooperated with (partial) work resumption in those countries.

These notable differences, which are seen also in the empirical findings, have implications for the conclusions that might be drawn concerning "successful" interventions. It may be that an intervention that was found to be successful from the point of view of work resumption in one country was successful because of the context in which it was performed, and its adoption in a different context in a different country would not produce the same outcome.

Training and Education

Impaired health during a long period of sickness, alone or combined with other circumstances, often prevents employees from returning to their ordinary job. Finding other suitable tasks at the existing workplace, or another suitable job, may then become a prerequisite for work resumption. This is not always possible without first gaining new vocational skills, either through training on one's own or at another workplace, or through vocational education directed toward a specific job. Moreover, especially employees with limited formal education may have to complete their schooling before participating in a vocational education program.

Two categories of training and education were used with the national cohorts in this project: general education and vocational education/job training. General education refers to schooling that is not preparatory for an occupation or a specific type of job. Job training refers to training without compensation from social security (sickness or disability benefit), at one's own or another workplace, that aims at work resumption in a specific job. Vocational education is a job-oriented specific education, irrespective of receiving a benefit from social security.

Training and Education Measures

Generally speaking, both general education and vocational education/job training were rare interventions in the six cohorts. In most cohorts, vocational education/job training was more common than general education. The only exception was the cohort from the United States. During the study period, general education was used most frequently in the Danish (13%), Swedish (10%) and American cohorts (19%); it was hardly used at all (2%) in the Dutch and German cohorts. Surprisingly, general education was used to a much greater extent in Denmark, where cohort members were more educated, than in Israel and Germany, where the cohorts were characterized by lower education levels.

TABLE 8.2
General Education, Vocational Education, and Job Training
at T2 and T3 (%)

	Denmark	Germany	Israel	N'lands	Sweden	US
General education						
T2	7	2	3	0	4	12
T3	9	0	4	2	6	8
T2 or T3	13	2	6	2	10	19
Vocational education/Job training						
T2	7	3	2	5	15	11
T3	16	9	6	6	15	7
T2 or T3	20	9	7	8	26	15

Vocational education/job training was a relatively common intervention in all of the cohorts. In Germany, Israel, and the Netherlands, seven to nine percent of the subjects were provided with vocational education or job training. In Denmark, Sweden, and the United States, the rate of participation was 15 to 26 percent.

When Training and Education Started

Early interventions are more likely to result in work resumption than late interventions. Results from a study conducted in Sweden indicate that work motivation of employees suffering from musculoskeletal diseases, especially back pain, decreased considerably during the first year due to work incapacity. After three months of absence, their motivation had decreased to 75 percent of their motivation at the onset of work incapacity, and after six months it had decreased to 30 percent. The motivation became critically low some time during three to six months of absence. Such a low motivation is expected to have a negative impact on a prognosis of work resumption (Öberg, 1989).

As seen in Table 8.2, both general education and vocational education/job training were provided in most cohorts more often during the second year. However, the opposite was the case in the American cohort. In view of the research on motivation discussed above, the provision of education and training as late as during the second year is not optimal.

Detailed information about the start of education and training for the cohorts is available only during the first year. General education in the American cohort, and general education and vocational education/job training in the Swedish cohort, were started earlier than in the other cohorts, at a median of seven months. Vocational education/job training started later in the Danish, Dutch, and American cohorts, at nine to ten months after the onset of the work incapacity period.

TABLE 8.3
Timing of Education: Number of Months after Reporting Sick before Interventions Started (Median) at T2

	Denmark	Germany	Israel	N'lands	Sweden	US
General education	10	*	.	.	7	7
Vocational education/ Job training	10	*	.	10	7	9

* data missing
. less than 16 observations

Relationship to Work Resumption

There were only a few significant relationships between general education and vocational education/job training on the one hand, and work resumption on the other.

A negative relationship was found between general education and work resumption during the first year in the Swedish cohort (p=0.01) and in the Danish cohort during both years (p=0.03 and p=0.00, respectively). Those who attended ordinary school returned to work more seldom than those who did not. Considering the rather late starting time, it is not surprising that negative relationships were found between the provision of these interventions and work resumption. General education is, by definition, a rather long intervention that is expected to provide employees with possibilities to complete their schooling before participating in vocational education, rather than to improve directly the chances of obtaining a new job.

In the American and Swedish cohorts, it was more common that an employee had both general education and vocational education/job training (5 to 6%, compared with 0 to 2% in other cohorts). Pursuing both general and vocational education is also a lengthy procedure, which is unlikely to be completed during the two-year follow-up period used in this project. No corresponding negative relationship was detected, however, in the American cohort. This may indicate that the American cohort was provided with short-term job training rather than long-term vocational education. No significant relationship was found between vocational education/job training and work resumption in any cohort.

It is not possible to draw any reliable conclusion from the relationship between the pattern of training and education on the one hand and work resumption on the other. Several other factors that may have influenced the process towards work resumption are analyzed together with outcomes in Chapter 10. Both individual characteristics and strategies to promote work resumption are included in that analysis; however, some can be discussed already at this point in this chapter.

The German subjects were older, less educated, and had poorer health than most subjects in the national studies, which may have reduced their possibilities to participate in general education and vocational education or job training. The Israeli subjects also had a relatively low level of education. They also had poorer health, which may have been caused by their work injuries. The Danish subjects, by contrast, had a relatively high level of education and were relatively healthy.

Despite the differences, the Danish, German, and Israeli cohorts had one important common feature that may have had implications on education and training. In these three cohorts, only 25 percent, 28 percent and 38 percent of the subjects, respectively, were convinced, when answering the first questionnaire, about their future possibility for work within their usual sphere of employment. In the Dutch, Swedish, and American cohorts, as many as 57 to 75 percent of the subjects expected to be able to return to their ordinary job and continue to work in the same field. A majority of

Danish and Israeli subjects faced the necessity of getting a new type of job, whereas many German subjects (32%) expected not to be able to work at all. In Denmark, employers may dismiss employees who have been absent from work for four months due to sickness; 62 percent of the Danish subjects faced unemployment due to dismissals during the first year and had to find a new job or change occupation.

What strategy was used in the Danish, German, and Israeli cohorts to promote changes of occupation? The relatively high frequency of general education and vocational education/job training in the Danish cohort may indicate that both types of interventions were regarded more often as a prerequisite for changing occupation in Denmark than in Israel or Germany.

Low frequencies of work resumption, especially during the first year, may have been caused either by the late start of education and training or by the lack of interventions during the first year. Moreover, general and vocational education may have been available only at certain periods of the year. Differences in waiting periods may be one of the causes of the observed variation in the frequencies of use among the cohorts and between year one and year two.

Work Accommodations and Employer Motivators

Changes in working conditions, such as adaptation of workplace and working hours, job redesign and change of workplace, transportation to the workplace, and job training with compensation from social security (sickness or disability benefit), are interventions that can be used to facilitate the work resumption at the old employer. Employer motivators, such as wage subsidy and exemption of wage payment, also aim mainly at work resumption with an old employer. Employees may, however, be provided all these interventions at a new employer as well. Sheltered workshops, by contrast, refer to work in a special protected workplace.

Employer motivators and most work accommodations are quite different from education and training in one important respect. They are applied when the employee returns to work and therefore coincide with the outcome of work resumption. This is the case with respect to all interventions in this section, except job training with compensation from social security and sheltered workshops. Therefore, the statistics presented have been calculated for those who have resumed work at least for a shorter period.

In this section, first the occurrence and the timing of the main work accommodations will be presented. Due to low frequencies, transportation to the workplace, sheltered workshops, and wage subsidy are commented on only briefly. Remaining subsections discuss the occurrence of a combination of several interventions and the relationship with work resumption.

Work Accommodations

In all six cohorts, work accommodations were much more frequent interventions than education and training.

Adaptation of working hours, such as changes in the number of hours or pattern of hours, was the most common of all work accommodations in the German and American cohorts (20% and 43%, respectively). Adaptation of hours was most frequent in the Israeli and Dutch cohorts (59% and 62%, respectively) and relatively infrequent in the German and Swedish

TABLE 8.4

Work Accommodations (% of Working Respondents) at T2 and T3

Intervention	Denmark	Germany	Israel	N'lands	Sweden	US
Adaptation of workplace						
T2	20	14[1]	11	19	20[2]	17
T3	15	14[1]	9	23	20[1]	15[1]
T2 or T3	24	14	15	31	24	23
Adaptation of working hours						
T2	32	16	52	62	27[2]	41
T3	36	13	36	18	28[1]	15[1]
T2 or T3	45	20	59	62	31	43
Job redesign/Change of workplace						
T2	51	15	61	30	15[2]	42
T3	50	14	38	30	28[1]	9[1]
T2 or T3	61	19	65	46	28	40
Job training with compensation						
T2	2	3	.	77	32[1]	3
T3	2	.	2	11	13	5[1]
T2 or T3	4	2	2	75	37	6

[1] 20% - 39% missing
[2] 40% - 59% missing
. less than 16 observations

cohorts (20% and 31%, respectively). The subjects in Israel, the Netherlands, and the United States were provided with other hours primarily during the first year.

Job redesign/change of the workplace was also a common vocational intervention in all of the cohorts. Many people suffering from low back pain cannot continue to work in their previous job or occupation. Some changes in their tasks or finding another job may therefore become a prerequisite for work resumption. Job redesign/change of the workplace was the most frequent work accommodation in the Danish and Israeli cohorts (61% and 65%, respectively), far more frequent than in the other cohorts.

As mentioned before, the great majority of the Danish and Israeli subjects expected that they would work in another occupation in the future. Furthermore, many subjects in Denmark (62%) had to change workplace after being dismissed. For the Israeli subjects, work incapacity was caused by work injuries which may have necessitated changes in working conditions. In the American and Dutch cohorts, 40 percent and 46 percent of the subjects, respectively, were provided with job redesign or change of workplace; in the Swedish and German cohorts, it was less than 30 percent. In the Israeli and American cohorts, this intervention was applied most often during the first year, whereas in the other cohorts those interventions were used roughly the same amount during both years.

The results seen in the Danish and Israeli cohorts were obvious, considering the circumstances. Work accommodation was necessary for many cohort members, but they also had the opportunity either to get another job or to have changes made in their ordinary tasks at the existing workplace. In the German and Swedish cohorts, by contrast, only a relatively small minority were provided this intervention. In Sweden, employers have an explicit primary responsibility to rehabilitate their employees and to facilitate their work resumption. Therefore, the Swedish subjects were expected to return to their old workplace in the first place. This may have influenced the pattern of interventions for the Swedish cohort and even "prevented" subjects from seeking suitable jobs. Many German subjects (32%) felt unable to resume work at all, and a change of workplace or job redesign were not a solution for them.

In Denmark, Sweden, and the United States, about 24 percent of the subjects were provided workplace adaptation with technical aids, such as special chairs, special tools, and lifting aids. In the Netherlands, 31 percent of the cohort received these interventions. In the German and Israeli cohorts, adaptations were less common. There were no large differences between the first and second years, except that Danish subjects were provided with workplace adaptations more often during the first year.

Job training with compensation from social security was a common intervention in the Swedish and Dutch cohorts, at 37 percent and 75 percent, respectively. These interventions were applied mainly during the first year in both cohorts. In Sweden, job training may also be applied on a part-time basis and successively lead to ordinary work resumption in full-time employment. This type of job training was uncommon in the other cohorts.

When Work Accommodations were Applied

As mentioned before, some interventions were used primarily as a first-year intervention. The cohorts in Israel, the Netherlands, and the United States were provided with other hours, and the cohorts in Sweden and the Netherlands with job training with compensation from social security, mainly during the first year. The Israeli cohort was also provided with job redesign or change of workplace more often during the first year than during the second year. Similarly, adaptation of the workplace usually took place during the first year in the Danish cohort. Other interventions in these cohorts, and all the interventions in the German cohort, were equally distributed between years.

Information is available about the start of the interventions used only during the first year. Generally, work accommodations started earliest in the Dutch cohort and latest in the American cohort.

TABLE 8.5

Timing of Work Accommodations: Number of Months after Reporting Sick before Interventions Started (Median) at T2

Intervention	Denmark	Germany	Israel	N'lands	Sweden	US
Adaptation of workplace	6	*	7	7	6	6
Adaptation of working hours	8	*	8	6	8	10
Job redesign/ Change of the workplace	8	*	8	6	.	9
Job training with compensation	.	*	.	5	6	.

* data missing
. less than 16 observations

Job training with compensation from social security was a rather early intervention, starting in the Dutch and Swedish cohorts on the average at a median of five to six months after the onset of a period of work incapacity.

Adaptation of the workplace took place on the average after six to seven months; adaptation of working hours and job redesign/change of workplace took place on the average after eight months in most cohorts. About 50 percent of the subjects who received job training with compensation started the intervention later than five to six months after the onset of their work incapacity period. Therefore, according to the motivation research discussed earlier, work motivation of half of the cohort members may have decreased and their opportunities for work resumption may have deteriorated considerably during the waiting period of five to six months.

Transportation to Workplace and Sheltered Workshops

Transportation to the workplace by taxi or commuting service from home to work, compensation for using one's own car, and a subsidy for buying a car or adapting a car were infrequent interventions in all of the cohorts. They were most commonly used in the Danish, Israeli, and Swedish cohorts, providing four to five percent of the subjects with transportation.

Sheltered workshops and work in a protected workplace or protected work environment for employees who are not able to work in open employment or who cannot compete with "normal" workers were also an infrequent intervention in all of the cohorts. In Denmark and Sweden, three percent of the subjects started to work in a sheltered workshop during the study period. In the other cohorts, this intervention was not applied at all or only in one single case. In the Danish cohort, there was a positive significant relationship ($p = 0.04$) between participation in a sheltered workshop and work resumption.

Employer Motivators: Wage Subsidy and Exemption of Wage Payment

Two types of employer motivators were included in the studies. Wage subsidy refers to a subsidy provided to an employer for employment of an impaired employee, at a maximum amount of 100 percent of the employee's wage, usually for a limited period. If the employer is entitled to pay only a partial wage, a wage below the normal wage level in the occupation, or no wage at all, the motivator is called an exemption of wage payment.

These two types of motivators are similar to job training with compensation from social security in one important respect. They may be an attractive alternative for employers to employ persons with impaired health on the condition that they are provided with job training with compensation from social security, a wage subsidy, or an exemption of wage payment. For a limited period, the employer will have no costs at all, or will have lower costs than normally, for the employee's wages. It makes a difference for employees, however, which one of these interventions is used. If employees are subject to exemption of wage payment, they may loose in economic terms by getting lower than a "normal" pay. If employers are provided with a wage subsidy or job training with compensation from social security, employees may loose only a minor amount, or not at all. Therefore, the choice of intervention is important to employees, especially as an incentive for work resumption.

Wage subsidy and exemption of wage payment were applied in the Danish cohort (14%), but hardly ever in the other cohorts. However, the subjects may have been unaware if a wage subsidy was provided, which may have lead to underreporting. This intervention was started in the Danish cohort on the average after a median of seven months. Due to low frequencies, reliable results are not available for the other cohorts.

TABLE 8.6
Wage Subsidy and Exemption of Wage Payment (% of Working Respondents) at T2 and T3

	Denmark	Germany	Israel	N'lands	Sweden	US
T2	12	2	.	0	0	.
T3	8	4	0	2	1	0[1]
T2 or T3	14	3	0	2	1	0

[1] 20% - 39% missing
. less than 16 observations

Combinations of Training, Education, and Work Accommodations

Several interventions may be used, either simultaneously or sequentially, during a period of work incapacity. As mentioned earlier, some cohorts were provided with a combination of general education and vocational education/job training more often than were others. Work accommodations, such as adaptation of the workplace and working hours, may be applied at the same time as well, aiming not only at work resumption but also at restoring work capacity.

There were considerable differences in frequencies of combined interventions among the six cohorts. The combinations illuminate some of the existing differences in the strategies for promoting work resumption. As mentioned in the preceding sections, the German cohort was provided with fewer interventions than the other cohorts. Combinations of interventions were, needless to say, also very rare in the German cohort.

TABLE 8.7
Major Combinations of Training, Education, and Work
Accommodations (% of Working Respondents) at T2 and T3

Interventions combined	Denmark	Germany	Israel	N'lands	Sweden	US
General education, vocational education/Job training[1]	2	1	1	0	6	5
Vocational education/Job training,[1] adaptation of workplace	5	2	2	3	9	4
Vocational education/Job training,[1] Job redesign/Change of workplace	17	1	5	6	8	8
Vocational education/Job training,[1] adaptation of working hours	10	3	5	5	6	10
Adaptation of workplace, job redesign/Change of workplace	17	7	12	19	7	11
Adaptation of workplace and working hours	12	0	12	24	8	14
Adaptation of workplace, job training[2]	1	0	1	27	10	2
Job redesign/ Change of workplace, adaptation of working hours	35	2	52	33	14	30

TABLE 8.7 *(Cont'd)*

Interventions combined	Denmark	Germany	Israel	N'lands	Sweden	US
Job redesign/ Change of workplace, job training[2]	2	0	2	36	13	4
Adaptation of working hours, job training[2]	2	0	2	56	12	4
Adaptation of workplace, Job redesign/ Change of workplace, adaptation of working hours	9	0	11	15	0	9
Job training,[2] job redesign/ Change of workplace, adaptation of working hours	1	0	2	29	8	3

[1] Without compensation from social security.
[2] With compensation from social security.

Other cohorts were, by contrast, provided with a great variety of combinations of interventions. Different types of work accommodations were often mixed together, especially in the Netherlands. Combinations of work accommodations and vocational education/job training without compensation from social security were generally less common, and were used primarily in the Danish and American cohorts.

Regarding all cohorts except the cohort from Germany, the most common combination was job redesign/change of the workplace and adaptation of working hours. This combination was used in 14 percent of the cases in the Swedish cohort, 30 to 35 percent of the cases in the Danish, Dutch, and American cohorts, and in as much as 52 percent of cases in the Israeli cohort.

Relationship to Work

Work accommodations were more frequent than training and education in all cohorts. Job redesign/change of the workplace and adaptation of working hours were the most common interventions, followed by adaptation of workplace. Job training with compensation from social security was quite common in the Dutch and Swedish cohorts. There were no significant positive relationships between job training with compensation from social security and work resumption in any country. The only almost-significant relationship, a negative one, was during the first year in the German cohort. Work resumption was less frequent among those German subjects who trained on the job with compensation than those who did not ($p=0.06$).

Bivariate relationships between most other work accommodations and employer motivators on the one hand, and work resumption on the other, are not meaningful because the cohort members could not be provided with work accommodations and employer motivators unless they returned to work. At that point, the intervention and the outcome coincide. Furthermore, there is no information available about possible offers of work accommodations that subjects refused to accept. Moreover, the results indicate that those who resumed work for a period but did not work at the time of respective measurement were provided with interventions to the same degree that those who were working at those times.

Employee Motivators: Disciplinary Actions and Labor Relationships

Disciplinary intervening actions taken by employers might shorten the period of work incapacity by reducing work disincentives inherent in income replacement arrangements, e.g. by threat of dismissal if a period of work incapacity lasts too long or if the employee does not cooperate with rehabilitation procedures. Also included here is an employee's contact with his or her employer/colleagues during absence from work, which might relate to work resumption.

This section focuses on three topics: the occurrence and timing of warnings of dismissal and actual dismissals, contact with colleagues and the employer, and the relation between employee motivators and work resumption.

Warning of Dismissal and Dismissal

Absences from work due to work incapacity that last a long period of time and/or are frequent, may cause the employer serious problems and expenses. A substitute worker may be expensive and difficult to find, especially for a short or unknown period of time. These facts may influence the employer to threaten the work incapacitated employee with dismissal. From the point of view of the incapacitated employee, warning of dismissal by the employer may accelerate work resumption if the employee does not wish to lose his or her job. On the other hand, actual dismissal postpones work resumption since the worker has to look for and find another job. Dismissal due to work incapacity is forbidden in the Netherlands and is restricted in Sweden, especially in large companies, for a certain period of time.

TABLE 8.8
Warning of Dismissal and Dismissal (%) at T2 and T3, and Timing (Median) at T2

	Denmark	Germany	Israel	N'lands	Sweden	US
T2						
Warning	10	7	18	10	*	16
Timing	3	*	4	.	*	2
Dismissal	62	7[1]	31	8	*	20
Timing	4	*	5	11	*	5
T3						
Warning	2	87	8	7	4[1]	5
Dismissal	5	9	5	13	8[1]	6
T2 or T3						
Warning	13	70	23	15	4[1]	19
Dismissal	65	9[1]	34	17	8[1]	23

[1] 20% - 39% missing
* data missing
. less than 16 observations

Warning of dismissal during the two years of the follow-up period was very frequent in the German cohort, where 70 percent of the subjects received such warning. It was quite frequent in the Israeli and the American cohorts, as well; about one-fifth of the subjects in those cohorts were warned that they might be dismissed. In the Danish and the Dutch cohorts, 13 to 15 percent of the subjects were warned, while in Sweden only four percent were warned.

Actual dismissal was high in the Danish cohort, where 65 percent were dismissed during the two years following the onset of work incapacity. The reason is that in Denmark many employees may be dismissed 120 days after onset of work incapacity. In the Israeli and the American cohorts, substantial numbers of subjects were dismissed as well (34% and 23%, respectively), as no protection against dismissal due to work incapacity existed in those countries.

Surprisingly, most of the many warnings of dismissal in Germany were not carried out, and only nine percent of the subjects that were warned with dismissal in that country were actually dismissed. Warning of dismissal was carried out regularly in the Netherlands and the United States, and most of the subjects who were warned in those countries were actually dismissed. In Denmark, Israel, and the United States, most of the many subjects that were dismissed were not warned.

In Sweden only eight percent of the subjects were dismissed, as in that country dismissal was allowed only after all possibilities of rehabilitation and work resumption at the original place of work were tried and found unsuccessful. This restriction especially protected subjects who worked in large places of employment.

In the Netherlands, 17 percent of the subjects reported dismissal. Since it is forbidden in the Netherlands to dismiss work incapacitated employees during the first two years after onset of work incapacity, it may be that subjects reported being dismissed if they received a notice even if the actual date of dismissal was not yet reached.

Timing of dismissals, like their frequency, reflected the structure of job protection in each of the participating countries. Most of the warnings and actual dismissals occurred during the first year in Denmark, Israel, and the United States, and they took place close to the onset of work incapacity. Half of the warnings were given before five months (median) in the cohorts from Denmark, Israel, and the United States. In the Swedish cohort, the few warnings and dismissals occurred during the second year. In the Dutch cohort, dismissal was reported to take place only toward the end of the first year after work incapacity, rising a little during the second year.

Contacts With Colleagues/Employer

Contacts with colleagues or the employer during the period of work incapacity may be a sign of an effort to resume work, or it could be a catalyst to work resumption. In Sweden and the Netherlands, the employer is required to initiate contact with work incapacitated employees in order to plan rehabilitation. All cohorts had high incidence of contacts with people from their place of work during the period of work incapacity, but there is unfortunately no data on the nature of these contacts—social or other—or as to the identity of the initiator.

More than 80 percent of the subjects in the Netherlands, Denmark, Germany, and Sweden, and 72 percent of the subjects in Israel, reported contacts with people from their former place of work during both the first and second year following the onset of work incapacity.

Around 80 to 90 percent of the subjects who were not working had such contacts during the first year after onset of work incapacity in all cohorts except Germany; the German subjects had such contacts in two-thirds of the cases (no data for United States for this year). During the second year, contacts dropped for the subjects in Israel and in the Netherlands, but remained high for the subjects in Germany and Sweden.

TABLE 8.9
Contacts with Colleagues/Employer (%) at T2 and T3[1]

	Denmark	Germany	Israel	N'lands	Sweden	US
T2	83	67	80[2]	90	84	*
T3	*	81	.	29	62	.
T2 or T3	83	83	72[2]	85	83	.

[1] At T3: By not working subjects
[2] 20% - 39% missing
* data missing
. less than 16 observations

Relationship to Work Resumption

Dismissal played a significant role in connection with work status at the end of the follow-up period. For all cohorts except for the one from Germany, those who were dismissed had significantly lower rate of work resumption $(p = .01)$, compared to those who were not.

Threat of dismissal also played the expected role: subjects in Denmark, Germany, Israel, and United States who were threatened by dismissal but were not actually dismissed, had a higher rate of work resumption at the end of the follow-up period. It may be concluded, therefore, that this warning was effective in these cohorts. As for Sweden and the Netherlands, which had strong job protection, it may be that the subjects in those countries did not really believe that warning of dismissal could be carried out; therefore, the warning did not encourage them to resume work.

Most of the subjects who had contacts with employers/colleagues during the period of work incapacity were not working at the end of the follow-up. However, it is not likely that these contacts prevented work resumption. Rather, the explanation probably lies in the fact that most of the subjects who were working at the end of the second year were working already at the end of the first. The question concerning contact with colleagues was addressed only to non-working subjects. In other words, the question was addressed to subjects who had inherently more difficulties in resuming work.

Work Incapacity Assessment, Benefit Withdrawal, and Rehabilitation

Various administrative procedures relating to eligibility for benefits and rehabilitation can have a significant impact on work resumption, including which actors are responsible for implementing these procedures and the timing of their actions. This section covers consequently the interventions that arise out of the benefit administration process, including medical examinations for sickness benefit eligibility, threat and actual withdrawal of this benefit, rehabilitation inquiry and planning, tests of vocational capacity, testing eligibility for disability benefits, and capitalization of benefits for purpose of establishing self-employment. Finally, some findings are discussed regarding the relationship between these different phases and interventions on the one hand, and work resumption on the other hand.

Medical Examinations for Sickness Benefit Eligibility

In all of the cohorts, medical examinations were conducted during the process of assessment of work incapacity in order to establish short-term sickness benefit eligibility. Thus, it was expected that all of the subjects would report having undergone examinations of this type, at least by the first year after the onset of work incapacity. However, this was the case only for the subjects from Sweden and the Netherlands.

TABLE 8.10
Medical Examinations for Sickness Benefit (%) at T2 and T3

	Denmark	Germany	Israel	N'lands	Sweden	US
T2	68	48	63	96	100	35
T3	17	48	48	30	100	35
T2 or T3	70	64	72	95	100	54

The median number of medical examinations during the first year after work incapacity was seven for the subjects from Sweden and five for those from the Netherlands, and less than one for the rest. During the second year, the number of medical examinations dropped to less than one in all of the cohorts except for the cohort from Sweden, where also there were fewer examinations than during the first year.

Threat and Actual Withdrawal of Sickness Benefit

Threat of withdrawal of short-term sickness benefits could motivate a work incapacitated person to intensify efforts toward work resumption. Actual withdrawal of sickness benefits might force a beneficiary to resume work. Neither threat nor withdrawal of benefit was frequent in any cohort.

In Denmark, 15 percent of the subjects said that they were threatened by benefit withdrawal during first year. For the subjects from Sweden and Germany, the rate ranged from five to seven percent. During the second year, the threat rate decreased in the cohorts from Denmark and the United States, and rose somewhat in the cohorts from Germany and Sweden. The timing of these threats in Denmark, Sweden, and the United States ranged from a median of nine to eleven months after the onset of work incapacity.

TABLE 8.11
Threat of Withdrawal of Short-Term Benefit (%) at T2 and T3, and Timing (Median) at T2

	Denmark	Germany	Israel	N'lands	Sweden	US
T2	15	7	*	1	5	*
T2 Timing	11	*	*	*	9	*
T3	9	12	2	1	7	*
T2 or T3	21	13	2	1	9	*

* data missing

Actual withdrawal of benefits was quite rare in all of the cohorts. It was reported at the end of the first year after work incapacity by six percent of the subjects in Denmark, and by three percent of the subjects in Sweden. Actual withdrawal of benefit decreased during the second year in all of the

TABLE 8.12
Withdrawal of Short-Term Benefit (%) at T2 and T3

	Denmark	Germany	Israel	N'lands	Sweden	US
T2	6	.	*	0	3	*
T3	5	9	4	0	4	*
T2 or T3	9	11	4	1	5	*

* data missing
. less than 16 observations

cohorts, except for the cohort from Sweden. It was reported by nine percent of the subjects from Germany, and by less than five percent of the subjects from Denmark, the Netherlands, Israel, and Sweden.

Rehabilitation Inquiry and Plan

Rehabilitation inquiry aims at assessing the needs of a work-incapacitated person in order to return to work, including the possibility of rehabilitation and what directions it should take, e.g. changes in the work environment, vocational rehabilitation, etc. This intervention was quite frequent in the first year after work incapacity in the Swedish, Danish, and Dutch cohorts (66%, 52%, and 48%, respectively). In these three cohorts, the process of rehabilitation inquiry and planning preceded the process of disability benefit eligibility inquiry, and its timing was set by law to be close to the onset of work incapacity. Therefore, it was substantial during the first year in these three cohorts, usually during the first half of the first year, and dropped to a great extent during the second year. In Israel and the United States, rehabilitation inquiry followed eligibility for disability benefits. Therefore, for subjects from these countries, this intervention was rare and late all along the follow-up period, especially in Israel (6%). In Germany, rehabilitation was also decided upon in connection with determining eligibility for disability benefits; therefore, rehabilitation inquiry was late frequently for the German subjects, at T3 (34%). But it was not as rare as in the Israeli and American cohorts.

TABLE 8.13
Rehabilitation Inquiry and Plan (%) at T2 and T3,
and Timing (Median) at T2

	Denmark	Germany	Israel	N'lands	Sweden	US
T2	52	23	1	48	66	11
T2 Timing	5	*	.	6	3	7
T3	5	34	6	10	6	13
T2 or T3	58	41	6	50	66	21

* data missing
. less than 16 observations

Rehabilitation inquiry was more frequent for subjects who were dismissed from their place of work in all of the cohorts except Germany, as those subjects were in need of help to find a new line of work. The rate of rehabilitation inquiry in the Danish cohort was 66 percent among dismissed subjects, compared to 44 percent among those who were not dismissed (significant, p=.00). This difference was significant in the Dutch cohort as well (p=.03).

Not all of the Danish and German subjects who underwent rehabilitation inquiry cooperated with these procedures. This conclusion may be drawn from the fact that the rate of warning of benefit withdrawal in these cohorts was higher among subjects who underwent rehabilitation inquiry and planning (significant, p=.00).

Warning of benefit withdrawal was given to subjects under rehabilitation inquiry more often than was the case with their counterparts in Denmark, Germany, and Israel. This was not the case in Sweden, as the main actor responsible for these two interventions was not the same. The employer in Sweden had a substantial part in the responsibility for rehabilitation inquiry, while the benefit was the responsibility of the social security agencies.

Test of Vocational Capacity

Testing of vocational capacity usually is carried out in a special institution that examines the work incapacitated person's working habits and capacities in a sample of simulated work situations. In Denmark and Israel, this was done usually in order to assess the possibility of rehabilitation and its most appropriate direction. In the Netherlands, it was a part of the assessment of eligibility for disability benefits, while in Sweden it could be done in both contexts. In the United States, it could be done in the context of benefit eligibility assessment or even as part of certain treatments, such as physiotherapy.

TABLE 8.14
Test of Vocational Capacity (%) at T2 and T3,
and Timing (Median) at T2

	Denmark	Germany	Israel	N'lands	Sweden	US
T2	10	4	5	5	11	7
T2 Timing	7	*	.	9	8	6
T3	17	4	5	3	7	13
T2 or T3	23	7	8	7	17	18

* data missing
. less than 16 observations

During the first year of follow-up, testing of vocational capacity was reported by 10 and 11 percent of the subjects from Denmark and Sweden, respectively. The rate of this intervention for the rest of the subjects ranged from four to seven percent. As for timing, it took place earlier for the American cohort, at a median of six months after the onset of work incapacity, than for the rest of the cohorts, which reported testing at seven to nine months after onset. The frequency of these tests increased in the second year for the subjects from Denmark and the United States, and decreased for those from the Netherlands and Sweden—as in these last two countries, most of rehabilitation assessments were done close to the onset of work incapacity. In Germany and Israel, the frequency of these tests in the second year remained similar to the rate in the first year.

Altogether, 23 percent of the Danish subjects underwent this type of testing during the two years covered, compared to 18 percent for the American subjects, 17 percent for the Swedish subjects, and about seven percent for the rest.

Assessment of Eligibility for Disability Benefit

Assessing eligibility and qualifying for disability benefits is a turning point, indicating that the person involved has chosen, or has been forced, to exit from the labor force. This is done by placing a claim in Denmark, Germany, the United States, and Israel, or by remaining on sickness benefits past a certain point in Sweden and the Netherlands.

During the two years of follow-up, more than 40 percent of the subjects in the Netherlands, the United States, and Israel were tested for disability benefits. The rates were 34 percent for the subjects in Germany, 23 percent for the subjects in Denmark, and only 13 percent for the subjects in Sweden. In Sweden, eligibility for disability benefits is considered usually only after it is established that all possibilities of rehabilitation were not feasible, a process which might take some time.

In the Netherlands and Denmark, most of these tests were done during the first year after the onset of work incapacity. In the United States, Germany, and Sweden, most were done during the second year. In the Dutch cohort, the rate of testing at the first year was double the rate of most of the other cohorts. In the Netherlands, social security authorities are required to invite beneficiaries to assess their qualifications for disability benefits after receiving seven months of sickness benefits. This explains the relatively high proportion of these tests for the Dutch subjects in the first year. It should also be mentioned that this process could have motivated the Dutch subjects to resume work, since eligibility criteria for disability benefits are generally more stringent than those for sickness benefits.

TABLE 8.15
Testing of Eligibility and Qualifications for Disability Benefit (%) at T2
and T3, and Timing (Median) at T2

	Denmark	Germany	Israel	N'lands	Sweden	US
T2						
Tested	17	19	59	39	3	16
Timing	7	*	6	9	.	5
Benefit qualified out of total	8	12	26	20	3	17
Benefit qualified out of tested	48	72	44	53	100	15
T3						
Tested	8	29	42	22	10	34
Benefit qualified out of total	10	20	22	17	10	14
Benefit qualified out of tested	58	76	52	75	98	42
T2 or T3						
Tested	23	34	69	43	13	44
Qualified	18	25	35	25	13	25

* data missing
. less than 16 observations

Most of the subjects that were assessed at the first year were found qualified for partial or full benefits in Germany. In Sweden, all of the subjects tested were qualified. In the rest of the cohorts, around one-half of the subjects who were tested qualified, except for those from the United States, where only 15 percent qualified.

The rate of qualifying for benefits, among those tested, rose in the second year in most of the cohorts, as by that time the decision procedures could be completed. The rate was nearly 100 percent in the cohort from Sweden, 75 percent in the cohorts from Germany and the Netherlands, more than 50 percent in the cohorts from Denmark and Israel, and 40 percent in the cohort from the United States.

Dismissed subjects were assessed for eligibility for disability benefits more than their counterparts who were not dismissed in Denmark (27%, compared to 13%), the Netherlands (58%, 40%), and the United States (56%, 41%). This difference was significant for all these cohorts (p=.01). In Israel, dismissed subjects were also assessed more than the others, but the difference was not significant. The reverse was found for Germany; perhaps in this cohort, dismissed subjects were referred for another benefit, such as early retirement. None of the few dismissed subjects in Sweden were assessed for disability benefits.

Assessments for eligibility for disability benefits were also connected to rehabilitation inquiry. This connection was expected in the Israeli cohort, because only disability benefit recipients can get rehabilitation services (significant, p=.04). This connection was found in the cohorts from the Netherlands and the United States as well (p=.00).

Capitalization of Benefit

Capitalization of disability benefits in order to enable a work incapacitated person to establish his or her own business was very rare, since it existed as a public measure only in Israel. In Sweden and Denmark, there was a special subsidy for self-employment.

TABLE 8.16
Capitalization of Benefit (%) at T2 and T3

	Denmark	Germany	Israel	N'lands	Sweden	US
T2	0	*	3	0	0	1
T3	0	*	3	0	1[1]	1[1]
T2 or T3	0	*	6	0	1	1

[1] 20% - 39% missing
* data missing

Relationship to Work Resumption

All measures connected with benefit and rehabilitation processes, including the disciplinary ones, did not improve chances of work within the two years covered by this study.

Persons who reach the point of taking action toward obtaining long-term income replacement might be expected to halt (or not begin) work resumption efforts, whatever their motivational or health status background. Findings verify this hypothesis. In all participating countries, subjects who were tested for eligibility for disability benefits worked less than their counterparts who were not tested. This difference was significant in all participating cohorts (p=.00), at both T2 and T3. Certainly, all those who qualified for a disability benefit worked less. Of the vocational and other non-medical interventions covered by this study, this process was found to be the most significant indicator for non-work at the end of the follow-up period.

Rehabilitation inquiry was found to decrease work resumption within two years. Subjects who underwent rehabilitation inquiry had lower rates of work resumption at the end of the follow-up period in all of the cohorts. This finding was significant for the cohorts from Denmark, Israel, the Netherlands, and the United States, (p=.00). This result is consistent with the observation that persons who require rehabilitation are less qualified for immediate work resumption, and that while this process can be started through the two years of the follow-up period, usually it cannot reach a successful conclusion within that time frame.

Since vocational capacity testing is a part of the process of assessment of rehabilitation potential or eligibility for disability benefits, those who were tested—and who probably were in need of rehabilitation and/or benefits, had lower rates of work at the end of the follow-up period (significant for the cohorts from Denmark, Israel, the Netherlands, and Sweden: p=.01). This was found in all cohorts except the cohort from the US, where sometimes this test is conducted in different contexts.

Disciplinary measures connected to sickness benefits did not produce the expected result either. Contrary to expectations, the rate of work at the end of the follow-up period for subjects who were threatened with withdrawal of a short-term sickness benefit was lower than for the others. The same was true for those whose benefit was actually withdrawn in Germany, Israel, the Netherlands, and Sweden, although most of these differences were not significant. It may be that in these cohorts, the less motivated subjects received such threats and "punishments." Only in Denmark did those subjects whose benefit was withdrawn work to a greater extent. Another possible explanation for these unclear findings is that at least some of the subjects in the respective cohorts may have understood the questions concerning withdrawal of sickness benefits to refer not to a threat of shortening the period of benefit payment as a punishment for uncooperation, but to the regular expected end of the benefit.

Job Services and Other Services

This category of interventions includes mainly support services for finding new jobs, such as job counseling, job club, job offers, and job searches (which, although not a service, might include use of social services). Also included here are changes in day-care arrangements for children, counseling, and reduction of waiting periods for medical treatments.

The frequency and timing of the different job and other services are presented in the next group of subsections. The last subsection deals with the relationships between these services and work resumption.

Job Counseling

Individual job-related counseling existed as a service to work incapacitated persons only in Denmark, where 10 percent of the subjects received this intervention during the covered period. In spite of the absence of job counseling as a service in the rest of the cohorts, 44 percent of the subjects in Germany said they had received such counseling. Some of these subjects may have received it privately, as was reported by nine percent of the subjects in the United States. In Sweden, this service existed for all job searchers, and 17 percent of the subjects in that country received it during the two years covered.

TABLE 8.17
Job Counseling (%) at T2 and T3, and Timing (Median) at T2

	Denmark	Germany	Israel	N'lands	Sweden	US
T2	5	33	1	1	20^2	5
T2 Timing	7	*	.	.	7	.
T3	6	33	5	2	11^1	5
T2 or T3	10	44	6	3	17^2	9

[1] 20% - 39% missing
[2] More than 80% missing
* data missing
. less than16 observations

Job counseling was provided usually during the second half of the first year after the onset of work incapacity.

Job Search

In all of the cohorts, except the cohort from Sweden, 20 to 30 percent of the subjects reported searching for work during the first year after the onset of work incapacity. In the Swedish cohort, job search was quite rare both in the first and second year after work incapacity, as most subjects still maintained their original jobs. In the second year, 18 to 25 percent of the subjects searched for a job in Germany, Denmark, and the Netherlands, compared to 34 to 36 percent of the subjects in the United States and Israel. The median timing of the start of the job search was seven to nine months after the onset of work incapacity.

TABLE 8.18
Job Search (%) at T2 and T3, and Timing (Median) at T2

	Denmark	Germany	Israel	N'lands	Sweden	US
T2	26	26	22	21	4^2	30
Timing	7	*	7	8	.	9
T3	25	18	34	21	2^1	36
T2 or T3	34	29	45	29	4^2	49

[1] 20% - 39% missing
[2] more than 80% missing
. less than 16 observations
* data missing

As might be expected, subjects who were dismissed searched for a job at much higher rates than those who were not (significant, except for the cohort from Sweden). Also, subjects who reported that they still maintained their right to return to their original place of work looked for a new job less than those who could not return to their old job. However, there were quite a number who looked for a new job in spite of being able to resume their old job.

Rehabilitation plans encouraged job search in the cohorts from Germany, the Netherlands, Israel, and the United States (significant for Germany and the Netherlands, $p = .00$). Subjects who underwent rehabilitation inquiry and planning searched for a job more than their counterparts who did not, indicating that job search may have been part of their rehabilitation.

Job Offer

The rate of receiving a job offer was quite low in all of the cohorts. During the two years covered, only four to eight percent of the subjects received such offers, except for the cohort from Germany, in which 17 percent of the subjects had job offers. Most of the subjects who received a job offer said they had searched for a job, but not all of them. Some received the offer from social security authorities, especially in Denmark and the Netherlands.

Job offers reported at T3 were made mostly by public authorities in Denmark, and by friends in Israel. For the American cohort, the sources were diverse. (In the other cohorts, and for offers reported at T2, there is no data concerning this issue.)

TABLE 8.19
Job Offer (% of Job Searchers) at T2 and T3

	Denmark	Germany	Israel	N'lands	Sweden	US
T2						
Offer (out of total)	6	12	*	2	11[2]	2
Offer (out of searched)	23	44	*	9	*	6
T3						
Offer (out of total)	3	11	8	5	5[1]	3
Offer (out of searched)	14	68	22	24	*	8
T2 or T3						
Offer (out of total)	7	16	8	6	7[2]	4

[1] 20% - 39% missing
[2] more than 80% missing
* data missing

Job Club

Activation groups, or a "job club," are usually workshops at which people learn and practice searching for a job. This service was very rare in all cohorts. Only two to four percent of the subjects in Sweden, the United States, and Denmark received this intervention during the first year after the onset of work incapacity, compared to one percent or none in the other cohorts.

Job search, job offer, job counseling, and job club were found to be interconnected in the cohorts from Denmark, Germany, the Netherlands, and the United States. In these cohorts, services like job counseling and job club were more likely provided to job searchers than in Israel and Sweden.

TABLE 8.20
Job Services – Correlations

	Job counseling	Job search	Job offer	Job club
Job counseling		Den (.18) Ger (.24) Neth (.13) US (.20)	Den (.22) Ger (.39)	Den (.28) Neth (.28) US (.34)
Job search			Den (.28) Ger (.40) Neth (.26) US (.12)	Den (.16) Neth (.21) US (.25)
Job offer				Ger (.20) Neth (.21) US (.25)
Job club				

Change in Day Care Arrangements for Children

Change in day care arrangements for children could be a consequence of work incapacity; for example, if these arrangements are offered by the employer. In such cases, it may motivate earlier work resumption at the former workplace and postpone work resumption at a new one. These arrangements could also be a service provided by rehabilitation authorities in order to enable work resumption.

Compared to the period before the onset of work incapacity, all subjects in Germany received less day care for their children during the first and second year. In Denmark, nine percent of the subjects received more day-care for their children during the first year following the onset of work incapacity than before, and seven percent received less. In the other cohorts, there were only very minor changes in day care for children after the onset of work incapacity.

Counseling

Social or psychological counseling may be a part of the rehabilitation process. In Denmark, nine percent of the subjects received this service during the first and second years after the onset of work incapacity. In the United States, seven percent of the subjects received psychological counseling during the first year; during the second year, this rate rose to 13 percent. In Germany, six percent of the subjects received social or psychological counseling during the first year, and this rate rose to 21 percent during the second year.

TABLE 8.21
Social/Psychological Counseling (%) at T2 and T3, and Timing
(Median) at T2

	Denmark	Germany	Israel	N'lands	Sweden	US
T2	9	6	1	1	3^2	7
Timing	7	*	.	.	.	8
T3	9	21	1	2	4^1	13
T2 or T3	14	21	2	4	4^2	16

[1] 20% - 39% missing
[2] more than 80% missing
. less than 16 observations
* data missing

Reduction of Waiting Periods for Health Care

Some subjects managed to obtain a reduction of waiting periods for medical treatment, especially in Denmark. In the first year after the onset of work incapacity, 29 percent of the subjects in the Danish cohort received this service, compared to two to five percent of the subjects in Sweden, the Netherlands, and the United States. This service was obtained very close to the onset of work incapacity in Denmark (after a median of one month). In the second year, 11 percent of the Danish subjects reported priority in medical care; in the other cohorts, the rate was less than three percent.

TABLE 8.22
Reduction of Waiting Periods (%) at T2 and T3

	Denmark	Germany	Israel	N'lands	Sweden	US
T2	29	*	*	4	5^2	2
T3	11	*	0	3	3^1	1
T2 or T3	32	*	0	5	5^2	2

[1] 20% - 39% missing
[2] more than 80% missing
* data missing

Relationship to Work Resumption

Job searches and receipt of a job offer, like dismissal, divided the participating cohorts into two groups. Each of these groups had a different pattern of frequencies of use of these services and of their correlation with work resumption at the end of the follow-up period. For the cohorts in which most of work resumption at T3 was returning to the original employer, that is, those from Sweden, the Netherlands, and Germany, these interventions were less frequent, especially in Sweden, and were not connected to work resumption. For the cohorts from Denmark, Israel, and the United States, where a considerable proportion of work resumption was with a new employer, job searches were more frequent and those subjects who searched for a job and/or had a job offer worked at the end of the follow-up period at higher rates than the others.

Job search was related positively to work resumption at the end of the follow-up period for the Danish and Israeli subjects (significant for the Danish), while it made only a slight difference for the American subjects. For the rest of the cohorts, subjects who searched for a job worked less at the end of the follow-up period, since in those cohorts work resumption at T3 was mostly with previous employers with whom the subjects had worked at the onset of work incapacity.

Receipt of a job offer increased work prospects for the subjects from Denmark, the United States, and Israel, since many of the work resumers in these cohorts worked with a new employer (significant for the United States and Israel). In the rest of the cohorts, where most of the subjects who were working at end of the follow-up period resumed their old jobs, job offer was not connected to work resumption. On the contrary, those who received an offer worked less (significant for Germany and the Netherlands). The reason for this may be that in those cohorts where most of work resumption was by resuming old jobs, the subjects who did not resume their old jobs were less motivated or had lower health status.

Subjects who received job counseling worked less than their counterparts who did not, except for those in the Danish cohort (significant for Germany and the Netherlands, $p = .00$). This finding may suggest that this counseling was a different service in Denmark, compared to the rest of the countries.

Subjects who received social or psychological services worked less at the end of the follow-up period compared to those who did not receive counseling (significant for the United States, the Netherlands, and Sweden). The period covered by this project probably was not long enough in order for this therapy to be completed. Certainly, those who did not need this intervention, and therefore did not get it, were more fit for immediate work resumption.

Summary and Conclusions

Rehabilitation Inquiry and Plan

Many vocational and other non-medical interventions are "tailor-made" services, provided upon careful examination of individual need and suitability. Therefore, some of the interventions monitored were not used very frequently.

The "gate" for applying many of the interventions to the subjects was the rehabilitation inquiry and plan. There was a great difference between two groups of cohorts concerning the timing, responsibility, and execution of this process. In Sweden, the Netherlands, and Denmark, its timing was defined by law, which was close to the onset of work incapacity and during the sickness benefit payment period. The employer was involved in initiation—and even execution—of this intervention, especially in the Netherlands and Sweden. On the other hand, in the United States, Israel, and Germany, this intervention was confined to disability benefit recipients, with no obligation to provide; this was especially the case in Israel and the United States. In line with these differences, rehabilitation inquiry and plan procedures were more frequent and close to the onset of work incapacity for the subjects in Denmark, the Netherlands, and Sweden, where recipients of sickness benefits were entitled to this service. In the United States and Israel, where only recipients of disability benefits were eligible for rehabilitation, they were rare and late. But in neither group of countries did this intervention lead to work resumption during the two years covered by the study—perhaps because the process of assessment, planning and executing these interventions lasted beyond the two-year follow-up period, even for the cohorts for which this process began close to the onset of work incapacity.

Education and Training

Education and training without compensation from social security were rare interventions in all of the cohorts. They were most widely used in the Danish, Swedish, and American cohorts. Only a few significant relationships, mostly negative ones, were found between education and training on the one hand and work resumption on the other. Those who participated in education and training had lower work resumption rates than those who did not. This does not mean, however, that education and training were unsuccessful interventions. General and vocational education started late and are, by definition, lengthy procedures which were unlikely to finish during the follow-up period of two years.

Work Accommodations

Work accommodations were far more frequent than education and training in all of the cohorts. However, in the German cohort they were used very little compared to the other cohorts. Job redesign/change of the workplace and adaptation of working hours were the most common work accommodations in all of the cohorts, and were used extensively in the Danish, Israeli, and Dutch cohorts. In the Dutch and Swedish cohorts, job training with compensation from social security was frequent as well. A great variety of combinations of work accommodations were used to promote work resumption in many countries, especially in the Netherlands.

Threat and Actual Loss of Work, and Job Services

Threat of loss of work may reduce disincentives inherent in the sickness benefit. Actual loss of a job will postpone work resumption. Rate of dismissal and its timing reflected the degree of job protection for work incapacitated persons in the respective cohorts.

Dismissal was high in the cohort from Denmark; 65 percent of the subjects were dismissed in this cohort during the two years covered, nearly all of them in the first year after the onset of sickness. This fact derives from Danish law by which employees may be dismissed after a given period of work incapacity. In Israel and the United States, a substantial percent of subjects (34% and 23%, respectively) were dismissed, since there is no job protection for work incapacitated workers in those countries. On the other hand, job protection for work incapacitated workers was quite strong in Sweden and the Netherlands, which resulted in a low percentage of dismissals for the subjects from those countries. Dismissals were not frequent for the German subjects either, although warning of dismissal was quite common in this cohort.

For all of the cohorts, dismissed subjects resumed work less than those who were not dismissed. In Denmark, Germany, Israel, and the United States, subjects who were threatened with dismissal but were not actually dismissed resumed work more than their counterparts who were not threatened with dismissal. This suggests that the warning did encourage work resumption in these cohorts. On the other hand, this connection was not found in Sweden and the Netherlands; perhaps those subjects did not take these warning seriously, as they were relying on their job protection rights.

Job search was frequent in Denmark, Israel, and the United States, where the cohorts also had higher rates of dismissals. Job search and related services did promote work resumption in these cohorts, which had substantial work resumption with a new employer. In the cohorts which had work protection for work incapacitated persons (the Netherlands and

Sweden), and also in the cohort from Germany, the main course of work resumption was with the original employer. In these cohorts, job searchers resumed work less than did the others. It may be that in these cohorts, those who did not follow the "major" course of work resumption—and therefore searched for a new job—were less motivated or harder to place.

Return to Former Work

In the Dutch, Swedish, and American cohorts, a majority of the subjects expected to return to their old workplace; in the other cohorts, it was a minority. There were different strategies to promote work resumption for those who felt obliged to change tasks or occupation. In the Danish cohort, a great variety of efforts were made: subjects were provided with general education, vocational education/job training, as well as job redesign and change of workplace—to a greater extent than in most other cohorts. Change of workplace/redesign of tasks were also common in the Israeli cohort. The intervention pattern of the Danish and Israeli cohorts is understandable; it was necessary for many of the subjects and they also had the opportunity either to get another job or to have changes made in their ordinary tasks at the workplace. This also applied to many subjects in the Dutch and American cohorts, and, to a minor extent, to those in the Swedish cohort. The German situation and strategy differed clearly from the others. Some 30 percent of the subjects in the German cohort did not expect to be able to work at all, and another 30 percent had to find another type of job. Education and training were, however, surprisingly rare. Low education, high age, and poor health of the German cohort may account for a substantial part of the pattern. Infrequent job redesigns and changes of workplace may indicate the presence of other, system-specific, characteristics as well. The German cohort may have faced a greater tendency for inflexibility in their labor market than was the case for the other cohorts.

Disability Benefit

The most important intervention from the point of view of work resumption was the test and eligibility for disability benefits. This was the only intervention that was significantly connected to work resumption in all of the cohorts; those subjects who were tested and/or granted disability benefits worked less than the others. This is not surprising, since establishing—or trying to establish—a prolonged or permanent wage-replacement may indicate a person's intention to refrain from work resumption, because of either health or motivational reasons. By granting this benefit, the system confirms this perception.

TABLE 8.23
Main Characteristics of Vocational and other Non-Medical Interventions

Intervention	Occurrence	Timing	Relationship to work resumption
Education and training	Most cohorts 2–20%, mainly the second year. Most common in Denmark, Sweden and US.	During the first year after 7–10 months.	Few significant relationships. Lower work resumption rates for subjects in general education in the Danish and Swedish cohorts.
Work accommodations	Most cohorts 28–65%, mainly the first year, often in combinations with each other. Adaptation of hours, job redesign, change of workplace most common in Denmark, Israel, Netherlands, US.	During the first year after 6–8 months.	Most interventions coincide with work resumption. Subjects participating in sheltered workshops had higher work resumption rates in Denmark.
Employer motivators	Very uncommon in five cohorts. 14% in Denmark.	During the first year after 7–10 months (Denmark).	Coincide with work resumption.
Employee motivators/ disciplinary actions and labor relationships	Dismissal was very high in Denmark (65%) and in US and Israel. The rest of the countries have job protection for work incapacitated subjects, so dismissal was rare, especially in Sweden.	Mostly during first year for cohorts with high dismissal and vice versa.	Dismissed subjects had lower work resumption rates.

Intervention	Occurrence	Timing	Relationship to work resumption
Work (in)capacity assessments/ benefit and rehabilitation procedures	More than 40% were assessed for disability benefit in Israel, Netherlands and US. In the rest of the cohorts, 13-34% were assessed. Rehabilitation inquiry was frequent in Denmark, Sweden and Netherlands (50-65%). In Israel and US – it was rare. In Germany – 42%.	Mostly during first year for Netherlands, Denmark and Israel. Close to onset of sickness for cohorts with high incidence. In Israel, US and Germany – it occurred later.	Assessing disability benefit qualification and rehabilitation inquiry had negative relation to work resumption.
Job services and other services	20-30% searched for a job in all cohorts, but Sweden. Job offer was not frequent, up to 8%, except for Germany with 16%.	Second half of first year.	Positive relation to work resumption for Denmark and Israel. For the rest - negative (except for US).

Tests for disability benefits were quite frequent in the cohorts from the Netherlands, the United States, and Israel (40% or more), and also in the cohort from Germany (34%); they were less so in the cohorts from Denmark (23%) and Sweden (13%). In the Netherlands and Denmark, testing was carried out earlier than in the other countries. The proportion of subjects eligible for a benefit out of those tested was higher in the second year, and amounted to over three-quarters of the subjects from Germany, the Netherlands, and Sweden, more than half of the subjects from Denmark and Israel, and about 40 percent of the subjects from the United States.

Relevance of Policy Context and Timing of Interventions

On the basis of the statistical tests performed, it is not possible to draw any reliable conclusion regarding the relationship between the interventions or incentives/disincentives on the one hand, and work resumption on the other, because several factors always have an impact on the outcome. Furthermore, bivariate relationships between most work accommodations or employer motivators and work resumption are not meaningful because work accommodations and employer motivators cannot be provided unless the employee returns to work. In this case, the intervention and the outcome coincide. In addition to the effect of the intervention or incentive/

disincentive itself, the procedure for selecting candidates for interventions or as targets of incentives affect the outcome in a way that is not well known. An analysis is presented in Chapter 10 where the combined effects of personal characteristics and interventions are evaluated.

At this point, it may be said that the different patterns of work resumption found in the different cohorts may suggest that it is the entire context of related policies, and also their timing and placement in the series of procedures aimed at return to work, that determine the content of an intervention. Therefore, it is difficult to draw conclusions as to the "success" (from the point of view of work resumption) of an isolated element of a vocational or other non-medical intervention. This means that it might be quite risky to recommend any fragmented element of policy.

Reference

Öberg, T. (1989). Den farliga sjukskrivningen. *Socialmedicinsk tidskrift nr*, 7, 344–348.

Appendix 8.1

Vocational and Other Non-medical Interventions in the Six Cohorts

Following is a list of 26 interventions covered by the WIR Project, including notes about the main differences among participating countries as they existed at time of the cohort creation. For each intervention, it is specified mainly whether it was a public service in the respective countries, which "actors" were involved, its place in the "career" of a work incapacitated person, and the source of financing.

A. Training and Education

1. Vocational Education and Job Training:

Career/vocation or job-oriented specific education in a school or education/training center, irrespective of receiving benefit. Training at the workplace, or in-company, directed towards a specific job and/or work resumption (own work or other work) without compensation from social security.

All countries except the United States had vocational training and/or job training as an intervention taken in order to facilitate work resumption of work incapacitated workers. The financing of the intervention was by public authorities. In Sweden, it was mostly job training and sometimes it was the obligation of the employer. The initiator mostly was the social security agency in Denmark, the Netherlands, and Israel. In Sweden, it could be the client, employer, or social security.

2. General Education:

General education in various subjects, not directed specifically towards a job.

This intervention was not included in the "rehabilitation basket" in any cohort, except for completion of education in Denmark, Sweden (up to one year), Germany, and Israel, if it was necessary in order to enable the client to find a job. The responsibility for initiation and financing here was similar to that for vocational education and job training, as described above.

B. Work Accommodations and Employer Motivators

3. Adaptation in Workplace:

Adaptations include any technical aids, such as special chair or table, special tools, adapted transport, etc., which are provided in order to facilitate work resumption.

Existed practically in all participating countries. In Sweden, the employer was required to adapt the workplace; therefore, initiation and financing was primarily the employer's responsibility. In the Netherlands, initiation was diverse and financing was usually by the employer. In specific situations (when several specific strict conditions are fulfilled), social security paid for these adaptations in the Netherlands and Sweden. In Denmark, the initiation was diverse and financing was by social security. In the United States, this intervention was not an action of rehabilitation, but rather an obligation of the employer to give equal chances of work to every individual, including the handicapped.

4. Special Transportation to Workplace:

Special transport from home to work, such as taxi service or commuting service, car expense pay, adaptation of one's own car, subsidy for buying a car, etc. Subsidy for other public transport was not included here.

Existed as an intervention aimed at work resumption mainly in Sweden. Initiation could be by diverse actors, financed by social security. Existed also in Denmark and Germany. In the United States, some states have special transportation arrangements for all work incapacitated persons. In Israel, mobility-handicapped workers could get a special mobility benefit instead of the disability benefit, but this was irrelevant for this research population.

5. Change of Workplace and/or Job Redesign:

Changes of work tasks, including minor changes such as not having to carry things; change of workplace.

Existed as a defined service in the Netherlands only, initiation was diverse and financed by the employer. Certainly, it might happen in all countries. The feeling was that the combination of job redesign with change of place of work together had created a variable, which was not clearly defined. However, information concerning change of place of work at the moment of the second or third interviews (T2 and T3) was requested in another question.

6. Change in Working Hours:

Changes in number and/or pattern of working hours: different shifts, less or more hours, more variation in hours, etc.

Existed in the Netherlands, Sweden, Germany, and Denmark as a service under the heading of "partial work resumption," which also included wage supplement by a partial benefit; financed by social security, initiation by different actors. Change in work hours might certainly happen in all countries, without a partial benefit to back it up.

7. Sheltered Workshop:

Work in a protected workplace or protected work environment for employees who are not able to work in open employment or who cannot compete with "normal" workers.

Existed in Sweden, the Netherlands, and Israel, but was not particularly relevant to the study population as it was confined usually to the mentally and developmentally handicapped. Financing was public (in the United States, mostly charity) and initiation diverse.

8. Job Training with Compensation from Social Security:

The employee "works" but the social security office paid the full sickness or disability benefit. The work can be the normal work, but also different: fewer tasks, slower, fewer hours, etc. This included also on-the-job training with compensation from social security.

Existed in all countries except Israel. The initiation was by social security in Denmark, the United States, and Sweden, and by the employee or employer in the Netherlands. Financing was by social security (in the Netherlands, it was by the employer since 1996).

9. Wage Subsidy:

The employer got a subsidy for employment of the sick employee, with a maximum of 100 percent of wages, usually for a limited time. Also if the employer was entitled to pay only partial/no wage or under normal wage level.

Existed in the Netherlands, Sweden, Denmark, and Germany. The responsibility for initiation was on the employer in the Netherlands, and diverse in the rest. Social security financed this service in the Netherlands and Denmark. In Sweden, the employment agency financed it for unemployed work incapacitated persons. In Germany, it was financed by social security or the employment agency.

C. Employee Motivators/Disciplinary Actions and Labor Relationships

11-12. Warning and Realization of Dismissal:

In the Netherlands, it was forbidden to dismiss a work incapacitated employee for two years on grounds of work incapacity. As some Dutch subjects reported dismissal, it seems that sometimes they said that they were dismissed when they got this notice even if the date of dismissal was not yet reached. In Sweden, dismissal was possible only after all steps toward work resumption in the original place of work were exhausted. This process usually took about a year. Dismissal certainly can and did happen in all other participating countries.

15. Contact with Employer/Colleagues:

Contacts between employees and their employer/colleagues during period of work incapacity.

In Sweden and the Netherlands, these contacts could happen in the framework of work resumption measures, as the employer was required to initiate contacts with work incapacitated employees in order to plan rehabilitation. Contacts with employer/colleagues could also happen out of social or other motives, in all participating countries.

D. Work Incapacity Assessment/Benefit Withdrawal and Rehabilitation Procedures

17. Medical Examination for Sickness Benefit Eligibility:

All evaluation of work incapacity for qualification for a sickness, disability, or work injury benefit. Performed by a qualified physician, not necessarily resulting in a medical certificate.

Existed in all countries; the responsibility for initiation and financing was practically by social security in all countries except the Netherlands. For this cohort, the employer financed and implemented the intervention, and the occupational doctor was responsible for initiation. In the Netherlands, examinations for benefit qualification were separated from those for treatment. In the rest of the countries, the same examination could serve both purposes.

13-14. Threats and Actual Withdrawal of Benefit:

The social security office warned or threatened the client with a reduction of benefit, discontinuation or withdrawal of benefit, and the realization of this threat.

Existed under special conditions mainly in Denmark and Netherlands. This question was not asked in the United States. In Israel, it was theoretical, as a practical matter.

18. Rehabilitation Inquiry and Plan:

Assessment of possibilities for rehabilitation and creating a plan for this purpose, detailing the measures necessary in order to enable the employee to resume work.

Existed in all countries as an obligation of the service provider, except the United States. Initiation was the responsibility of an occupational doctor in the Netherlands. In Israel, the claimant had to request rehabilitation and then social security made the assessment and plan. In Sweden, the employer had the primary responsibility for the rehabilitation of the employee. In the rest of the countries, social security initiated this service. Financing was by social security in Denmark, Germany, and Israel; by social security or the employer in Sweden; and by the employer in the Netherlands.

16. Test of Vocational and Work Capacity:

A technique of vocational capacity assessment: the client is tested in a real, work-like environment (e.g. in a kind of laboratory). Usually by having the client perform samples of work.

Existed in all participating countries, by social security initiation. In Sweden, could be initiated by the employer as well. Financing in Israel and Denmark was by social security; in Sweden, by social security or the employer. In the rest of the countries, it was diverse.

19. Assessments and Eligibility for Disability Benefit:

Existed in all participating countries. The initiation of this intervention was on the claimant, who had to request the benefit. After the benefit was requested, social security was responsible for initiating and financing the assessment and the benefit. Although in all participating countries the claimant should have requested the benefit, in the Netherlands, Denmark, and Sweden, social security was involved in advising them to do so at a fixed time following work incapacity. In the Netherlands, for example, the client is invited to claim eligibility for disability benefits seven months after the onset of work incapacity. Sometimes this might encourage work resumption as the conditions of those benefits are not as favorable as with sickness benefits. In Sweden, eligibility for disability benefits was assessed only after all possibilities for returning to original or a new place of work were exhausted. This usually happened around one year after the onset of work incapacity. Sometimes social security would initiate transition from sickness to disability benefit in Sweden.

In the United States, a sick employee was not in contact with the social security authorities before claiming disability benefits. Also, eligibility for sickness benefits involved a means test in one of the two state programs covered in the national study.

10. Capitalization of Benefit/Subsidy for Self-employment:

Award of a lump sum instead of benefits or a special subsidy, e.g. to start one's own business.

The possibility of capitalization of a disability benefit in order to establish self-employment existed only in Israel. Subsidy for self-employment existed also in Denmark and Sweden.

E. Job Services and Other Services

20. Job and Benefit Counseling:

All kinds of job-related or benefit-related individual counseling from employment service, occupational therapist, social security, etc.

This variable did not have the same content in the different countries. In the Netherlands, referred to as "support directed at work." In Sweden and the United States, referred to as "general employment counseling." Only Denmark had special counseling service for work incapacitated employees.

21. Job Search:

By the employee himself or herself. All kinds of ways the employee could use to search for jobs (through employment services, newspapers, friends, family, etc.). The third interview included also a question on the ways of job search.

22. Job Offer:

Suitable job offer given to the employee by rehabilitation authorities, employment service, or social security office. Offer may be presented even without a job search on the part of the employee, especially in Denmark.

23. Activation Group/Job Club:

Mostly workshops aimed at promoting job search qualifications, such as skills of application for a job; group activities, such as visits to place of work in Sweden, group therapy aimed at rehabilitation, etc. (The United States questionnaire referred to the latter only.)

24. Change in Day Care Arrangements for Children:

Any change in day care for children, including canceling the provision of day care because of work incapacity; provision of day care for children in order to encourage work resumption.

Did not exist as a defined service for work incapacitated persons in any of the participating countries. Might certainly happen anywhere.

25. Psychotherapy/Counseling:

Social counseling by welfare organization, psychotherapist, etc. Not primarily benefit- or job-oriented.

Existed in Denmark, financed by social security as a service connected to rehabilitation. (Existed in all countries as a medical service, one might presume.) In Israel, the rehabilitation officer could give short-term therapy.

26. Reduction of Waiting Period in Health Care:

The social security office, employer, or other relevant actors, could seek ways to speed up the medical treatment of the employee in case of waiting lists for medical treatment.

Did not exist as a defined service in any cohort. In the Netherlands, social security or the employer could initiate.

Appendix 8.2

Summary of Work Incapacity Procedures

TABLE 8A2.1: Denmark

	Client	Employer	Doctor	Social Security
Day 1	Informs employer	May ask for doctor's certificate. Pays sickness benefit (100% up to ceiling).	Examines, treats and gives certificate.	May ask for doctor's certificate
Week 2	Informs municipality, has to cooperate with treatment and rehabilitation (towards return to work).	End of sickness pay on employer's account. Private employer may pay wage and refund it. Government pays wage or benefit. Reports to municipality if still ill.		Finances benefit to employees in private sector
Month 2		Reports to municipality if still absent.		
Month 3			Assesses work resumption probability.	Assesses possibilities and rehabilitation needs for work resumption at old employer, new employer or disability benefit. Re-assessment every 3 months.
Year 1		End of sickness pay for civil servants.		End of sickness pay.

TABLE 8A2.2: Germany

	Client	Employer	Doctor	Social Security
Day 1	Informs employer	Pays sickness benefit until day 42		
Day 3	Gives doctor's certificate to employer		Certificate	
Day 21	Should contact doctors to get medical rehabilitation		Can testify the need for medical rehabilitation	Sickness fund should send the client its medical review board
Day 43		End of sickness pay		Sickness fund/health insurance starts paying about 70% of the last wages; consulting for rehabilitation program
Week 72				Decision about the future working status and kind of income should be made: - disability pension - unemployment benefit - social welfare - public assistance - additional rehabilitation program (temporary)

TABLE 8A2.3: Israel

	Client	Employer	Doctor	Social Security
Day 1	Informs employer. Claims work injury allowance from social security. If denied – gets sick pay from employer. Can claim (work) disability benefit any time.	Pays first day, if no work injury allowance – pays sick pay.	Examines and determines work incapacity and number of days of work incapacity and disability.	Determines entitlement for work injury allowance. If granted – pays this allowance.
Day 90	Claims general disability benefit (if was not entitled to work injury allowance).	End of sickness pay (for those denied work injury allowance).	Advises for disability and rehabilitation	Determines general disability benefits for those not entitled to work injury allowance.
Day 186			Advises for disability and rehabilitation	End of work injury allowance. Work disability benefit may be decided upon even before end of injury allowance. After disability benefit entitlement is established (either one) starts rehabilitation

TABLE 8A2.4: Netherlands

	Client	Employer	Doctor	Social Security
Day 1	Informs employer. Answers social security questionnaire	Informs social security.		
Week 2 –3	Examination by occupational doctor.	Rehabilitation plan. Agreement on date of return to work.	Invitation to occupational doctor. Assesses work incapacity.	
Week 13		Informs social security.		Assessment of employers' efforts in rehabilitation.
Month 7			Assesses work incapacity.	Inquires about earning ability, entitlement to benefit and rehabilitation plan.
Month 12		End of responsibility		Invitation to assess entitlement to disability benefit.
Year 2		End of obligation to re-hire.		
Every three years				Re-assessment of entitlement to disability benefit.

TABLE 8A2.5: Sweden

	Client	Employer	Doctor	Social Security
Day 1	Informs employer.	Pays sickness benefit until day 14.		
Day 8	Gives doctor's certificate to employer.		Examines, treats and gives certificate.	
Day 15		Informs social security about the sickness case. Additional sickness benefit (10%) is paid until day 90 from insurance (collective labor agreement).		Entitlement to sickness benefit.
Week 4	Informs social security stating medical situation and reasons for not working. Submits a special doctor's statement to social security.	Performs rehabilitation inquiry. Has primary responsibility for rehabilitation measures.	Gives a special statement to the client, stating medical status and rehabilitation needs and possibilities.	Entitlement to sickness benefit (thorough assessment).
Week 8	Cooperates with social security in rehabilitation plan.	Informs social security about rehabilitation inquiry.		Rehabilitation plan and execution (coordination with employer, doctor etc.), pays eventual rehabilitation benefit (no mandatory timing).
Month 12	May apply for disability benefit any time (no mandatory timing).			Entitlement for disability benefit, temporary or permanent, by initiative from client or social security (no mandatory timing, usually after 1 year).

TABLE 8A2.6: United States

	Client	Employer	Doctor	Social Security
Day 8	Receives form and fills in	Gives form	Adds details to form	Sends form to TDI
Day 14	Starts receiving pay			Starts paying
Week 26	End of pay NJ; claim long term benefit			End of pay NJ
Week 52	End of pay Calif.			End of pay Calif.

9

A Closer Look at Work Resumption

John Kearney

The primary objective of this chapter is to provide cross-national comparisons for a number of variables in relation to outcomes recorded at the end of the two-year follow-up period (T3), including occupation, vocational rehabilitation intervention, reasons for not working, changes in hours worked or wages, type of medical provider, and type of medical treatment. Additionally, the chapter discusses patterns of work resumption throughout the course of the Project and the characteristics of workers who returned to work at different points, as well as those of workers who returned to work and later stopped working. Some additional tables and a technical note on the statistical analysis used in the chapter are included as appendices.

Characteristics of Work Resumption

This section considers the influence that certain variables may have had on the level of work resumption. Specifically, it discusses the proportions of work resumers from each national cohort who resumed working either for a new employer or their previous employer, the percentages of work resumption by occupational group, and the proportions of resumers from each occupational group who changed their occupation.

Type of Employer

One factor which may be important to many workers in helping them to resume working is their employer's willingness to retain them throughout a period during which they are work incapacitated, and to provide necessary accommodations to enable them to return to work successfully. Table 9.1 shows the proportion of subjects who had resumed working for their old employer at T3, in comparison to those who found a new employer.

TABLE 9.1
Work Resumption by Type of Employer (%) at T3

	Denmark	Germany	Israel	N'lands	Sweden	US
Working at T3 (% of all subjects	39.7	35.1	60.4	71.6	62.6	62.6
Old Employer	42.3	94.2	45.6	81.9	86.2	56.4
New Employer	50.9	3.5	51.3	17.7	7.1	37.6
Self Employed	1.7	2.3	3.1	0.4	2.1	4.7
Other	5.1	0.0	0.0	0.0	4.6	1.3

$p \leq .001$

The patterns among the country cohorts were highly divergent. Over 90 percent of work resumers from the German cohort returned to work for their old employer. This was also the preferred avenue to work resumption for the Dutch and Swedish cohorts. By contrast, more than half of the subjects who returned to work from the Danish and Israeli cohorts, as well as more than one-third of those from the American cohort, found a new employer. This finding is consistent with data on dismissal presented in Chapter 8. Significant percentages of subjects were dismissed by their employers in Denmark, and, to a lesser degree, in Israel and the United States. However, dismissal was rare for subjects in Germany, Sweden, and the Netherlands, due to job protection provided to work incapacitated workers in those countries.

Occupation

The type of occupation appears to be significant in the decision to resume working, since it is related to the demands of work. Cohort data on work resumption by occupation for five of the participating countries (all except Germany) are as shown in Table 9.2.

TABLE 9.2
Rates of Work Resumption by Occupation (%) at T3

	Denmark	Israel	N'lands	Sweden	US
Working at T3 **(% of all subjects)**	39.7	60.4	71.6	62.6	62.6
Manager	.	.	87.5	.	60.0
Professional	75.0	.	.	66.7	81.3
Technical[1]	60.8	92.3	77.8	81.3	59.6
Clerical[1]	37.1	69.2	75.0	62.3	72.7
Sales/Services[1]	28.0	61.5	61.8	65.2	57.1
Crafts/Trades[1]	51.7	63.9	75.9	63.2	71.7
Factory worker/ **Truck driver**[1]	38.7	51.9	72.3	51.6	40.6
Unskilled[1]	27.1	54.7	51.1	60.0	61.1

[1] $p \le .05$
. less than 10 observations

There were not enough observations from several cohorts to determine the rate of work resumption among managers and professionals. However, in those instances where data were sufficient, generally the rate of work resumption was well above the average for all occupations. Technicians, clerical workers, sales workers, service providers, and those involved in the crafts and trades industries returned to work at a rate that ranged from average to above average for most cohorts. The exception to this trend was the Danish cohort, where the rate of work resumption among clerical workers, sales workers, and service providers was less than the average for all occupations. In all of the cohorts, factory workers, truck drivers, and unskilled workers returned to work at a rate that ranged from average to well below average.

TABLE 9.3
Change in Occupation by Occupational Group (%) at T3

	Denmark	Israel	N'lands	Sweden	US
Working at T3 (% of all subjects)	39.7	60.4	71.6	62.6	62.6
Manager/Professional					
Different occupation	58.3	.	26.9	26.1	27.8
Same occupation	41.7	.	73.1	73.9	72.2
Technical					
Different occupation	45.2	66.7	22.9	36.0	46.4
Same occupation	54.8	33.3	77.1	64.0	53.6
Clerical[2]					
Different occupation	53.9	.	22.2	34.4	28.1
Same occupation	46.1	.	77.8	65.6	71.9
Sales/Services[1]					
Different occupation	47.1	79.2	29.4	29.1	66.7
Same occupation	52.9	20.8	70.6	70.9	33.3
Crafts/Trades[1]					
Different occupation	56.7	77.4	39.1	17.5	60.6
Same occupation	43.3	22.6	60.9	82.5	39.4
Factory worker/Truck driver					
Different occupation	70.8	63.0	48.5	53.3	23.1

	Denmark	Israel	N'lands	Sweden	US
Factory worker/Truck driver *(Cont'd)*					
Same occupation	29.2	37.0	51.5	46.7	76.9
Unskilled[1]					
Different occupation	84.2	79.3	39.1	38.5	36.4
Same occupation	15.8	20.7	60.9	61.5	63.6

[1] $p \leq .001$
[2] $p \leq .05$
. less than 10 observations

Although the patterns of work resumption showed some variation by cohort, the general trend was that the rate of work resumption was higher for those occupations that involve fewer physical demands. In an effort to determine whether workers in physically demanding occupations changed jobs in order to resume working, Table 9.3 presents the proportions of work resumers from each occupational group who returned to work in an occupation different from the one in which they were employed at the time they became work incapacitated.

Most clerical workers in the cohorts from Sweden, the Netherlands, and the United States returned to work at the same occupation, while more than half of those in the cohort from Denmark changed occupations. Large percentages of sales and service workers in the Israeli and the American cohorts changed their occupation, in contrast to the Swedish and Dutch cohorts, where few made such a change. The same pattern was evident among workers in the crafts and trade industries. Most unskilled workers in the cohorts from Denmark and Israel changed occupation, while less than 40 percent of those in the cohorts from Sweden, the Netherlands, and the United States did so.

There is no statistically significant difference between country cohorts in proportions of managers and professionals, technical workers, factory workers, and truck drivers who changed occupation. However, it is noteworthy that over 70 percent of managers and professionals in the cohorts from Sweden, the Netherlands, and the United States remained in the same occupation.

No consistent pattern of job change by type of occupation is evident among the six country cohorts. This may be due in part to differences in job demands, but it is also apparent that change in occupation was much more common in countries where workers were more frequently dismissed from their jobs. It appears that most subjects who changed occupation did so as a result of being dismissed, rather than to seek an occupation with fewer physical demands.

Changes in Hours Worked, Wages, and Occupation

Work incapacitated workers often have to make considerable adjustments in order to resume working. Table 9.4 provides some indication of the extent of these adjustments in terms of hours worked, wages, and occupation.

TABLE 9.4
Change in Hours Worked, Wages and Occupation for
Resumers (%), T0 – T3

	Denmark	Germany	Israel	N'lands	Sweden	US
Working at T3 (% of all subjects)	**39.7**	**35.1**	**60.4**	**71.6**	**62.6**	**62.6**
Hours Worked						
Fewer	32.9	8.8	55.6	16.0	68.2	27.5
More	11.6	2.5	4.4	9.9	31.8	19.9
No Change	55.5	88.8	40.0	74.1	0.0	52.5
Wages						
Higher	33.3	8.6	9.4	32.3	59.4	42.4
Lower	24.4	7.4	55.4	11.8	40.6	24.6
Same	42.3	84.0	35.2	55.9	0.0	33.1
Occupation						
Same	40.8	96.2	26.3	65.0	68.6	58.5
Different	59.2	3.8	73.8	35.0	31.4	41.5

$p \leq .001$ for hours worked, wages and occupation

There was no change in hours worked for most of the resumers from the German and Dutch cohorts. By contrast, approximately 40 to 50 percent of resumers from the Danish, Israeli, and American cohorts reported that there was no change in work hours, and all of the resumers from the

Swedish cohort reported some change in hours worked. There was a similar pattern for all cohorts with respect to the type of change in hours of work. A much higher proportion from each cohort reported working fewer hours, as opposed to more hours.

The pattern of change in wages corresponded in most instances to reported changes in hours worked. The highest proportions of resumers who reported no change in wages were identical to those from the cohorts that most frequently reported no change in hours worked (Germany and the Netherlands). Nevertheless, for every cohort except the cohort from Israel, resumers who reported a change in wages reported receiving higher wages more frequently than receiving lower wages. By contrast, 55.4 percent of resumers from the Israeli cohort reported lower wages, and only 9.4 percent reported receiving higher wages. The high proportion of workers from most cohorts who received higher wages could be due to wage increases that took place between T0 and T3, or to occupational changes.

Changes in occupation were rare for resumers from the German cohort; only 3.8 percent reported a change in occupation. However, a significant proportion of resumers from each of the other cohorts reported a change in occupation, ranging from 31.4 percent for the Swedish cohort to 73.8 percent for the Israeli cohort.

Work Resumption and Vocational and Other Non-medical Interventions

Table 9.5 displays the participation in various vocational rehabilitation (VR) programs and other non-medical interventions for those subjects who were working at T3. The values in this table represent VR participation at any point during the survey (T1-T3).

For each country cohort from which there were sufficient observations, 80 percent or more of work resumers reported that they had an adapted workplace. Over 85 percent of resumers from the Israeli and American cohorts reported that they received job placement services, but this intervention did not appear to have that significant an effect on any other cohort. Workers from only one cohort (Denmark) reported receiving an employer wage subsidy; more than 70 percent of the subjects in that country received a subsidy. A large number of work resumers from the American, Swedish, and Dutch cohorts reported that they were working for therapeutic reasons (job training with compensation, volunteer work, etc.), but there were less than 10 observations from the other country cohorts on this intervention. Work resumers from only two cohorts (Israel and the United States) reported in significant numbers that they had received general education.

TABLE 9.5
Rates of Work Resumption for Subjects Receiving Vocational
and Other Non-Medical Interventions (%) at T3

Interventions	Denmark	Germany	Israel	N'lands	Sweden	US
Working at T3 (% of all subjects)	39.7	35.1	60.4	71.6	62.6	62.6
Adapted workplace	82.5	.	93.3	90.9	91.7	81.4
Applied for disability benefit [1]	6.0	5.9	54.9	50.3	19.6	42.2
Vocational capacities tested[1]	28.7	18.8	30.0	48.0	52.4	65.2
Rehabilitation plan[1]	28.2	30.3	26.7	59.7	62.4	29.1
Job training/ Vocational education[1]	43.2	18.2	68.4	67.7	63.3	66.7
General education[1]	22.4	.	80.0	.	52.6	62.0
Employer wage subsidy	70.6	.	.	.	.	.
Therapeutic work resumption[2]	.	.	.	82.1	79.3	83.3
Job placement services[1]	50.0	20.0	95.0	40.9	52.4	87.5

[1] p ≤ .001
[2] p ≤ .01
. less than 10 observations

Subjects were asked whether they had applied for disability benefits. There was considerable variation in the responses, which may be a reflection of differences in the social insurance programs for each of the country cohorts.

Work Resumption and Medical Interventions

One of the primary objectives of this project was to identify those medical interventions that are most successful in helping work incapacitated persons to resume working. This section looks at work outcomes in relation to the types of medical providers seen by work resumers and the various types of medical treatments they received.

Type of Medical Provider

Subjects were asked what types of medical providers (family doctor, company doctor, specialist, or physical therapist) they had seen for their back condition. As shown in Table 9.6, the responses were quite similar for each cohort in relation to the proportion of respondents who were working at T3. The only variations were that work resumers from the German cohort were more likely to have been treated by a company doctor, and resumers from the Danish and American cohorts were less likely to have seen a company doctor.

TABLE 9.6
Consultation of Medical Providers and Work Resumption (%) at T3

	Denmark	Germany	Israel	N'lands	Sweden	US
Working at T3 (% of all subjects)	**39.7**	**35.1**	**60.4**	**71.6**	**62.6**	**62.6**
For those having seen...						
Family Doctor	39.3	31.2	60.7	71.5	62.1	59.9
Company Doctor	28.0	47.1	63.0	71.0	61.9	44.9
Specialist	38.4	35.0	60.2	69.9	62.1	60.1
Physical therapist	39.6	34.9	59.9	72.0	63.8	59.3

p ≤ .001 for each medical provider

Table 9.7 shows the types of medical providers seen by work resumers who remained with their old employer, in comparison to those who were working for a new employer. There were only two noticeable trends. First, resumers who returned to work with their old employer were more likely to have been treated by a company doctor. This trend was very pronounced

TABLE 9.7

Consultation of Medical Providers and Working at Old or New Employer (%) at T3

	Denmark		Germany		Israel		N'lands		Sweden		US	
	Old	New	Old	New	Old	New	Old	New	Old	New	Old	New
For those having seen...												
Family Doctor	44.7	55.3	95.1	4.9	47.0	53.0	82.3	17.7	92.1	7.9	58.0	42.0
Company Doctor	.	.	100.0	0.0	55.2	44.8	82.0	18.0	91.3	8.7	65.6	34.4
Specialist	48.9	51.1	96.0	4.0	47.4	52.6	80.9	19.1	94.6	5.4	59.2	40.8
Physical Therapist	46.6	53.4	95.4	4.6	47.5	52.5	82.5	17.5	92.3	7.7	55.7	44.3

. less than 10 observations

for the Dutch and Swedish cohorts, and was universal for the German cohort. The second trend was that few resumers from the German, Swedish, and Dutch cohorts who returned to work with a new employer were treated by a medical provider of any kind.

Medical Treatments

The various medical treatments reported by subjects who had resumed work at T3 are shown in Table 9.8. This table reflects treatment at any point during the course of the survey (T1-T3). The large percentages of resumers who received various types of medical treatment in each of the six country cohorts is indicative of the importance of medical treatment to relieve back pain. A description of medical treatments applied to all subjects is included in Chapter 7.

If we now concentrate on those who returned to work, the following picture can be seen (not in table). There were very few instances in which

TABLE 9.8
Work Resumption at T3 for Subjects Receiving
Medical Treatments (%)

Treatments	Denmark	Germany	Israel	N'lands	Sweden	US
Working at T3 (% of all subjects)	**39.7**	**35.1**	**60.4**	**71.6**	**62.6**	**62.6**
X-Rays	40.0	31.0	60.3	69.4	65.6	62.0
Hospitalization	41.8	33.8	57.9	70.7	71.8	63.8
Back surgery	52.9	30.4	54.9	76.9	77.6	66.3
Acupuncture	39.0	33.3	74.5	63.0	57.5	48.2
Pain relieving injections/ Medicine	38.9	32.1	60.2	72.0	62.1	61.0
Passive treatments	39.3	32.6	60.0	70.7	63.2	61.8
Muscle training/Range-of-motion	39.9	35.0	61.3	71.2	64.1	61.3
External support	36.0	29.9	59.3	62.0	64.5	58.5

$p \leq .001$ for each treatment

an unusually high proportion of work resumers reported that they had received any one particular treatment. Work resumers from the Danish, Swedish, Dutch, and American cohorts had back surgery much more frequently than any other treatment. Acupuncture was comparatively the most frequently reported treatment received by work resumers from the Israeli cohort; by contrast, a relatively low percentage of resumers from the Dutch and American cohorts received acupuncture. With these few exceptions, both resumers and non-resumers reported the same types of medical treatments in approximately equal proportions.

Work Resumption Patterns

The WIR Project measured work status at one and two years following the onset of work incapacity (T2 and T3). In Chapter 6, Table 6.2 provides data on four work resumption patterns: 1) continuous working (those who were working at T2 and T3); 2) late resumers (those who were not working at T2, but were working at T3); 3) relapse (those who were working at T2, but not at T3); and 4) non-resumers (those who were not working at T2 or T3).

This section explores the association between various demographic characteristics, health indicators, and job characteristics, and those patterns of work resumption. Tables 9.9 through 9.11 show the significance of these characteristics for late resumers and relapsed resumers, by comparison to continuous resumers; and for non-resumers, by comparison to late resumers. Table 9.12 shows the comparative significance of these characteristics for all four groups. Additional data on these characteristics for all four groups are provided in tables presented in Appendix 9.1 at the end of this chapter.

"Continuous" Versus "Late Resumers"

In the Danish cohort, there was a considerably higher proportion of males who returned to work at T2; by contrast, most late resumers were female. See Table 9.9. A strong association between household composition and the pattern of work resumption was identified in the Israeli cohort. While resumers in most types of households were working both at T2 and T3, more than half of those in "other" household situations were late resumers. There was some difference in the Swedish cohort between resumers who were native born and spoke the native language, and those who were foreign born and spoke a different language; the latter group were more likely to be late resumers. In the American cohort, there was some association between a higher level of back function (as reflected in the Hannover ADL score) and work resumption at T2.

TABLE 9.9
Continuous vs. Late Resumers: Patterns of Work Resumption and
Selected Characteristics (Significant Associations)

	Denmark	Germany	Israel	N'lands	Sweden	US
Demographic characteristics at T1						
Age	—	—	—	—	—	x
Gender	xx	—	—	—	—	—
Educational level	—	—	—	—	—	—
Household composition	—	—	xxx	—	—	—
Mother language (native/other)	—	—	—	—	x	—
Nationality (native/ foreign)	—	—	—	—	x	—
Health indicators (T3)						
Pain intensity	—	—	—	—	—	—
Back function	—	—	—	—	—	x
Job characteristics (T1)						
Weekly working hours	—	—	—	—	xx	—
Physical job demands	—	—	—	—	—	—
Job strain	xx	—	x	—	—	—

Legend: xxx: p ≤ .001   xx: p ≤ .01   x: p ≤ .05
— not significant

In the area of job characteristics, only a few variables in one or two cohorts showed a relationship with work resumption patterns. In the Swedish cohort, most of the resumers who were working less than 20 hours per week were among those who returned to work at T3. A similar pattern was found in the Danish and Israeli cohorts with the level of job strain; in both cases, resumers who reported a low level of job strain were more likely to have returned to work at T2 than those who reported higher levels of strain. Job strain includes such factors as the levels of skill and creativity required, the amount of work, and the speed at which work must be performed. As indicated in Table 9.9, no individual characteristic is associated with the pattern of work resumption in more than two country cohorts.

"Continuous Resumers" Versus "Relapse"

The significance of association between continuous work and relapse (work at T2, but not at T3) is shown for the same characteristics in Table 9.10.

Relatively small proportions of subjects from each of the six cohorts (between 5% and 10%) were working at T2 but not at T3. Few associations between this group and continuous resumers were found relative to demographic characteristics. Females from the Danish cohort were more likely than males to have stopped working at T3, but the opposite pattern was found for the German cohort. The level of education was associated with relapse among the Israeli cohort; resumers with a moderate level of education were less likely to have relapsed than those with either lower or higher levels of education.

Strong associations were found, however, relative to health indicators, job strain, and the tendency to stop working at T3. There was a significant correlation for the Swedish and Israeli cohorts between relapse resumers and a level of pain described as intense. Additionally, resumers from the Dutch, Swedish, Danish, and American cohorts who were no longer working at T3 reported greater difficulties in functioning than those who continued to work. Job strain was associated with relapse for resumers in the Dutch, Danish, and Swedish cohorts. Resumers from the Dutch cohort who reported a high level of job strain were more likely to have stopped work; the same tendency was seen among those from the Danish and Swedish cohorts who reported moderate job strain or greater.

Late Resumers" Versus "Non-resumers"

Table 9.11 shows the association between the same demographic characteristics and work resumption at T3, as compared to non-resumption (not working at T2 and T3). There were few associations between these two patterns and the demographic characteristics. The most prominent were a correlation between non-resumption and a low level of education for the Danish cohort, and a strong association for the Israeli cohort involving household composition. A considerably higher proportion of Israeli workers living in "other" household situations were late resumers, by comparison to those living alone, with a partner, or with children.

TABLE 9.10
Continuous Resumers vs. Relapse Group: Patterns of Work
Resumption and Selected Characteristics (Significant Associations)

	Denmark	Germany	Israel	N'lands	Sweden	US
Demographic characteristics at T1						
Age	—	—	—	—	—	—
Gender	xx	x	—	—	—	—
Educational level	—	—	x	—	—	—
Household composition	—	—	—	—	—	—
Mother language (native/other)	—	—	—	—	—	—
Nationality (native/ foreign)	—	—	—	—	—	—
Health indicators (T3)						
Pain intensity	—	—	xx	—	xxx	—
Back function	xx	—	—	xxx	xxx	x
Job characteristics (T1)						
Weekly working hours	—	—	—	—	—	—
Physical job demands	—	—	—	—	—	—
Job strain	xx	—	—	xx	x	—

Legend: xxx: p ≤ .001   xx: p ≤ .01   x: p ≤ .05
— not significant

TABLE 9.11
Late Resumers vs. Non-Resumers: Patterns of Work Resumption and Selected Characteristics (Significant Associations)

	Denmark	Germany	Israel	N'lands	Sweden	US
Demographic characteristics at T1						
Age	x	—	—	—	x	—
Gender	—	—	—	x	—	—
Educational level	xx	—	—	—	—	—
Household composition	—	—	xxx	—	—	—
Mother language (native/other)	x	—	—	—	—	—
Nationality (native/foreign)	—	—	—	—	—	—
Health indicators (T3)						
Pain intensity	xxx	—	xxx	xxx	xxx	xx
Back function	xxx	—	xxx	xxx	xxx	xx
Job characteristics (T1)						
Physical job demands	—	—	—	—	—	—
Job strain	—	—	—	x	—	—

Legend: xxx: p ≤ .001   xx: p ≤ .01   x: p ≤ .05
— not significant

The association between health indicators and work resumption was very strong for all of the country cohorts, except for the German cohort. The pattern was similar for each of those cohorts: the more intense the level of pain and the lower the functional capacity, the more likely it was that the person had not returned to work.

Work Resumption and Selected Baseline Characteristics

Table 9.12 combines all work resumption patterns in order to present a more complete picture of the relationship between the various patterns and the selected characteristics. The most prominent trends identifiable from this table are discussed below.

Age: There was a strong association between age and the patterns of work resumption for five of the six country cohorts, and the trend was similar in each one. Non-resumers and, to a lesser extent, relapsed workers were considerably older than continuous resumers and late resumers. Over 80 percent of the subjects from the Danish cohort who were 55 years of age or older, and over 70 percent of the subjects in the same age group from the German cohort, were non-resumers.

Gender: Continuous resumers from the Danish and Dutch cohorts were predominantly male, and non-resumers were predominantly female.

Educational Level: Subjects from the Danish and Israeli cohorts with less than a high school education were predominantly non-resumers.

Pain Intensity: The association between the intensity of pain and the pattern of work resumption was strong for five of the six country cohorts. In each instance, the pattern was similar: continuous resumers and late resumers reported lower levels of pain than relapsed workers or non-resumers.

Back function (Hannover ADL Score): Continuous and late resumers from all six cohorts reported considerably better levels of functioning than relapsed workers and non-resumers.

Physical Job Demands: Higher proportions of non-resumers and relapsed resumers from three country cohorts (the Netherlands, Sweden, and the United States) reported considerably higher levels of physical job demands than those reported by continuous resumers. Approximately two-thirds of the American subjects who reported low physical job demands were continuous resumers, and only 16 percent were non-resumers.

Job Strain: A much higher proportion of non-resumers from the Danish and Dutch cohorts reported high levels of job strain than did other subjects.

TABLE 9.12
Patterns of Work Resumption (Continuous/Late
Resumer/Relapse/Non-Resumer) and Selected Characteristics
(Significant Associations)

	Denmark	Germany	Israel	N'lands	Sweden	US
Demographic characteristics at T1						
Age	xxx	xxx	—	xx	xx	xxx
Gender	xxx	x	—	xx	—	—
Educational level	xx	—	xx	x	—	—
Household composition	x	—	xx	—	—	—
Mother language (native/other)	—	—	—	x	—	—
Nationality (native/ foreign)	—	—	—	—	—	—
Health indicators (T3)						
Pain intensity	xxx	x	xxx	xxx	xxx	xxx
Back function	xxx	xxx	xxx	xxx	xxx	xxx
Job characteristics (T1)						
Weekly working hours	—	—	—	xx	x	—
Physical job demands	—	x	—	x	xxx	xxx
Job strain	xxx	—	—	xxx	x	—

Legend: xxx: p ≤ .001   xx: p ≤ .01   x: p ≤ .05
— not significant

Reasons Reported for Not Working

Workers who reported that they were not working at T3 were asked why they had not returned to work. As shown in Table 9.13, those who reported that they had not returned to work due to back problems ranged from 62.7 percent to 78.8 percent for five of the six cohorts. However, only 50.5 percent of those from the Dutch cohort gave this response.

TABLE 9.13
Reason for not Working (%) at T3

	Denmark	Germany	Israel	N'lands	Sweden	US
Not Working at T3 (% of all subjects)	60.3	64.9	39.6	28.4	37.4	37.4
Back problems	68.6	62.7	74.3	50.5	78.8	74.1
Other health problems	11.8	9.3	6.7	15.5	8.7	7.9
Other circumstances	19.6	28.0	19.0	34.0	12.5	18.0

$p \le .002$

The proportion of workers who reported that they did not resume working due to other health problems was relatively low—ranging from 6.7 percent to 15.5 percent. A considerably higher proportion from each of the cohorts (as high as 34% in the Netherlands) reported that they had not returned to work due to reasons not related to their back condition or other health problems. Among the other reasons for not returning to work were school attendance and pregnancy.

Summary and Conclusions

This chapter addressed outcomes at T3 in relation to selected variables and the demographic characteristics of the subjects, and in relation to the pattern of work resumption. The following is a summary of findings and some concluding remarks.

Employer and Occupation

The proportion of resumers who returned to work with their previous employer, rather than a new employer, was highly divergent and appears to be related to the level of job protection provided in each of the participating countries. There is no evidence that such policies had any effect on the overall rate of work resumption.

There does appear to be a relationship between work resumption and the type of occupation, in that generally the rate of work resumption was greater for those occupations that involve fewer physical demands. However, there was no evidence that resumers were inclined to change occupation in order to go back to work. Rates of occupational changes appeared to be related to the percentage of job dismissals.

Vocational and Other Non-medical Interventions

There was no clear pattern of any vocational intervention being utilized effectively across country cohorts, with the exception of workplace adaptations. In five of the six country cohorts, a high percentage of resumers received workplace adaptations. It is not known, however, how frequently the adaptation was critical to work resumption, nor how many non-resumers could have returned to work if a particular adaptation had been provided. The role of workplace adaptations is a subject that merits additional research.

Reasons for Non-resumption

It cannot be assumed that all workers who stop working due to a back impairment, and do not resume working, do so solely because of the back impairment. A significant proportion of non-resumers were not working at T3 due to other health problems or unrelated circumstances.

Medical Providers and Treatments

No relationship between the type of medical provider and work resumption at T3 was identified. Nor were there any conclusive findings with respect to medical treatments. Numerous medical treatments were applied to the subjects from all cohorts. Acupuncture was used infrequently in the Israeli cohort, but subjects working at T3 received this treatment more than did subjects who were not working. This treatment was applied most frequently in Sweden, but it was no more effective for working subjects than for subjects who were not working at T3. Resumers from the Danish, Swedish, Dutch, and American cohorts had back surgery more frequently than any other treatment. This was not the case in the German and Israeli cohorts, where back surgery was performed as often on resumers as it was on non-resumers.

Patterns of Work Resumption

The baseline characteristics of continuous resumers and late resumers were generally similar, while the characteristics of relapsed resumers more closely resembled those of non-resumers. Age (55 years or older), the intensity of pain, the degree of functional capacity, and the level of physical job demands were the characteristics most closely associated with work resumption or non-resumption.

Indications of Successful Interventions

The data collected for this project show that in all of the participating countries, a great many interventions are furnished by medical practitioners, VR providers, employers, and others to assist people with lower back pain to return to work. Some indications of the success of these efforts are: in four of the six country cohorts, more than 60 percent of the subjects returned to work at T3 or earlier; in five of the six country cohorts, over 80 percent of employers provided workplace adaptations to facilitate work resumption; and numerous forms of medical treatment, ranging from pain medication to surgery, were provided by a variety of medical practitioners in all of the participating countries.

Careful measurement of job strain, functional capacity, and employer-provided workplace adaptations seem critical in assisting people with disabilities to return to work. Synergizing the medical, VR, and other services with the individual and his or her employer regarding the key determinants of work ability seem equally important.

Technical Note

SAS (Statistical Analysis System) was used for all statistical calculations. Chi square test and Fisher's exact test were used for comparing variables. P-values <0.05 were regarded as statistically significant. For each professional category (Table 9.2 and Table 9.3) and each treatment received (Table 9.8), the Chi square test was done to determine if the outcome variable (working/not working) varied within the six national cohorts. Similarly, for each medical provider (Table 9.7), the Chi square test was calculated to determine if the outcome variable (old employer/ new employer) for those respondents working at T3 varied within the six cohorts. In Table 9.9 through Table 9.11, Fisher's exact test was used to measure the relationship between characteristics and the outcome variables. In like manner, both Chi square test and Fisher's exact test were used to measure the relationship between the characteristics and the outcome variables in Table 9.12. The characteristics for Table 9.9 through Table 9.12 were categorized as shown in Table 9A1.1 through Table 9A1.12 in Appendix 9.1 of this chapter. However, the variable "weekly working hours" was categorized as shown in Chapter 5.

Appendix 9.1

Additional Data on Work Resumption Patterns

TABLE 9A1.1
Demographic Characteristics (%) of Continuous Resumers

	Denmark	Germany	Israel	N'lands	Sweden	US
Continuous Resumers (% of all subjects)	**26.1**	**30.8**	**41.1**	**63.5**	**50.3**	**54.1**
Age						
≤ 24	22.2	.	26.3	42.1	.	54.6
25-34	34.0	23.1	51.4	70.9	52.7	66.2
35-44	30.8	55.3	44.0	70.3	59.8	53.4
45-54	23.2	41.1	33.9	50.5	48.8	54.8
≥ 55	8.9	13.3	30.4	68.4	41.9	32.4
Gender						
Male	37.0	31.0	42.6	69.8	47.2	59.0
Female	18.3	30.6	36.5	53.9	52.1	50.7
Household composition						
Living alone	21.1	14.3	.	50.0	47.1	44.9
Living with partner only	18.0	27.1	38.5	67.6	42.4	56.2
Living with partner and children	32.6	38.6	43.5	64.6	59.0	60.1
Living with children only	35.7	.	.	.	50.0	48.2
Other	42.9	.	30.6	52.0	.	48.0

. less than 10 observations

TABLE 9A1.2
Health Indicators (%) at T3 of Continuous Resumers

	Denmark	Germany	Israel	N'lands	Sweden	US
Continuous Resumers (% of all subjects)	**26.1**	**30.8**	**41.1**	**63.5**	**50.3**	**54.1**
Pain intensity						
None	52.9	25.0	.	78.1	77.5	81.0
Mild	33.3	66.7	58.7	72.0	67.3	71.4
Moderate	17.2	34.3	48.0	52.5	45.9	45.7
Severe	11.1	22.4	13.5	35.9	18.6	25.3
Back function (Hannover ADL)						
Low	10.6	18.8	32.1	26.7	24.7	24.2
Moderate	19.6	32.1	47.1	58.9	43.6	64.7
Good	47.6	60.0	59.6	81.4	74.2	72.9

. less than 10 observations

TABLE 9A1.3
Job Characteristics(%) of Continuous Resumers

	Denmark	Germany	Israel	N'lands	Sweden	US
Continuous Resumers (% of all subjects)	**26.1**	**30.8**	**41.1**	**63.5**	**50.3**	**54.1**
Physical job demands						
Low (≥7)	32.3	33.3	52.9	77.6	69.3	66.9
Moderate (4-6)	28.3	30.5	39.5	67.5	52.9	52.8
High (≤4)	18.0	31.3	29.7	55.6	38.9	40.5
Job strain (imbalance demand/control)						
Low (<1)	36.5	34.6	50.0	73.6	58.9	58.9
Moderate (1 - 1.3)	14.6	29.0	38.2	55.4	44.3	48.9
High (>1.3)	16.4	28.6	31.3	32.6	43.6	44.7

TABLE 9A1.4
Demographic Characteristics (%) of Late Resumers

	Denmark	Germany	Israel	N'lands	Sweden	US
Late Resumers (% of all subjects)	13.6	5.0	19.3	8.1	14.5	18.5
Age						
≤ 24	29.6	.	36.8	15.8	.	9.1
25-34	13.0	0.0	18.1	10.7	20.0	2.8
35-44	13.5	2.6	16.5	7.0	15.5	13.5
45-54	12.8	7.8	23.7	6.9	14.6	6.4
≥ 55	8.9	4.1	4.4	0.0	8.1	8.8
Gender						
Male	12.5	3.2	18.8	8.9	15.0	7.1
Female	14.4	8.2	20.6	6.4	14.2	9.5
Household composition						
Living alone	9.9	0.0	.	0.0	11.8	8.2
Living with partner only	16.7	8.4	19.2	10.5	12.8	9.6
Living with partner and children	11.6	2.4	13.5	7.7	16.7	6.5
Living with children only	17.9	.	.	.	13.6	18.5
Other	14.3	.	42.9	8.0	.	8.0

. less than 10 observations

TABLE 9A1.5
Health Indicators (%) at T3 of Late Resumers

	Denmark	Germany	Israel	N'lands	Sweden	US
Late Resumers (% of all subjects)	**13.6**	**5.0**	**19.3**	**8.1**	**14.5**	**18.5**
Pain intensity						
None	18.6	2.8	.	9.6	15.0	6.9
Mild	18.8	0.0	20.6	8.8	14.9	7.1
Moderate	9.4	5.1	24.4	5.1	16.4	11.6
Severe	9.7	7.1	9.5	5.1	10.0	6.3
Back function (Hannover ADL)						
Low	6.4	5.2	15.7	1.3	12.9	8.9
Moderate	13.1	3.8	25.7	8.9	15.4	9.2
Good	21.1	8.6	21.3	10.4	15.6	7.5

. less than 10 observations

TABLE 9A1.6
Job Characteristics (%) of Late Resumers

	Denmark	Germany	Israel	N'lands	Sweden	US
Late Resumers (% of all subjects)	**13.6**	**5.0**	**19.3**	**8.1**	**14.5**	**8.5**
Physical job demands						
Low (≥7)	13.9	9.5	14.3	7.9	10.7	7.4
Moderate (4-6)	12.0	5.3	20.2	6.1	15.5	8.3
High (≤4)	15.3	3.0	23.4	9.4	15.8	10.3
Job strain (imbalance demand/control)						
Low (<1)	11.9	4.8	14.1	8.0	12.7	7.8
Moderate (1-1.3)	18.2	5.8	19.1	9.5	17.7	10.6
High (>1.3)	12.7	4.8	25.3	6.5	12.9	8.5

TABLE 9A1.7
Demographic Characteristics (%) of Relapse Resumers

	Denmark	Germany	Israel	N'lands	Sweden	US
Relapse (% of all subjects)	5.4	10.0	7.9	9.2	8.4	8.5
Age						
≤ 24	11.1	.	10.5	21.1	.	9.1
25-34	9.0	0.0	8.3	5.8	1.8	15.5
35-44	5.3	10.5	7.7	9.4	10.3	9.0
45-54	3.2	10.0	5.1	9.9	8.1	5.6
≥ 55	1.8	11.2	13.0	10.5	11.3	2.9
Gender						
Male	3.3	13.6	8.4	7.6	9.5	5.8
Female	7.0	3.5	6.4	11.4	7.8	10.4
Household composition						
Living alone	4.2	17.9	.	25.0	7.8	6.1
Living with partner only	3.2	5.6	11.5	6.7	11.2	4.1
Living with partner and children	8.7	13.3	7.1	8.6	6.9	10.5
Living with children only	0.0	.	.	.	4.6	3.7
Other	7.1	.	8.2	12.0	.	12.0

. less than 10 observations

TABLE 9A1.8
Selected Health Indicators (%) at T3 of Relapse Resumers

	Denmark	Germany	Israel	N'lands	Sweden	US
Relapse (% of all subjects)	5.4	10.0	7.9	9.2	8.4	8.5
Pain intensity						
None	5.7	11.1	.	6.9	0.0	5.2
Mild	6.8	11.1	11.1	10.4	5.0	9.2
Moderate	5.0	10.1	4.9	10.1	11.5	10.9
Severe	4.2	9.4	10.8	15.4	12.9	6.3
Back function (Hannover ADL)						
Low	5.7	9.4	8.6	12.0	12.9	8.9
Moderate	5.9	10.4	4.3	13.4	11.1	7.6
Good	4.8	11.4	10.6	5.5	3.1	9.0

. less than 10 observations

TABLE 9A1.9
Job Characteristics (%) of Relapse Resumers

	Denmark	Germany	Israel	N'lands	Sweden	US
Relapse (% of all subjects)	5.4	10.0	7.9	9.2	8.4	8.5
Physical job demands						
Low (≥7)	4.6	21.4	11.4	5.3	5.3	9.5
Moderate (4-6)	5.0	9.5	7.0	7.0	10.6	7.4
High (≤4)	6.7	4.0	6.3	11.7	7.9	7.8
Job strain (imbalance demand/control)						
Low (<1)	4.1	13.5	8.7	7.5	5.7	8.2
Moderate (1 - 1.3)	9.1	7.3	7.4	6.8	13.3	8.5
High (>1.3)	4.6	4.8	8.1	17.4	6.5	8.5

TABLE 9A1.10
Demographic Characteristics (%) of Non-Resumers

	Denmark	Germany	Israel	N'lands	Sweden	US
Non-resumers (% of all subjects)	54.9	54.2	31.7	19.2	26.9	28.9
Age						
≤ 24	37.0	.	26.3	21.1	.	27.3
25-34	44.0	76.9	22.2	12.6	25.5	15.5
35-44	50.4	31.6	31.9	13.3	14.4	24.1
45-54	60.8	41.1	37.3	32.7	28.5	33.3
≥ 55	80.4	71.4	52.2	21.1	38.7	55.9
Gender						
Male	47.3	52.3	30.2	13.8	28.4	28.2
Female	60.3	57.7	36.5	28.4	26.0	29.4
Household composition						
Living alone	64.8	67.9	.	25.0	33.3	40.8
Living with partner only	62.2	58.9	30.8	15.2	33.6	30.1
Living with partner and children	47.1	45.8	35.9	19.1	17.4	22.9
Living with children only	46.4	50.0	.	.	31.8	29.6
Other	35.7	.	18.4	28.0	.	32.0

. less than 10 observations

TABLE 9A1.11
Health Indicators (%) at T3 of Non-Resumers

	Denmark	Germany	Israel	N'lands	Sweden	US
Non-resumers (% of all subjects)	54.9	54.2	31.7	19.2	26.9	28.9
Pain intensity						
None	22.9	61.1	.	5.5	7.5	6.9
Mild	41.0	22.2	9.5	8.8	12.9	12.2
Moderate	68.3	50.5	22.8	32.3	26.2	31.9
Severe	75.0	61.2	66.2	43.6	58.6	62.0
Back function (Hannover ADL)						
Low	77.3	66.7	43.6	60.0	49.5	58.1
Moderate	61.4	53.8	22.9	18.8	29.9	18.5
Good	26.5	20.0	8.5	2.7	7.0	10.5

. less than 10 observations

TABLE 9A1.12
Job Characteristics (%) of Non-Resumers

	Denmark	Germany	Israel	N'lands	Sweden	US
Non-resumers (% of all subjects)	54.9	54.2	31.7	19.2	26.9	28.9
Physical job demands						
Low (≥7)	49.2	35.7	21.4	9.2	14.7	16.2
Moderate (4-6)	54.7	54.7	33.3	19.3	21.1	31.5
High (≤4)	60.0	61.6	40.6	23.4	37.4	41.4
Job strain (imbalance demand/control)						
Low (<1)	47.5	47.1	27.2	10.9	22.8	25.1
Moderate (1-1.3)	58.2	58.0	35.3	28.4	24.8	31.9
High (>1.3)	66.4	61.9	35.4	43.5	37.1	38.3

10

Work Resumption and the Role of Interventions

Theo J. Veerman & Edward Palmer

Introduction

Each of the previous chapters devotes specific attention to various aspects of the WIR Project. They have examined the characteristics of the country cohorts at the onset of the national studies, their patterns of work resumption, the different kinds of medical, vocational, and other non-medical interventions employed, and how often they have been used. This chapter brings the threads of the previous chapters together to analyze what affected the outcomes of the Project.

Normally, people who stop work due to lower back pain are away for only a short period of time. The current recommended therapy for patients with back pain is to encourage physical activity, and to minimize time spent away from work. In light of this, patients who have not returned to work within 90 days are not typical back pain patients. Many factors contribute to "pushing" and "pulling" people back to work, but experience shows that the longer people are away from work, the less likely it is that they will return as time progresses. Therefore, whatever conclusions might be drawn from the Project, while relevant to the specific group targeted for study because they had been unable to work for at least 90 days, may not be particularly relevant for back patients in general.

Since the path to a permanent disability benefit begins with these 90-day patients, it is especially important for social security planners to understand the processes at work at this juncture in the progress of work in-capacity. As seen in Chapter 6, roughly half of the subjects followed in the national studies eventually returned to work (varying across countries from 35% to 72%), but the rest did not, at least not within two years. Thus, in the context of attempting to understand the process low back patients fol-low toward disability versus work resumption, the subjects studied in the Project can be considered "typical."

The two central questions to be answered by the analysis presented in this chapter are: How do factors such as individual lifestyle, health and em-ployment history, socio-economic circumstances, and work environment of the individual affect work resumption, work ability, and perceived health? Is it possible to distinguish separate effects for medical, vocational, and other non-medical interventions, over and above these factors?

The first group of factors are the baseline factors that are fixed in the short two-year time period of the studies. They describe the subjects and their work environment at 90 days after the onset of work incapacity. The purpose of the interventions is to affect health and/or work resumption pos-itively. Figure 10.1 is a schematic presentation of how the baseline factors and interventions fit together.

FIGURE 10.1
General Model for the Analysis

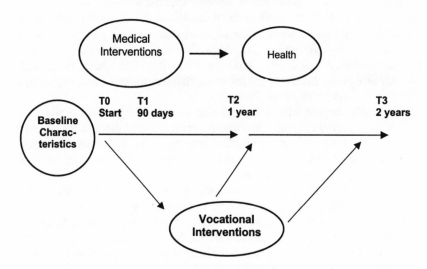

T1 : First questionnaire
T2 : Second questionnaire
T3 : Third questionnaire

The data compiled during the Project do not contain detailed information on the exact timing or sequence of interventions. Instead, information was collected on measures taken prior to returning the initial questionnaire, after the subject was selected for the study at 90 days of work incapacity, and for measures occurring in the subsequent intervals of one and two years. This is the information that is analyzed in this chapter.

The analysis undertaken in this chapter is a first step in creating insights into the interrelationship among all of the factors included in the Project's research design. Hopefully, the results will invite further analysis casting further light upon mechanisms determining work resumption. Some opportunities for such future analysis are noted in this chapter.

This chapter outlines an analytical approach to integrating the combined results of the six national studies, using a recently developed model that describes the factors influencing work ability and brings together the main features of the studies. The chapter then turns to multivariate statistical analyses to assess the influence of interventions in recovery of work capacity and return to work. Finally, the results are discussed in light of the main research questions of the Project.

Work Capacity

The social security systems in the six countries that participated in the Project all require that an individual's work capacity be reduced significantly in order to receive sickness or disability benefits. In other words, the occurrence of back pain alone is not sufficient to receive benefits, and recovery from back pain alone may not be sufficient to resume work or to leave the benefit rolls. A systematic view of factors underlying work capacity will be helpful for interpreting the results from the combined analysis. The initial theoretical model for this study was presented in Chapter 3.

The analysis in this chapter recognizes the especially important role of individual motivation and attitudes. Therefore, a second model in which these factors have a more prominent place can be a useful tool in interpreting the findings. This model is a general model of work ability formulated by Ilmarinen, in which human resources, or human capital, are determined by an individual's health status and his or her skills acquired through education and training (Ilmarinen, 1999). Human resources, together with individual motivation and the characteristics of the work environment, determine work ability. Using Ilmarinen's model, work capacity at a specific time can be viewed as being determined by a combination of: more long-term factors, e.g. an individual's education and acquired skill level; commonly shared values about work and health; the specific workplace; the individual's perceived current health and attitude towards work; and the willingness of the employer to adapt the workplace or accommodate the employee's specific needs.

Work capacity in the context of sickness and disability benefit eligibility is also very much a function of how gatekeeping criteria and administrative procedures are applied. The roles of employers, doctors, claim adjusters, and other actors in the social security system are all important, as is the amount of earnings replacement provided by the relevant sickness and disability benefit schemes. The individual's own economic situation may also be important.

Ilmarinen's model combines the central hypotheses on "work ability" of a number of disciplines, including health care, economics, psychology, sociology, and social medicine. Each is discussed briefly below.

Health: One must be sufficiently healthy to work. What is sufficient health varies from work situation to work situation and from individual to individual. The goal of medical interventions is to prevent health deterioration and to promote health improvement, with the implicit goal of maintaining normal quality of life. Normal quality of life implies the ability to work.

Economics: In economics, a central hypothesis is that education and training create human capital and determine individual work ability and earnings careers. People work, according to this theory, as long as the marginal return of work is greater than that of non-work (leisure). There is a selection effect that is important in the present context: higher earnings are likely to be associated with higher education (training) and normally less physically demanding work.

Psychology: Motivation, itself a function of social values and individual attitudes, is central in psychology for determining how individuals act in a given situation. What people do with normal health and education, i.e. normal human resources, depends nevertheless on their individual motivation.

Sociology and Social Medicine: Physical and psychological demands associated with a given job or work place determine how good a fit there is between the individual and the work place. Physical demands at the work place, such as heavy lifting and repetitive movements, and psychological demands, such as the relationship between demands and the ability to control one's situation, are all potential factors determining work ability. The literature in sociology also emphasizes the importance of social support and social networks for well being.

Medical interventions aimed at improving the health of a person who is work incapacitated can improve work ability and, indirectly, work resumption. The aim of vocational and other non-medical interventions is to influence work resumption more directly. According to the above paradigm, it is possible to influence work resumption by improving human resources (education and training), but also by working through motivation, values, and attitudes. Most of the vocational and other non-medical interventions used in the countries involved in the Project are focused on helping through education and training, by accommodating the work place, or by aiding in finding a new place of work or a new occupation.

FIGURE 10.2
Factors Influencing Work Ability

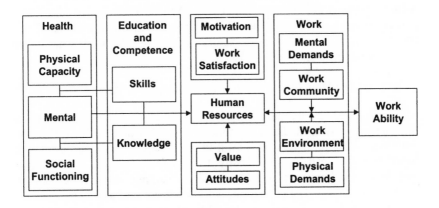

Source: Ilmarinen (1999)

Motivation is generally believed to be important, but is not well understood in the present context. What is more, it is difficult to measure. Antonovsky presents the hypothesis that some people simply have the built-in generator that drives them forward, whereas others do not (Antonovsky, 1987). It is fair to say that most people succeed in dealing with moving along in life. When necessary, for whatever reason, most people change jobs; sometimes the reason is health, or health demands of a specific work task. Furthermore, people usually deal with personal and family crises without interventions from the public sector. What Antonovsky's insights suggest in the context of work incapacity and reintegration is that in the absence of a built-in generator, some people may need some help.

It was shown in Chapter 6 that increasing age, beginning at the age of 45, was associated with lower return-to-work rates at the end of two years in all of the cohorts but the cohort from the Netherlands. This can be taken as an indicator of the significance of many of the factors in the above figure. Possible explanations are reduced physical capacity, outdated knowledge or skills, a change in attitude regarding the importance of work after age 45, and a lower ability to cope with job demands.

Other findings presented in Chapter 6 also fit well with the work ability model, such as the finding that higher return-to-work rates are related to better perceived health, higher educational levels, and a "better" work environment (lower physical job demands). Income development, which showed substantial variation across the six cohorts, can also be expected to influence return-to-work rates.

In sum, the data from the six national studies suggest that the information on health, education and skill levels, motivation, and work environment all support the hypothesis that each of these alone is correlated with perceived work ability and, hence, return to work. Later sections of this chapter will analyze how these factors affect return to work when taken into consideration simultaneously.

Overview of the Model and Strategy for Analysis

The general idea behind the analysis is that given an individual's baseline characteristics, medical, vocational, and other non-medical interventions will be more or less successful in promoting work resumption. The baseline characteristics are mostly fixed characteristics. In the short two-year period covered by the national studies, age varies little; gender, mother tongue, level of education, work environment, and individual and family income prior to sickness are all fixed. Health and employment history prior to sickness are, by definition, fixed as well. These are characteristics that describe the individual's initial status in important respects, and were measured with the first questionnaire that was sent out shortly after subjects were included at 90 days of work incapacity.

There are two groups of variable factors. One, subjectively determined health status, is a key variable for the analysis. A second is individual expectations; self-perceived work ability will be used as an indicator. Expectations may, in fact, also reflect motivation to return to work. Even though expectations and motivation could have changed during the two-year follow-up period, only their values at the baseline measurement (90 days) will be included in the following analysis. Analyzing changes in expectations/motivation is one area for promising further analysis.

Interventions span the entire period of work incapacity, and beyond. Typically, medical interventions come first, usually much before the baseline point of 90 days, and are followed after a period of several months by vocational and other non-medical interventions. The exception is surgery. On the other hand, as shown in Chapter 8, vocational and other non-medical interventions get started typically after six to ten months of work incapacity. Medical interventions can occur even after return to work and, more importantly, vocational rehabilitation may coincide with return to work.

Vocational and other non-medical interventions can be both started and completed in the first year, e.g. wage subsidies, work place adaptation, and taking on new job tasks with the same employer. On the other hand, many of these interventions can take longer and continue into the second year, and some may not get started until into the second year. This means that work status at both one and two years, and the role of vocational and other non-medical interventions, both in the first and the second year of observation, will be important to examine. As shown in Chapter 7, medical interventions are concentrated heavily within the first year, and improvements in self-reported health status usually come within the first year. For this reason, correlations between medical interventions and improvement in health status will be examined only for the first year.

Thus, the analysis will cover the effects of both medical and vocational and other non-medical interventions on first-year outcomes, taking the baseline characteristics into consideration. It will also examine whether vocational and other non-medical interventions contribute further to work status at the end of two years, given an individual's work status at the end of the first year. A description of the multivariate regression analysis technique used is presented at the end of this chapter.

Thus, the four questions to be answered by this analysis are: How do the baseline characteristics affect health and return-to-work outcomes? Do medical interventions during the first year contribute to the improvement of health status? Do vocational and other non-medical interventions during the first year contribute to work resumption after one year? Do vocational and other non-medical interventions during the second year contribute further to work resumption, given the work status after one year?

Medical Interventions and Health in the First Year

According to the information provided in Chapter 7, there was a positive correlation in all six national cohorts between better health and work. The back function (Hannover ADL score) was significantly better for subjects who resumed work within a year than for the non-resumers. This was also true of scores measuring social functioning, vitality, and mental health. Also, subjects not working at one year indicated they had more pain than those who were working. Since the ADL score measures how well people function physically, it could be viewed as the most objective of the scores used in measuring health connected with back pain.

The first line of analysis focuses on the effect of medical interventions on health status. Five possible indicators of health status at T2 were considered as possible dependent variables in this analysis: 1) back function (Hannover ADL); 2) pain intensity; 3) general health; 4) vitality; and 5) mental health. For choosing the best indicator of health status at T2, these indicators were analyzed to determine which was the best predictor of work status (working/not working) at T2. For all cohorts, the ADL score was the best predictor, and other health indicators added little or nothing to the explained variance in work status. Table10.1 summarizes the results in terms of explained variance.

TABLE 10.1
Percent of (Additional) Variance Explained by Back Function (ADL) and Other Health Measures on Work Status at T2

	Denmark	Germany	Israel	N'lands	Sweden	US
Back function	18	11	18	20	13	11
Hannover ADL T2						
Pain intensity T2	2	–	–	5	6	–
General health T2	–	2	–	–	2	2
Vitality T2	–	–	–	–		*
Mental health T2	–	–	2	2	–	*

Legend:
–: no significant contribution
*: data missing
Note: Method: Multiple regression entering ADL first and other measures as a block second.

In the next step, all baseline characteristics and medical interventions were screened for inclusion in the multivariate analysis at T2.[1] All health indicators at T1, including the T1 ADL score, were also included as baseline characteristics. This means that the analysis will not explain the absolute ADL score at T2, but the change in the ADL score relative to the initial health status. Thus, by analyzing the effects of medical interventions on the ADL score at T2 given the health status at T1, it can be seen whether medical interventions explained any improvement in ADL scores between T1 and T2.

Medical interventions undertaken both prior to inclusion at 90 days (T0-T1) and between 90 days and one year (T1-T2) were included in the multivariate analysis aimed at explaining the improvement of ADL status at the end of one year. Early medical interventions during the first three months of work incapacity could both have affected the ADL score at T1 and have contributed to an improvement in ADL scores between T1 and T2.

This analysis was done using multiple regression with the ADL scores at T2 as the dependent variable. The independent variables were entered stepwise in three blocks. First, all baseline characteristics (including health indicators at 90 days (T1)), were entered; those with no significant correlation with the ADL score were excluded prior to the next step. Second, the "early" medical interventions (T0-T1) were entered (dichotomized as not applied vs. applied). Third, all medical interventions in the period T0-T2 were entered.

Variables that were statistically significant in at least one of the countries are shown in Table 10.2. All results of the statistical analysis are presented in their entirety in Appendix 10.1 to this chapter. The relative importance of the baseline characteristics is indicated by their order of inclusion in the regression model (1 = most important, 2 = second important, etc.); the direction of their influence is indicated by + or - (the characteristic is positively or negatively related to health improvement at T2).

These results show, in sum, that health (ADL score at T2) is explained mainly by the ADL and other health indicators at T1, and partly by several other background factors. The main demographic characteristic—age—played an independent role in four cohorts, where increasing age had a negative effect on the improvement of ADL. Gender had an independent correlation with health improvement in the cohorts from Denmark and the Netherlands, with females showing less improvement in ADL. Other baseline characteristics, such as educational level, job characteristics, or sickness history, if they had any independent contribution at all, had so only in one of the cohorts.

Generally, the introduction of medical interventions added hardly any additional explanation to what was predicted already by initial health and the few significant baseline characteristics. In three countries, there was no significant further contribution from any of these interventions in either direction. The only positive effect of medical interventions was found in the Swedish cohort, where surgery during the first three months provided a small contribution to ADL improvement. Given the fact that the frequency of early surgery in the cohort from Sweden was the lowest of all six cohorts, this may indicate that the selection process for back surgery, and/or the way it is administered, is more successful in Sweden, as was discussed in Chapter 7.

Finally, according to these results the other health interventions did not have the expected positive relationship to improvement of ADL. Pain relieving medication in several instances was negatively related to improvement of ADL scores. In the German cohort, medicinal baths during a later

TABLE 10.2
Prediction of Back Function Scores (ADL) at T2 by ADL-T1, Baseline Characteristics (T1) and Medical Interventions

	Denmark	Germany	Israel	N'lands	Sweden	US
Block 1. Baseline characteristics at T1						
Back function T1 (Hannover ADL) (good)	1+	1+	1+	1+	1+	1+
Pain intensity (high)	2 -	2 -	3 -	0	3 -	0
General health (good)	4+	–	4+	2+	2+	2+
Social functioning (good)	0	0	5+	0	0	0
Perceived work ability (high)	0	3+	0	0	0	5+
Age (high)	5 -	–	2 -	–	4 -	3 -
Gender (female)	3 -	0	–	3 -	0	0
Educational level completed (high)	–	–	–	–	–	4+
Mother language (not the national language)	–	–	0	–	5 -	0
Active coping when still working (yes)	–	0	–	4 -	–	–
Passive coping when still working (yes)	–	4 -	–	–	0	0
Strain in old job (high)	0	0	–	–	6 -	0

	Denmark	Germany	Israel	N'lands	Sweden	US
Weeks sick in year before present spell (many)	0	0	–	–	–	6 -
Total % variance explained by baseline characteristics	45	57	16	36	51	60
Block 2. Medical interventions T0-T1						
Received pain relieving medication	0	neg	–	–	neg	0
Operation was done	0	–	–	0	pos	0
Additional % variance explained	–	2	–	–	2	–
Block 3. Medical interventions T0-T2						
Received medicinal baths, mud-packing	–	neg	–	–	–	0
Received pain relieving medication	0	0	–	–	0	neg
Additional % variance explained	–	1	–	–	–	1

Legend:

–: variable was not selected for multivariate analysis due to many missing values or insignificant zero-order correlation

0 : variable was entered in multiple regression analysis but had no significant contribution

1, 2,.. : variable had significant contribution; 1, 2 = order of inclusion in multiple regression

+ / - : characteristic is positively/negatively related to better functional capacity (ADL-score T2)

pos : intervention has positive contribution to functional capacity (ADL score T2)

neg : intervention has negative contribution to functional capacity (ADL score T2) stage (3-12 months) also showed a negative relationship to improvement of ADL scores.

Summing up, no positive relationship between the application of specific medical interventions and the improvement of back function was shown, with the exception of surgery in Sweden. However, this may not be taken as proving that medical interventions are not effective. Rather, poorer back function may have been a reason for, instead of the effect of, the treatment; if that is the case, even an effective intervention might result in an insignificant correlation with ADL improvement. Furthermore, some types of interventions may not be tested statistically, as a result of their high frequencies. This is why "interventions" like visiting a general practitioner or a specialist cannot be analyzed in a field study like this project; almost everyone in most of the cohorts received these interventions.

Finally, it may not only be the separate intervention as such which is important with respect to improvement of health. Other aspects of medical treatment are possibly more relevant, such as the timing of the intervention, the way it was administered, or specific sequences of interventions.

Baseline Characteristics, Vocational and Other Non-medical Interventions, and Work Status in the First Year

The repertoire of vocational and other non-medical interventions available in the six countries was quite large, but in each national cohort a specific intervention might have been applied only infrequently—or might not have been available in a particular country. For this reason, it was necessary to create a broader classification for the purposes of analysis by clustering separate interventions into groups. This classification is somewhat more detailed than the classification in Chapter 8, since the purpose of the analysis conducted here was more specific. The clusters created for the analysis are: education and training (includes job training/vocational education and general education); workplace accommodations (includes workplace and transportation adaptations, job redesign/change of workplace, adaptation of working hours, sheltered workshop); therapeutical work resumption; visiting a company doctor (occupational physician); employee motivators (includes warning of dismissal and actual dismissal, threat of negative sanctions and actual negative sanctions, and capitalization of benefits); wage subsidies for employers; contacts with colleagues and employer during sickness; case management (includes tests of vocational capacity, (re)evaluation of work incapacity, rehabilitation inquiry/rehabilitation plan); assessment for disability benefits; Job counseling, job search and placement; services (includes activation groups, increased day care for children, social or psychological counseling, reduction of waiting periods in health care).

The organizational responsibilities of the different actors involved in the rehabilitation process are discussed in Chapter 8. Organizational processes can be an important determinant of outcomes. To the extent that some countries seem to be more successful than others, differences in process may be an important factor, apart from the effect of separate interventions as such.

The analysis in this section was done using logistic regression models with work resumption at T2 (working no/yes) as the dependent variable. The independent variables were entered stepwise in two blocks. First, all baseline characteristics (provided they met some statistical criteria), including health indicators at 90 days (T1), were entered.[2] Second, all vocational and other non-medical interventions (grouped as above) in the period T0-T2 were entered together. Each of these interventions was dichotomized as applied/not applied.

As a measure of the respective importance of baseline characteristics and vocational and other non-medical interventions, the percentage of cases classified correctly are reported as follows: a priori (before entering any variables); after entering baseline characteristics; and after entering interventions in the first year. The greater the increase in the percentage classified correctly, the more important each set of variables is in predicting work resumption.

The results for significant variables are reported in Table 10.3. Further details of the analysis are given in Appendix 10.1 to this chapter.

The importance of baseline characteristics and the additional importance of vocational and other non-medical interventions are discussed below.

Baseline Characteristics

One or more of the health indicators (as measured already at T1) were among the strongest predictors of work resumption at T2 in all of the cohorts, with the strongest effects noted in the cohorts from the United States, the Netherlands, and Sweden. Health at the onset of work incapacity clearly determined a large part of work resumption after one year.

Generally, the demographic and income variables did not explain much. A notable exception was age: older age was related to less work resumption in four of the cohorts. Also notable was the importance of personal income in the Israeli cohort, where higher income was related to work resumption.

Job characteristics had significant outcome effects in all of the cohorts, except the cohort from the United States. Physical demands at work were important in three of the cohorts, those from Germany, Israel, and

TABLE 10.3
Prediction of Work Status T2 by Baseline Characteristics and Vocational Interventions T0-T2

	Denmark	Germany	Israel	N'lands	Sweden	US
Cases classified correct before regression model (%)	68	59	50	73	52	62
Block 1. Baseline characteristics at T1						
Health indicators T1						
Self-perceived work ability T1 (high)	1+	2+	0	5+	6+	1+
Pain intensity T1 (high)	2 -	0	2 -	2 -	1 -	5 -
General health (good)	0	–	–	1+	2+	0
Social functioning (good)	0	0	–	0	5+	2+
Demographics						
Age (older)	4 -	7 -	–	8 -	–	3 -
Total personal income before sickness (high)	0	0	1+	–	–	–
Received social support (high)	–	–	–	–	7 -	–
Job and employment history						
Physical demands in old job (high)	0	6 -	3 -	0	4 -	0
Social support in old job (high)	–	0	–	6+	0	–

	Denmark	Germany	Israel	N'lands	Sweden	US
Control over job demands (high)	0	–	–	4+	–	–
Job strain (old job) (high)	3 -	–	0	0	0	0
Still employed at T1? (yes)	6+	1+	–	–	–	4+
Layoffs in firm last year? (yes)	5+	0	–	–	–	–
Starting year in old job (started recently)	7+	–	4 -	0	–	–
Proportion of years worked since age 20 (high)	–	5+	–	–	–	–
Number of jobs since age 20 (high)	–	–	–	3 -	–	0
Attitude: Work should not interfere with life (agree)	–	3+	–	–	–	–
Sickness history						
Weeks sick in year before present spell (high)	–	4 -	–	7 -	–	0
Back treatments in year before present spell (yes)	–	0	–	–	3 -	–
Cases classified correct after Block 1 (%)	79	80	67	79	68	78

TABLE 10.3 *(Cont'd)*

	Denmark	Germany	Israel	N'lands	Sweden	US
Block 2. Vocational interventions T0-T2						
Education, training	neg	–	–	–	–	0
Workplace accommodations	pos	–	pos	pos	–	–
Employee motivators	neg	–	neg	0	–	0
Assessment for disability benefit, etc.	0	0	neg	neg	neg	–
Therapeutic work resumption	–	0	–	pos	–	pos
Job counseling, -search	–	0	–	neg	–	–
Case management	neg	neg	pos	–	–	neg
Wage subsidies	0	–	–	–	–	neg
Cases classified correct after Block 2 (%)	86	80	82	87	68	78

Legend:
– : variable was not selected for multivariate analysis due to many missings or insignificant zero-order correlation
0 : variable was entered in logistic regression analysis but had no significant contribution
1, 2,. : variable had significant contribution; 1, 2 = order of inclusion in logistic regression model
+ / - : characteristic is positively/negatively related to work resumption at T2
pos : intervention has positive contribution to work resumption T2
neg : intervention has negative contribution to work resumption T2

Sweden. This is not at all surprising for the subjects from Israel, given that the Israeli cohort was drawn from persons applying for work-injury benefits.

Still having a place of employment at T1 was important in the cohorts from Denmark, Germany, and the United States. Also noteworthy was the result for the German cohort that the attitude "I enjoy working but it shouldn't interfere with the rest of my life" was significant.

Finally, sickness and absence history in general had some influence in the cohorts from Germany, the Netherlands, and Sweden.

Vocational and Other Non-medical Interventions

In addition to the effects of baseline characteristics, vocational and other non-medical interventions during the first year had significant contributions to the prediction of work resumption in several countries, although not always in the expected positive direction.

Two types of these interventions had a positive relationship with work resumption in several cohorts: workplace accommodations and therapeutic work resumption (which was not available in all national systems). It should be noted, however, that those interventions are tied logically to resumption as such; adapting a workplace is hardly worthwhile if there is no resumer to use this workplace, and therapeutic resumption is a resumption by definition. It is unknown whether the fact that a person was still at work by T2 was caused by the workplace accommodation, or by the therapeutic resumption, as such.

Vocational measures may also retard work resumption or preclude it, as is witnessed by several negative effects in the statistical analysis. For example, claiming work incapacity, or "disability," is negatively related to work resumption, almost by definition, and this was significant already in the first year in three cohorts (Israel, the Netherlands, and Sweden). Thus, some interventions may not be the cause, but rather the effect of prolonged work incapacity.

Case management was also negatively related to work resumption in several cohorts; here the same selection mechanism—case management being used especially towards persons with prolonged work incapacity—may apply. A notable exception was the Israeli cohort, where case management positively predicted work resumption.

Education in the Danish cohort, job counseling in the Dutch cohort, and wage subsidies in the American cohort all seemed to have negative effects on work resumption. Apart from the possibility that here also the intervention might be an effect of longer work incapacity, this could also be explained by postulating that career change takes time (e.g. education will take some time before the employee has been re-educated for a new job). Since neither of these picked up a positive effect in the two-year analysis below, this possible explanation appears to be less probable.

Workplace accommodations and the opportunity for therapeutical work resumption (job training with compensation from social security) are the two types of interventions that contributed positively to the prediction of work resumption. As both types are tied logically to work resumption itself, it would be more accurate to state that these are specific modalities of work resumption that seem to contribute to earlier resumption.

Various vocational and other non-medical interventions tend to contribute negatively to resumption, which may be an effect of selection (interventions being applied mostly to the more "severe", and longer lasting spells) and/or related to the duration of the intervention itself (e.g. education).

Generally, interventions did less to predict work resumption after one year than did the baseline characteristics. The only cohorts where they really added to this prediction were those where the "positive" interventions (work accommodations, therapeutic resumption) seemed to be effective.

Baseline Characteristics, Vocational and Other Non-medical Interventions, and Work Status in the Second Year

The group considered in this section consists of persons who were respondents throughout the entire study. Because this group is smaller than those who participated only at T1 and T2, the data for both groups were compared to see whether the results as to work resumption at T2 for subjects who responded only at T1 and T2 were the same as those for the subjects who responded at T3 as well. The results were largely the same. Nonresponders are discussed generally in Chapter 5.

The procedure followed in this section was estimating the same type of logistic regression model as that used in the preceding section, with the important difference that vocational and other non-medical interventions undertaken in the first year could be distinguished from those undertaken in the second year. Thus, the procedure followed was as follows: first, work status at T2 plus all baseline characteristics (including health indicators) at T1 were entered; second, the interventions during the first year (T0-T2) were entered; third, the interventions in the second year (T2-T3) were entered.

In all cohorts, work status at T2 was by far the strongest predictor of work status at T3. Therefore, for all other factors considered, work status at T3 was analyzed given work status at T2. In other words, the question became: what do the baseline characteristics and vocational and other non-medical interventions (in the first and second year respectively) add to the probability of working at T3, given work/non-work status at T2? The results are presented in Table 10.4.

The importance of previous work status, baseline characteristics, and vocational and other non-medical interventions as to work status after two years are discussed below.

TABLE 10.4
Prediction of Work Status T3 by Work Status T2, Baseline
Characteristics and Vocational Interventions

	Denmark	Germany	Israel	N'lands	Sweden	US
Cases classified correct before regression model (%)	60	65	60	72	63	62

Block 1. Baseline characteristics at T1 and work status T2

Work status T2 (working)	1+	1+	1+	1+	1+	1+

Health indicators T1

Self-perceived work ability T1 (high)	2+	3+	0	7+	0	2+
Pain intensity T1 (high)	0	0	2 -	0	6 -	0
General health (good)	0	0	–	0	2+	3+
Mental health (good)	0	–	0	2+	0	–

Demographics

Age (older)	0	0	3 -	5 -	4 -	0
Gender (female)	0	–	–	3 -	–	–
Educational level (high)	4+	–	0	0	0	0
Total personal income before sickness (high)	3+	–	0	0	5+	–

Job and employment history

Physical demands in old job (high)	0	–	–	6 -	3 -	0

TABLE 10.4 *(Cont'd)*

	Denmark	Germany	Israel	N'lands	Sweden	US
Still employed at T1? (yes)	0	2 +	–	–	–	0
Working hours per week, old job (high)	–	–	–	0	–	4 -
Attitude: Work should not interfere with life (agree)	–	0	–	–	7 -	–
Sickness history						
Weeks sick in year before present spell	0	–	–	4 -	–	0
Cases classified correct after Block 1 (%)	82	87	74	84	79	83
Block 2. Vocational interventions T0-T2						
Education, training	–	–	pos	–	–	–
Contact with colleagues	pos	–	–	–	pos	–
Assessment for disability benefit, etc.	neg	neg	0	neg	neg	0
Job counseling, -search	pos	0	–	0	–	–
Case management	neg	0	–	–	–	0
Cases classified correct after Block 2 (%)	82	87	76	85	79	83

	Denmark	Germany	Israel	N'lands	Sweden	US
Block 3. Vocational interventions T2-T3						
Work accom-modations	pos	–	pos	pos		–
Employee motivators	neg	pos	–	neg	–	0
Assessment for disability pension, etc.	neg	0	neg	neg	neg	neg
Contact with colleagues	–	pos	–	–	–	–
Services	0	–	–	0	–	neg
Seen a company doctor	–	–	–	–	–	pos
Case management	0	0	0	neg	–	0
Cases classified correct after Block 3 (%)	86	91	82	88	80	83

Legend:
– : variable was not selected for multivariate analysis due to many missing values or insignificant zero-order correlation
0 : variable was entered in logistic regression analysis but had no significant contribution
1, 2,.. : variable had significant contribution; 1, 2 = order of inclusion in logistic regression model
+ / - : characteristic is positively/negatively related to work resumption T3
pos : intervention has positive contribution to work resumption T3
neg : intervention has negative contribution to work resumption T3

Work Status at T2

In all of the cohorts, work status at T2 was by far the best predictor of work status at T3. This implies that whatever is achieved toward work resumption in the first year is of crucial importance for the "final" work status after the second year. Nevertheless, other variables and interventions contributed further to T3 work status as well.

Baseline Characteristics

Perceived work ability (as perceived already at T1), remained one of the most important predictors of additional work resumption in the second year in three cohorts (Denmark, Germany, and the United States), where this was important at T2. This finding is consistent with the discussion of the work ability model at the beginning of this chapter.

Subjective health indicators were more important in the three other cohorts (Israel, the Netherlands and Sweden), where perceived work ability seemed less predictive. Possibly poor subjective health (at T1) expressed the same thing in these cohorts as poor subjective work ability did in the others.

Age came up as important (higher age diminishing the chances of return to work) in the cohorts from Israel and Sweden, where it was not significant during the first year. In all of the other cohorts, it was significant in the first year but obviously lost importance in the second year, except for the cohort from the Netherlands, where it was moderately significant during both years. Thus, higher age was related to less work resumption over the full two-year period, although the effect was sometimes stronger in the first year and sometimes stronger in the second.

Gender, which was insignificant in the first year, came up as being important in the second year in the Dutch cohort, with females having poorer chances of returning to work.

Total personal income before sickness was important in the cohorts from Denmark and Sweden. In the Danish cohort, 70 percent of non-workers experienced a decline in income; in the Swedish cohort the figure was 60 percent. In the American cohort, the figure was 80 percent and in the Dutch cohort it was 67 percent; however, these cohorts had fewer non-resumers. It is difficult to draw any conclusions among different countries from these data. The role of income and of (expected) loss of income in return to work is one of the issues raised by the Project that warrants more refined analysis.

Physical demands on the (old) job became significantly important in the cohorts from the Netherlands and remained important in the cohort from Sweden. However, they lost their relevance at two years in the cohorts from Denmark and Israel. With these exceptions, generally the importance of several job characteristics which were found in the first year vanished in the second year.

Still being employed at T1, which was significant in the cohorts from Denmark, Germany, and the United States at one year, had additional (even great) significance only in the German cohort at the two-year point.

The effect of health history showed some consistency at one and two years. The number of weeks sick prior to the "present spell" was significant only in the Dutch cohort, and it was significant at both measurement points. Back treatment prior to the "present spell" lost its significance in the Swedish cohort at the two-year point.

Vocational and Other Non-medical Interventions

After having taken the above-mentioned background variables into account, the vocational and other non-medical measures undertaken during the first year proved to be less important with respect to work resumption after two years than they were relative to resumption after one year. Vocational and other non-medical interventions during the second year had some more importance for work resumption after the second year, but again they did not always have the expected positive effect. Those interventions that showed any relationship at all are discussed below.

Education and training for the subjects in Israel during the first year had a significantly positive effect on the two-year outcome. Denmark and Israel were the two countries in which the largest percentage of subjects said at 90 days that they had good work prospects if they could change jobs (56% in Denmark and 58% in Israel, compared to 25 to 30 percent in the other countries). General educational measures were nevertheless most frequent with subjects from Denmark, Sweden, and the United States, but did not seem to contribute significantly to work resumption. However, as shown in Chapter 8, it normally takes up to 10 or 12 months in these countries for educational activities to be initiated, and the education program itself may take a long time as well.

Job counseling and job search during the first year became significant in the Danish cohort for work resumption after the second year. This seems logical, both because a large percentage of subjects responded that they needed to change jobs and because the threat of early dismissal was high in Denmark.

In spite of the fact that subjects in Denmark and Israel said to a greater extent that a job change was necessary, job counseling was a rarely employed measure in those countries compared to job search. Job counseling occurred by far most often in the cohort from Germany, followed by the cohort from Sweden. Job search activities were a frequent vocational measure in all of the other cohorts, except the cohort from Sweden, where the emphasis was on returning to the same workplace. Job counseling and job search taken together, however, did not have a significant effect on the outcomes in any cohort if applied in the first year, with the exception of the cohort from Denmark.

Assessment of work incapacity in the first year was negatively related to work resumption in the second year in the cohorts from Denmark, the Netherlands, and Sweden. The same was the case with assessments in the second year for all cohorts, except the cohort from Germany. Again, the explanation might be that such assessments (which are often assessments for long-term benefits) are made only if the work incapacity is prolonged and the prospect of work resumption is slim. Probably the same reversal of cause and effect exists with case management in either the first or second year, which was negatively related to work status in the Danish and Dutch cohorts.

Work accommodations had a significant positive relationship with work resumption in the first year in the cohorts from Denmark, Israel, and the Netherlands. This continued to be the case for the second year in those same countries in that work accommodations during the second year were related to additional work resumption in the second year. Again, it should be noted that work accommodations usually will occur only if there has been work resumption, and therefore the accommodations may not be the cause of resumption but rather a specific mode of resumption. Nevertheless, the accommodations used frequently for subjects in all three of those countries were adaptation of working hours and job redesign/change of jobs. Adaptation of working hours occurred for 62 percent of the subjects in the Dutch cohort, largely in the first year. Israel was close, with adaptation for 59 percent of the subjects; the figure for Danish subjects was 45 percent; for American subjects it was 43 percent. Even more frequent was therapeutic work resumption for the Dutch subjects, which occurred in 77 percent of the cases, and all within the first year. Sweden was second with respect to therapeutic work resumption, with 37 percent of the subjects receiving this intervention; the figure in the first year was 32 percent. In the other cohorts, this intervention was hardly available. Adapting the work place occurred much less frequently than changing work hours or job redesign in all of the cohorts (20-30% in Denmark, the Netherlands, Sweden, and the United States).

Employee motivators and contact with colleagues had a significant positive correlation with work status at T3 in the cohort from Germany, where vocational measures are, as a rule, less frequent than in other countries. These interventions did not have a significant effect in the other cohorts.

In sum, the data relative to vocational and other non-medical interventions suggest one reason why the Dutch cohort was more successful than the other cohorts in returning to work. The Dutch cohort, together with the Danish and the Israeli cohorts, used changes in work hours and job redesign extensively and successfully. What distinguished the Dutch cohort from the other two cohorts was that the Dutch cohort used therapeutic work resumption far more often as an intervention. Only the Swedish cohort came close in this respect, although the statistical results did not indicate a significant effect in Sweden. Finally, in the Dutch cohort (as well as in the Danish and the Swedish cohorts), benefits and work were combined much more than in the Israeli and the American cohorts. Thus, the Dutch cohort seems to have had the best results in using all of the available means for adapting work circumstances to their needs. On the other hand, the Dutch cohort may have been an "easier" cohort to work with. With respect to several indicators, the Dutch cohort looked more "promising" already at the outset, in light of the work ability model presented earlier in this chapter. This will be elaborated upon further in the following section.

The Cohorts Compared

The information from the various chapters in this book indicates that the cohorts recruited in the six countries differed considerably in ways that should be expected to affect the outcomes, and should be taken into account in evaluating the results. A number of important baseline characteristics describing work ability are brought together in Table 10.5.

What does the table indicate? A summary of the information in that table follows, relative to the work ability model presented at the beginning of this chapter.

Age: The German cohort was the oldest, with an average age of 49 and with 61 percent of the subjects 50 to 59 years of age. The Swedish cohort was the next oldest, with an average age of 44 and with 36 percent of the subject between 50 and 59 years of age. The Dutch and Israeli cohorts were the youngest.

Motivation and expectations: The Dutch cohort was by far the most optimistic about its chances of returning to work, when asked at 90 days. Only two percent of the subjects thought they could not return to work, compared to 32 percent of the subjects from Germany. In addition, 75 percent of the Dutch cohort predicted at 90 days that they could return to the same job. In contrast, only 25 percent of the Danish subjects and 28 percent of the Israeli subjects predicted that they could return to the same job. Notably, in all of the cohorts, the subjects were too optimistic at the outset about their prospects for returning to work. In every cohort, the percentage of non-resumers turned out to be much higher than the percentage of those who initially expected never to return to work.

Health: In the 90-day questionnaire, ADL scores, which can range from 0 (bad) to 100 (good), were between 47 and 53 in all of the cohorts—except for the cohort from Israel, which had a much lower score of 34. There were no large differences in perceived pain intensity as measured in the 90-day questionnaire. On a scale of 0 to 10, where 0 is no pain, subject scores ranged from 5.6 (Denmark) to 6.3 (Israel).

Whereas five of the six cohorts began with approximately the same average ADL score reported on the 90-day questionnaire, the Dutch cohort showed the greatest improvement in its average ADL score, from 48 to 65.

TABLE 10.5

Outcomes at Two Years and Baseline Indicators of the Work Capacity of the Country Cohorts

Country	Work Resumption T3, %	Average Age	Age 50–59, %	Education Low, %	Mother Language "no" %	Back Function (ADL) 90-days	Pain 90-days	Work Prognosis, %		
								Same Job	New Job	Can't Work
Denmark	40	41	14	45	8	48	5.6	25	56	19
Germany	35	49	61	95	3	47	6.5	38	31	32
Israel	60	39	18	58	34	34	6.3	28	58	14
N'lands	72	40	18	67	2	47	5.8	75	24	2
Sweden	63	44	36	36	18	53	5.9	61	23	16
US	62	42	27	11	18	52	5.9	57	30	14

The Dutch cohort was also the only cohort reporting substantial improvement, on average, in the Sciatica score, which measures pain radiating out into the legs. Similarly, the pain intensity scores for the Dutch cohort improved more than for the other cohorts.

Already at T1, the Dutch cohort scored much higher on the vitality scale than the other cohorts, and it was high on the mental health scale (together with the cohorts from Denmark and Sweden). This indicates that the Dutch cohort, although scoring similarly on pain and ADL functions, nevertheless was characterized by better vitality and mental health at the outset.

In sum, the Dutch cohort appears to have begun with about the same level of physical impairment as the cohorts from the other countries, except Israel, and then showed by far the greatest improvement in the impairment measures. On the other hand, other health indicators suggest that the Dutch cohort (apart from being relatively young) was in better general health at the outset than the other cohorts.

Education: The German cohort had by far the lowest educational level, followed by the cohort from the Netherlands.

Summing up across countries, the German cohort was older and poorly educated, and, for this reason, was less likely to succeed in terms of the work ability model. This was borne out in the outcomes of the German national study. A large percentage (56%) of the Danish cohort indicated that they needed to change jobs to resume work; otherwise, that cohort's average key baseline indicators did not differ greatly from those of the other cohorts. The Danish cohort did not stand out in terms of differing health, age, or education. Nevertheless the Danish cohort had a relatively poor outcome, perhaps because the system did not accomplish what was needed. The Danish job security arrangements, where employees may be, and often are, dismissed after 120 days of work incapacity, may have reduced chances for return to a subject's old job and thus lowered work resumption rates.

The remaining four cohorts had the best outcomes, with the Dutch cohort ending up on top. The Israeli cohort was drawn from a population with work injury, and, similar to the Danish cohort, 58 percent of the subjects indicated that they would need to change jobs in order to resume work. In addition, 34 percent of the Israeli cohort had another mother tongue. The Dutch cohort was in the middle of the cohorts in terms of age, but was the second highest cohort in terms of low education levels. On the other hand, all but two percent had Dutch as their mother tongue. The Swedish cohort was the second oldest (on average, 44 years old) and was five years older than the Israeli cohort, which was the youngest cohort. As many as 18 percent of the Swedish subjects did not have Swedish as their mother tongue, but the percentage of subjects with a low level of education was lower than in the other cohorts. The age structure of the American cohort was in the middle, but 18 percent of the American subjects had some other language than English as their mother tongue. The American cohort did not stand out from the others in any other respect that was measured.

Both the Israeli and the American cohorts stood out in one other respect that has to do with the benefit rules. Of the non-resumers, 51 percent of the Israelis and 73 percent of the Americans had no benefit at the end of two years, compared to 11 percent in the Danish cohort, 13 percent in the Dutch cohort, and 17 percent in the Swedish cohort. The tougher policy in Israel and the United States probably provides part of the explanation why many people did resume, especially in the United States, where statistical analysis reveals that neither medical nor vocational rehabilitation measures had a significant positive effect.

In sum, there was a dividing line between the four relatively more successful country cohorts and the two others, and then again between the Danish cohort and three of the four more successful cohorts. The cohorts in the Netherlands and Sweden had a higher frequency of work resumption. This is not surprising, as work resumption is central to the philosophy of the systems in those two countries. If people do not resume work, they are most likely to stay in a benefit chain, including unemployment benefits, with disability benefits being a benefit of last resort. As noted above, the Americans and Israelis were successful in getting people off benefits, but not as successful in returning people to work. The results for the Danish cohort indicated less success both in returning people to work and in getting them off benefits.

Conclusions: Major Determinants of Work Resumption

The core question of this study is whether interventions aimed at promoting return to work are effective. In view of the results presented in this chapter, it appears that their effectiveness is hard to prove. In so far as return to work can be predicted, baseline characteristics which were present already at the starting point used for the national studies (90 days after the onset of work incapacity) seem to be more influential than interventions. This holds both for the effect of medical interventions on improvement of back function (ADL score), which presumably is a prerequisite of work resumption, and for the effect of vocational and other non-medical interventions on return to work.

Viewing all national cohorts together, four factors appear to be especially important. Higher perceived work ability and lower pain intensity at the outset were important predictors of return to work at both one and two years, while advancing age and greater physical job demands operated against work resumption. Among interventions, work place accommodations appeared to be the most successful intervention across countries.

It should be emphasized that the WIR Project did not have an experimental design and thus cannot deliver scientific proof of the effectiveness or ineffectiveness of interventions. Furthermore, other ways of formulating the analytical model and more sophisticated statistical techniques might reveal more about the processes determining return to work and the significance of individual factors, including specific interventions. Nonetheless, several observations can be made on what the studies indicate about the importance of personal and work characteristics, medical, vocational, and other non-medical interventions, and incentives and disincentives for work resumption.

Personal and Work Characteristics ("Baseline Characteristics")

The first observation that stands out is the insignificance of most personal characteristics. Viewed across country cohorts, systems do not discriminate between lower and higher education, foreigners and non-foreigners, low and high income, or men and women. The few cases where these factors did influence work resumption may suggest interesting questions for the countries concerned. For example, why did the Dutch system give women a lower chance of return to work, whereas this was not the case in other country cohorts? Identifying these specific national mechanisms could be a useful task for national researchers. The only demographic factor that mattered to some extent in all of the cohorts was age. Older workers had less of a chance of returning to work. Age may be an indicator of the importance of skills and knowledge, but also perhaps of individual motivation and of workplace and societal attitudes towards older workers, as was set out in the work ability model discussed earlier in this chapter.

Second, health and self-perceived work ability are of obvious importance. The role of perceived work ability is of special interest. Work ability as perceived already in the 90-day questionnaire was predictive of return to work in the long run. This may indicate that already at an early stage of work incapacity, expectations and self-image are created that influence the process in the two years to follow. Return to work might well be a self-fulfilling prophecy, to some extent, where perceived work ability might also be an expression of the motivation and values factor from the work ability model.

Third, the role of limitations in back function (ADL score) is important. This was shown by the fact that the Dutch cohort, with the best resumption results in the first year—the most important year by far for eventual return to work—was also the one showing the best improvement in ADL scores. Conventional wisdom would be that improvement in ADL scores is a prerequisite for work resumption. Interestingly, the data suggest the mechanism might work partly the other way around. The Dutch system uses by far more, as well as a wider variety of, flexible and adapted work resumption interventions (therapeutic resumption, starting in reduced working hours, etc.). The data from the Dutch study would also support the hypothesis that work resumption itself helps to improve functional capacity.

Fourth, job characteristics generally do what they are expected to do. Most noteworthy is that the greater are the physical demands posed by the job, the smaller is the chance of returning to the job. This was especially the case within the first year; in the second year, job characteristics lost much of their importance for work resumption. Some other characteristics appear to be important for specific countries. For example, in Denmark, where it is easy to lose your job when work incapacitated, still having a job was significant for work resumption at one year.

Finally, returning to the model that initially guided the Project's research design described in Chapter 3, the data from the national studies provide significant information about the predictive value of specific individual and work-related characteristics.

Medical Interventions

Medical interventions did not seem to add much to the improvement of back function over and above the influence of baseline factors. The notable exception was surgery in the cohort from Sweden, where, with a much lower rate of occurrence than in, for example, the cohorts from the Netherlands and the United States, success seemed to be greater. The medical literature indicates generally that the timing of an intervention is important, with a less favorable outcome after three months; this may have been one of the contributing factors to the weak results.

However, it would not be reasonable to pass judgement on medical interventions on the basis of these results. Even insignificant statistical results might be interpreted as a positive outcome, given the probable selection effects (the worst patients possibly getting more intensive or specific treatments). Also, factors such as timing, sequence of specific treatments, and different ways of administering them may be of influence. In fact, during the 1990s, increasingly evidence from experimentally designed studies suggests that manipulation has a positive effect on chronic lower back pain. One conclusion of the WIR Project is that more scientific evaluation of treatments, with a randomized experimental design using well-defined control groups, is indispensable. This is the only way to move forward and identify best practices.

Two important aspects of medical interventions deserve mentioning, which distinguishes them from vocational and other non-medical interventions. First, it is reasonable to assume that no incentives are needed to apply such interventions; patients suffering from severe back pain will want to recover and will accept treatments aimed at recovery. Second, the patients themselves, with their wish of recovery, are the sole central actor; in return to work, both the employee and the employer play a part, and both may experience incentives or disincentives for using relevant interventions.

Vocational and Other Non-medical Interventions

For most of the vocational and other non-medical interventions, effectiveness is just as hard to prove as for medical interventions, and non-significant results do not necessarily mean ineffectiveness. Still, some positive results may be noted, especially with workplace accommodations and therapeutical work resumption.

To some extent, these results can be viewed as artificial. These interventions do not come before, but coincide with work resumption; they are modes of resumption. But the availability of these modes is important. The positive effect of work accommodations fits well with the significant influence of work characteristics—and both have their effect, especially within the first year, the period where most of the return process happens. And it is not simply coincidence that the country extensively using the whole battery of such flexible modes of returning to work—the Netherlands—ends up with the highest return rates.

The effectiveness of flexible return-to-work strategies is probably most pronounced relative to work resumption with the old employer, which was by far the most frequent way in which subjects returned to work in Germany, Sweden, and the Netherlands. In the other three countries, where work resumption with a new employer was more common, there was some positive influence from other types of interventions as well. Examples include job counseling/job search in the cohort from Denmark and education in the cohort from Israel. In a sense, it seems logical that interventions directed toward a new employment opportunity should show some effect, especially in countries where job protection for work incapacitated persons is less extensive.

Interventions, Incentives, and Disincentives

From the original model as presented in Chapter 3, it would seem as if incentives/disincentives and interventions are independent factors in work resumption. In reality, they are closely interconnected. Where there are strong incentives to resume work, relevant interventions (in so far as they are available in national systems) will often be applied; where there are strong disincentives, they will not.

What are relevant incentives and disincentives for return to work? Two kinds emerge from the national studies. First, job protection is important. In Sweden and the Netherlands, people seldom lose their jobs because they are sick and this was reflected both in higher return-to-work rates and in a high frequency of return to work with the old employer in the cohorts from those countries. In Denmark, Israel, and the United States, where job protection is more limited, work resumption was much more common with a new employer. For the Israeli and the American cohorts, this type of resumption was so frequent that the overall return-to-work rates came close to the rates for the Dutch and Swedish cohorts. The cohort from Denmark, where there is less job protection than in the Netherlands and Sweden but a more extensive benefit network for the jobless, did less well than the others.

This suggests a second incentive: the financial incentive built into the benefit system. It was not possible to construct relevant benefit-incentive variables as part of the Project. Nevertheless, a comparison of the six cohorts suggests their importance. Israel and the United States are the countries with more limited benefit opportunities. Chapter 6 showed that the non-resumers from those countries received no benefit whatsoever more frequently than those from the four European countries. This "forces" people back into work more strongly than in Denmark, where limited job protection is combined with a more extensive benefit system.

The combination of job protection and benefit regulations might well explain differences in work resumption rates and patterns, and the extent to which work resumption is aided by relevant vocational and other non-medical interventions. Limited job protection and less generous benefits might combine into an incentive to return to work, with the old or a new employer. More extensive job protection combined with a generous network of benefits will tend to result in more opportunities for return to work, especially with the old employer, but combined with continued receipt of benefits. For example, therapeutic work resumption may not necessarily lead to permanent, normal work resumption, although it is hoped that it will be a stepping stone moving people in the right direction. Limited job protection with a generous benefit network may reduce the overall return-to work rates because the opportunity to return with the old employer is worse, and the financial incentive to search for a new job with a new employer is less.

There might be a back side to this picture as well. Systems which more or less guarantee work resumption and/or a benefit may generate more long-term work incapacity. There are signs that the country seemingly most effective in returning persons to work who have been work incapacitated for three months—the Netherlands—is also the country with the highest frequency of three-month spells; whereas Denmark, with its lowest return-to-work rates, seems to "produce" fewer of these spells (Cuelenaere et al., 1999). The seemingly less successful Danish system might well have a positive combination of incentives within the first three months, leaving a smaller, and more difficult, group of three-month cases.

In sum, the analysis to this point provides several important insights. First, persons with higher subjective work ability evaluations from the outset do better. Second, health, and especially pain, is an important determinant of work resumption. Third, apart from age discrimination, evident in all but the Israeli and Swedish cohorts, there is very little discrimination. Fourth, high physical job demands operate against return to work, suggesting that this should be a focus in rehabilitation efforts. Fifth, the WIR Project has not provided general evidence of successful categories of interventions, with the exception of workplace accommodations and therapeutical resumption, which by definition involve returning to the workplace, job counseling and re-education in a few countries, and surgical practices in Sweden. This does not mean that there are no worthwhile interventions, but it does indicate that much sharper instruments—experimental studies—are needed to sort out best practices.

Finally, there is evidence that it matters for individual behavior how job protection and benefit networks are combined. A combination of strong job protection and an extensive benefit network promotes return to work, especially with the old employer. A combination of weak job protection and a weaker benefit network tends to lead to the same result, but with a higher frequency of changes in employers. On the other hand, weak job protection and a strong benefit network appear to work less well in returning people to work. The postlude is that we really do not know what happened in the participating countries during the first three months following the onset of work incapacity. The better systems are able to deal with cases of work incapacity in the first three months, the more likely it is that those cases that are left are more difficult to return to work. This suggests that a study that begins at the very outset of the work incapacity process is needed to learn the whole story.

Notes

1. Within each cohort, baseline characteristics for which over 15% of cases had missing values were eliminated; for the remaining variables, possible missing values were replaced with the (cohort-specific) mean of all valid cases. Of these remaining variables, those which had no significant zero-order correlation with the T2 ADL score were excluded from regression analysis.

2.   The variables measuring the baseline characteristics had to meet the statistical criteria in order to be used in the model, i.e. less than 15% missing values and a significant zero-order correlation with work resumption.

References

Antonovsky, A. (1987). *Unraveling the Mystery of Health*. San Francisco: Jossey-Bass Inc.

Cuelenaere, B., Veerman, T. J., Prins, R. & van der Giezen, A. M. (1999). *In Distant Mirrors: Work Incapacity and Return to Work*. Zoetermeer: College van Toezicht Sociale Verzekeringen (Ctsv).

Ilmarinen, J. (1999). *Aging Workers in the European Union*. Helsinki: Finnish Institute of Occupational Health.

Description of the Statistical Analysis Used

The following general approach was taken in performing the statistical analysis:

First, starting from a large set of baseline characteristics, for each national cohort those characteristics having more than 15 percent missing values were eliminated. For the remaining variables, in order to avoid cumulating missing values in multivariate analysis, missing values were converted into the mean score for that variable within the cohort.

Second, the complete list of baseline variables were run against the outcome variables—*health status* and *work status*. Within each national cohort, variables having no significant ($p < .05$) bivariate correlation with the dependent variable (i.e. health status for the analysis of medical interventions; work status for the analysis of vocational and other non-medical interventions) were excluded from further multivariate analysis.

Third, regression models were applied to the remaining variables for each national cohort. In the first step, all remaining baseline characteristics were entered into the analysis, and in the following steps, the relevant intervention variables were entered. The result should indicate what additional contribution these interventions have to improvement of health and work status, given the "baseline chances."

Appendix 10.1

Full Results of Statistical Analysis

For the analysis summarized in Tables 10.2 through 10.4, variables from all areas covered in the Project were inspected initially for inclusion in the multivariate analysis. From the set of variables initially inspected, only those variables which in the final model had a significant contribution to prediction of the dependent variables (back function scores, work status T2 and work status T3, respectively) are reported in those tables.

Tables 10A.2 – 10A.4 in this appendix report the full set of variables initially inspected, and the results.

For all three analyses, a set of "baseline characteristics" covering health indicators, demographical characteristics, job and employment history, and sickness history, were initially selected. "Baseline" refers to the variables *as measured at T1*. These characteristics, being either single items or scales/indexes, were taken from the international database directly.

Medical intervention variables were also taken as single items from the database directly, scored as "applied / not applied."

For the vocational interventions, some of these were taken as single items from the database as well; some others, having very low frequencies of application in some of the countries, were clustered into larger categories, as described below.

Clustering of vocational intervention variables

The following clustering in the vocational interventions was used (where a cluster of interventions was scored as "applied" if any of the underlying single items was applied):

-Job training/education: includes job training/vocational education and general education

-Work accommodations: includes workplace adaptations, adaptation of transportation, job redesign/change of workplace, adaptation of working hours, and sheltered workshop

-Employee motivators: includes warning of dismissal, actual dismissal, threat of negative sanctions, actual negative sanctions, and capitalization of benefits

-Case management/assessments: includes test of vocational capacity, (re-)evaluation of work incapacity, rehabilitation inquiry/rehabilitation plan

-Job counseling, including also job search and job placement

-Services: includes activation group, extended day care for children, social counseling, and reduction of waiting periods in health care

The following vocational interventions were taken as single items:
-Therapeutic work resumption
-Wage subsidy to employer
-Contact with colleagues or employer
-Assessment of eligibility for disability benefit
-Having seen a company doctor

First selection step: maximum of 15% missing values

All variables initially selected were screened for missing values. Variables having > 15% of missing values for a country were excluded from further analysis for that country, so as to avoid a cumulation of missing values in multivariate analysis. Variables not meeting this criterion are indicated as "-" in the tables below.

For the remaining variables, possible missing values were substituted by the mean of non-missing values for each country.

Second selection step: zero-order correlation of p < .05

The remaining variables were screened for non-significant zero-order correlations with the dependent variable. Variables having a non-significant correlation (p > .05) in a cohort were excluded from the multivariate analysis for that cohort. These variables are indicated as "−" in the tables below.

Third step: multivariate analysis

All remaining variables were submitted to a multivariate model. For the analysis of back function scores (ADL scores), traditional multiple regression models were used. For the analysis of work status (T2 and T3 respectively), logistic regression models were used.

Variables submitted to the regression model but not selected in the final solution of the model, are indicated as "0" in the tables below. For the remaining variables, selected in the final solution, either the standardized B (multiple regression) or the odd's ratio (logistic regression) are reported in the tables below.

TABLE 10A.1
Results of Multiple Regression Model Predicting
Back Function Scores (ADL) at T2

	Denmark	Germany	Israel	N'lands	Sweden	US
Number of cases	494	295	289	392	436	413
Dependent variable: Back function scores (ADL) at T2	**Standardized B's**					
BASELINE CHARACTERISTICS						
Age (high)	-.07	—	-.16	—	-.16	-.09
Gender (female)	-.13	0	—	-.19	0	0
Mother language (other than national)	—	—	0	—	-.14	0
Education completed	—	—	—	—	—	.08
Smoking index T1	—	—	-	—	—	-
Personal wage/Salary before sickness	0	-	—	0	—	0
Total personal income before sickness	0	0	—	0	—	0
Household income before sickness	-	—	-	-	-	-
Received support index T1	—	—	0	0	—	—
Others-depend-on-me index T1	0	—	-	—	0	-
Psychological job demand (old job)	0	—	0	—	—	0
Job decision latitude (control) (old job)	—	—	—	—	—	—
Social support at work (old job)	0	—	—	0	—	0
Job strain (old job)	0	0	—	—	-.07	0
Physical job demand (old job)	—	—	—	—	—	0
# of weekly working hours (old job)	—	0	—	0	—	—

	Denmark	Germany	Israel	N'lands	Sweden	US
Job: Still employed at T1?	—	0	-	-	-	0
Firm job certainty 1: Layoffs in last year?	—	—	0	—	—	—
Firm job certainty 2.1: Expected layoffs coming year?	—	—	—	—	—	—
Firm job certainty 2.2: Will patient possibly be laid off?	-	—	-	-	-	0
Sickness history: Weeks sicklisted last 12 months	0	0	—	—	—	-.07
Sickness history: # spells due to back pain last 12 months	-	-	-	-	-	-
Health problem duration: Back pain started when?	—	—	-	—	—	0
Received treatment before sicklisting?	—	—	—	—	0	—
Proportion of years worked since age 20	0	—	0	—	0	—
Number of jobs since age 20	0	—	—	—	—	0
Started in present job (recently)	0	—	—	—	—	—
Work moral: Financial motive to work	0	—	0	—	0	—
Attitude: Work shouldn't interfere with life	—	—	—	—	—	—
Attitude: Work is most important thing in life	—	—	0	—	0	0
Attitude: People report sick too easily	0	—	0	—	-	—
Passive coping before sicklisting	—	-.11	—	—	0	0
Active coping before sicklisting	—	0	—	-.11	—	—
Hannover ADL scale T1	.45	.40	.12	.38	.49	.54

TABLE 10A.1 *(Cont'd)*

	Denmark	Germany	Israel	N'lands	Sweden	US
BASELINE CHARACTERISTICS (Cont'd)						
Self-perceived work ability	0	.16	0	0	0	.11
Pain intensity	-.21	-.26	-.14	0	-.12	0
General health T1	.11	-	.16	.24	.12	.14
Vitality T1	—	—	—	—	—	-
Mental health T1	0	0	0	0	0	-
Social functioning T1	0	0	.13	0	0	0
Comorbidity: Interference with work resumption	-	—	-	-	-	-
MEDICAL INTERVENTIONS						
Operation T0-T1	0	—	—	0	.13	0
Passive treatments: Heat or cold T0-T1	—	-	—	—	—	—
Passive treatments: Ultrasound/Short wave T0-T1	—	-	—	—	—	—
Passive treatments: Acupuncture T0-T1	—	-	—	—	—	—
Pain relieving medication T0-T1	0	-.14	—	—	-.09	0
Passive treatments: Massage T0-T1	—	-	—	—	—	—
Passive treatments: Manipulation/Traction T0-T1	—	-	—	—	—	—
Passive treatments: Mud packing/Baths T0-T1	—	-	—	—	0	0
Active treatments: Gymnastics T0-T1	—	0	—	—	—	—
Active treatments: Pain school T0-T1	—	-	—	—	0	—
How many specialists seen T0-T1?	0	-	—	—	—	-

	Denmark	Germany	Israel	N'lands	Sweden	US
MEDICAL INTERVENTIONS (Cont'd)						
Visited physiotherapists T0-T1?	—	-	—	—	—	0
Operation T0-T2	—	0	0	-	-	—
Passive treatments: Heat or cold T0-T2	—	-	—	-	-	0
Passive treatments: Ultrasound/Short wave T0-T2	—	-	—	-	—	0
Passive treatments: Acupuncture T0-T2	—	-	—	-	-	0
Pain relieving medication T0-T2	0	0	—	-	0	-.07
Passive treatments: Massage T0-T2	—	0	—	-	—	0
Passive treatments: Manipulation/Traction T0-T2	—	-	—	-	—	0
Passive treatments: Mud packing/Baths T0-T2	—	-.08	—	-	-	0
Active treatments: Gymnastics T0-T2	—	0	—	-	-	—
Active treatments: Pain school T0-T2	—	-	—	-	—	—
How many specialists seen T0-T2?	0	0	0	-	0	0
Visited physiotherapists T0-T2?	—	0	—	-	—	0

Legend:

-: excluded due to $> 15\%$ missing values

—: excluded due to non-significant ($p > .05$) zero-order correlation with dependent variable

0: submitted to regression analysis but not entered in final solution of the model

TABLE 10A.2
Results of Logistic Regression Model Predicting
Work Status (Non-Working /Working) at T2

		Denmark	Germany	Israel	N'lands	Sweden	US
Number of cases		494	295	289	392	436	413
Dependent variable: Work Status T2 (not working/working)	Range		Odd's ratios in final model				
BASELINE CHARACTERISTICS							
Age (high)	19-60	.96	.97	—	.98	—	.95
Gender (male)	0-1	0	—	—	0	—	—
Mother language (other than national)	0-1	—	—	—	0	—	—
Education completed	0-6	0	—	—	0	—	0
Smoking index T1	0-92	—	—	.	—	0	.
Personal wage/Salary (national) before sickness		0	.	0	0	—	—
Total personal income before sickness	(national)	0	0	1.0003	—	—	—
Household income before sickness	(national)	.	—	.	.	.	—
Received support index T1	1-3	—	—	—	—	.69	—
Others-depend-on-me index T1	1-3	—	—	—	0	—	.
Psychological job demand (old job)	1-4	0	0	0	0	0	0
Job decision latitude (control) (old job)	1-4	0	—	—	.99	—	—
Social support at work (old job)	1-4	—	0	—	1.12	0	—
Job strain (old job)	0-4	.33	—	0	0	0	0

		Denmark	Germany	Israel	N'lands	Sweden	US
Physical job demand (old job) (scored high > low)	3-12	0	1.11	1.23	0	1.15	0
# of weekly working hours (old job)	0-90	—	—	0	0	—	0
Job: Still employed at T1?	0-1	1.65	10.5	-	-	-	2.70
Firm job certainty 1: Layoffs in last year?	0-1	3.89	0	—	—	—	—
Firm job certainty 2.1: Expected layoffs coming year?	1-3	—	—	—	—	—	—
Firm job certainty 2.2: Will patient possibly be laid off?	1-3	-	—	—	-	-	—
Sickness history: Weeks sicklisted last 12 months	0-52	—	.95	—	.99	—	0
Sickness history: # spells due to back pain last 12 months	0-32	-	-	-	-	-	-
Health problem duration: Back pain started when?	1-3	0	—	-	—	0	0
Received treatment before sicklisting?	0-1	—	0	—	—	.50	—
Proportion of years worked since age 20	0.01-1.00	—	7.09	—	—	—	—
Number of jobs since age 20	0-100	—	—	—	.80	—	0
Starting year present job	0-46	1.01	—	.92	0	—	—
Work moral: Financial motive to work	3-15	—	—	—	—	—	—

TABLE 10A.2 (Cont'd)

		Denmark	Germany	Israel	N'lands	Sweden	US
Attitude: Work should not interfere with life	1-3	—	1.73	—	—	—	—
Attitude: Work is most important thing in life	1-3	—	—	—	0	0	0
Attitude: People report sick too easily	1-3	—	0	—	—	-	—
Passive coping before sicklisting	1-3	—	0	—	—	—	—
Active coping before sicklisting	1-2.5	—	0	—	—	—	—
Hannover ADL scale T1	0-100	0	0	0	0	0	0
Self-perceived work ability	1-10	1.01	1.24	0	1.09	1.11	1.25
Pain intensity	1-10	.74	0	.84	.86	.86	.87
Comorbidity: Interference with work resumption	0-1	-	0	-	-	-	-
General health T1	0-100	0	-	—	1.04	1.01	0
Vitality T1	0-100	—	—	—	—	—	-
Mental health T1	0-100	0	0	—	0	0	-
Social functioning T1	0-100	0	0	—	0	1.01	1.02
VOCATIONAL INTERVENTIONS T0-T2							
Job training/ Education	0-1	.19	—	—	—	—	0
Work accommodations	0-1	21.77	—	20.95	2.46	—	-
Employee motivators	0-1	.48	—	.26	0	—	0
Case management/ Assessments	0-1	.40	.32	1.90	—	-	.54

		Denmark	Germany	Israel	N'lands	Sweden	US
Job counseling, -search, -placement	0-1	—	0	—	.44	—	—
Services	0-1	—	—	—	—	—	—
Therapeutic work resumption	0-1	—	0	-	5.66	—	3.86
Wage subsidy to employer	0-1	—	-	-	—	—	.00
Contact with colleagues/employer	0-1	—	-	-	0	—	-
Assessment for disability benefit	0-1	—	0	.29	.25	.002	—
Seen company doctor?	0-1	—	-	—	—	—	—

Legend:

-: excluded due to > 15% missing values

—: excluded due to non-significant (p > .05) zero-order correlation with dependent variable

0: submitted to regression analysis but not entered in final solution of the model

TABLE 10A.3
Results of Logistic Regression Model Predicting
Work Status (Non-Working/Working) at T3

		Denmark	Germany	Israel	N'lands	Sweden	US
Number of cases		441	245	265	370	382	377
Dependent variable: Work Status T3 (not working/working)	Range			Odd's ratios in final model			
Work Status T2 (not working/ working)	0-1	11.78	62.32	9.30	4.03	6.52	10.05

BASELINE CHARACTERISTICS

Age (high)	19-60	0	0	.98	.96	.98	0
Gender (male)	0-1	0	—	—	2.99	—	—
Mother language (other than national)	0-1	0	—	—	—	—	—
Education completed	0-6	1.19	—	0	0	0	0
Smoking index T1	0-92	—	0	—	—	0	-
Personal wage/Salary before sickness	(national)	0	-	0	0	—	—
Total personal income before sickness	(national)	1.0001	—	0	0	1.0001	—
Household income before sickness	(national)	—	0	-	-	-	-
Received support index T1	1-3	—	—	—	—	—	—
Others-depend-on-me index T1	1-3	—	—	—	—	—	-
Psychological job demand (old job)	1-4	0	0	—	0	0	0

		Denmark	Germany	Israel	N'lands	Sweden	US
Job decision latitude (control) (old job)	1-4	0	—	—	0	0	—
Social support at work (old job)	1-4	—	—	—	0	—	—
Job strain (old job)	0-4	0	—	—	0	0	0
Physical job demand (old job) (scored high > low)	3-12	0	—	—	1.25	1.25	0
# of weekly working hours (old job)	0-90	—	—	—	0	—	.98
Job: Still employed at T1?	0-1	0	4.99	-	-	-	0
Firm job certainty 1: Layoffs in last year?	0-1	—	-	-	—	-	—
Firm job certainty 2.1: Expected layoffs coming year?	1-3	—	—	—	—	—	—
Firm job certainty 2.2: Will patient possibly be laid off?	1-3	—	—	-	-	-	—
Sickness history: Weeks sicklisted last 12 months	0-52	0	—	—	.95	—	0
Sickness history: # spells due to back pain last 12 months	0-32	—	-	-	-	-	-
Health problem duration: Back pain started when?	1-3	—	—	-	—	0	0
Received treatment before sicklisting?	0-1	—	—	—	—	0	—

TABLE 10A.3 *(Cont'd)*

		Denmark	Germany	Israel	N'lands	Sweden	US
Proportion of years worked since age 20	0.01-1.00	0	—	—	0	—	—
Number of jobs since age 20	0-100	—	—	—	—	—	—
Years in old job	0-46	0	—	—	—	0	—
Work moral: Financial motive to work	3-15	—	—	—	—	—	—
Attitude: Work should not interfere with life	1-3	—	0	—	—	.72	—
Attitude: Work is most important thing in life	1-3	—	—	—	0	0	0
Attitude: People report sick too easily	1-3	—	0	—	—	·	—
Passive coping before sicklisting	1-3	—	—	—	—	—	—
Active coping before sicklisting	1-2.5	—	—	—	—	—	—
Hannover ADL scale T1	0-100	0	—	0	0	0	0
Self-perceived work ability	1-10	1.16	1.21	0	1.21	0	1.18
Pain intensity	1-10	0	0	.84	0	.90	0
Comorbidity: Interference with work resumption	0-1	·	0	·	·	·	·
General health T1	0-100	0	0	—	0	1.01	1.01
Vitality T1	0-100	—	—	—	—	0	·

		Denmark	Germany	Israel	N'lands	Sweden	US
Mental health T1	0-100	0	—	0	1.02	0	-
Social functioning T1	0-100	—	0	—	0	0	0

VOCATIONAL INTERVENTIONS T0-T2

		Denmark	Germany	Israel	N'lands	Sweden	US
Job training/ Education	0-1	—	—	2.96	—	—	—
Work accommodations	0-1	0	-	0	0	—	-
Employee motivators	0-1	0	-	0	0	—	0
Case management/ Assessments	0-1	.41	0	—	—	—	0
Job counseling, -search, -placement	0-1	2.27	0	—	0	—	—
Services	0-1	—	—	—	—	—	—
Therapeutic work resumption	0-1	—	0	-	0	—	—
Wage subsidy to employer	0-1	—	-	-	—	-	—
Contact with colleagues/ employer	0-1	2.97	-	-	—	2.55	-
Assessment for disability benefit	0-1	.24	.06	0	.49	.002	—
Seen company doctor?	0-1	—	-	—	0	—	0

VOCATIONAL INTERVENTIONS T2-T3

		Denmark	Germany	Israel	N'lands	Sweden	US
Job training/ Education	0-1	—	—	—	—	—	—
Work accommodations	0-1	6.71	-	9.39	12.56	-	-
Employee motivators	0-1	.27	71.10	—	.18	—	—

TABLE 10A.3 *(Cont'd)*

		Denmark	Germany	Israel	N'lands	Sweden	US
Case management/ Assessments	0-1	0	0	0	.53	—	0
Job counseling, -search, -placement	0-1	0	0	—	0	-	0
Services	0-1	0	—	—	0	-	.38
Therapeutic work resumption	0-1	—	-	—	—	-	-
Wage subsidy to employer	0-1	—	-	—	—	—	-
Contact with colleagues/ employer	0-1	—	19.10	-	-	-	-
Assessment for disability benefit	0-1	.0005	0	.31	.42	.22	.47
Seen company doctor?	0-1	—	-	—	—	—	2.48

Legend:

-: excluded due to $> 15\%$ missing values

—: excluded due to non-significant ($p > .05$) zero-order correlation with dependent variable

0: submitted to regression analysis but not entered in final solution of the model

11

Factors Influencing Work Resumption: A Summary of Major Findings

Boukje Cuelenaere & Rienk Prins

Aim and Background of the Project

As noted in Chapter 3, the available literature on work incapacity and interventions aimed at work resumption offers only limited information to policy makers interested in learning from experiences in other countries. Quite a bit has been written on social security arrangements in various countries, including descriptions of relevant regulations, organizational structures, and the use and expenditures of benefit schemes. One can also find overviews of rehabilitation and return-to-work measures used to stimulate work resumption in various countries, and there is also a good amount of cross-national data on various national repertoires of medical treatment and on the organization of health care in different countries. There are, however, no existing sources or methodologies for valid cross-national comparisons of currently applied return-to-work interventions and an assessment of their effectiveness. In many countries, there is little insight into the application of medical, vocational, and other non-medical interventions, and their impact on health and labor force participation.

The Work Incapacity and Reintegration (WIR) Project was designed explicitly to overcome some of these deficiencies in the comparative social security literature. One of the aims of the Project was to offer a closer, comparative look at measures taken to restore or improve health, to promote return to work, and to limit the payment of sickness and disability benefits. The national studies were designed to create sound descriptions of the interventions used in each participating country, and to provide solid insight into the effects of those interventions. The studies were also intended to compare health care measures undertaken on behalf of a similar category of persons in each country. The Project's prospective research design and its repeated measurement of treatments, return to work measures, and major elements of work incapacity and work resumption behavior have provided a wealth of information.

The aim of this chapter is to present and integrate the findings from earlier chapters, which covered various aspects of long-term work incapacity and work resumption, interventions applied, and client characteristics (base line characteristics). In doing so, conclusions will be drawn regarding the application and effect of interventions in relation to return to work and to other characteristics of the various social systems.

Ambitions and Restrictions

The Project's ambitious aim imposed several requirements on the design, methodology, and organization of the studies carried out in each country. However, it was clear from the beginning that it would not be feasible to create a fully representative sample of subjects in each country due to technical, organizational, and financial constraints. Instead, the national studies were set up using the same categories of subjects as to medical condition and work incapacity status, but with the subjects being monitored under different social security and health care systems, and different labor conditions. The Project was also designed to include sufficient personal and work characteristics to account for the impact of differences in socio-demographic and job variables known to affect health, recovery, and work resumption.

For the most part, these variables and the targeted interventions were measured at the same moment and with standardized instruments. The Project's design and methodology also allowed for some variations when local research conditions required flexibility. Each research team tried, within the financial and time constraints of their national project, to meet the methodological standards agreed upon. Nevertheless, local conditions sometimes required more flexibility than originally expected. Cross-national differences in cohort creation (e.g., as to regional variations), timing of measurements, and various degrees of loss of subjects could not always be prevented. Moreover, some variables proved not to be valid for all participating countries.

Despite these limitations, some of which resulted from this project being the first effort of its kind, important conclusions can be drawn regarding measures to reduce long term work incapacity. To a certain degree, conclusions regarding the vocational and other non-medical interventions and work resumption are restricted to persons with back disorders. However, the more fundamental mechanisms revealed in this study relative to supporting or inhibiting return to work also have implications for persons with other health restrictions.

Striking Differences in Work Resumption Rates and Patterns

Work status and benefit status were measured three times in the two-year observation period after the onset of work incapacity. From a social policy perspective, work resumption was the most desirable of the outcome variables. Work resumption is the specific goal of many of the interventions applied and it solves the problem of high numbers of benefit recipients and low labor market participation rates even more than does the reduction of benefit payments. The data show, however, that return-to-work rates differed considerably across the national cohorts after both one year and after two years. In Denmark and Germany, about 40 percent of the subjects returned to work within the two-year observation period. In Israel, Sweden, and the United States, about 60 percent of the subjects returned to work; in the Netherlands, the rate was over 70 percent. In the Netherlands and the United States, these high return-to-work rates were reached already within one year. Even when cohort differences are taken into account (e.g. age, occupational status), these differences, while reduced, are still striking.

As noted in Chapters 6 and 9, four patterns of work resumption can be discerned from the data: continuous resumers (without subsequent or new spells of work incapacity), late resumers, relapse resumers, and non-resumers. In all of the cohorts, the work resumption rates were much higher in the first year than in the second year of observation. Moreover, in some cohorts with high resumption rates, such as those from the United States and the Netherlands, there was no net increase in work resumption at all in the second year. In other cohorts, such as those from Sweden, Israel, and Denmark, the net return-to-work rate increased in the second year about 10 percent. The percentage of subjects who returned to work only in the second year—the late resumers—ranged from five percent in the German cohort to 19 percent in the Israeli cohort. The opposite group—relapse resumers who returned to work within one year but were no longer working one year later—was smaller, at about 10 percent overall and only five percent for the cohort from Denmark. Consequently, the first year appears to be decisive for successful work resumption; return to work actions taken in the second year added to work resumption rates only on a very limited scale.

Another striking difference was found in the employer status after work resumption. In the cohorts from Denmark and Israel, about one-half of the resumers were working at a new employer; in the United States, this figure was almost 40 percent. A totally different pattern was found in the cohorts from the Netherlands and Germany, where 80 percent or more of the subjects that resumed work returned to their old employer. In Sweden this was about 70 percent. In those countries, labor relations, employers' personnel management policy, or rehabilitation services (employer motivators) provide more opportunities for long-term work incapacitated persons to retain work. These contextual differences may also affect the need for certain interventions provided by social security or labor market institutions, as described below in the section on vocational and other non-medical interventions.

Finally, there were also some cross-national differences concerning the quality of work after resumption. Thus, certain categories of workers resumed work at lower quality jobs than they had before they became work incapacitated. This was particularly true in the cohort from Israel and, to a lesser extent, in the cohort from Denmark. In those cohorts 55 percent and 33 percent, respectively, of resumers were working at jobs with lower qualification levels.

The Role of Demographic, Health and Vocational Factors

The contrasts in return-to-work rates lead to a further analysis of personal characteristics of the cohorts that are related to work resumption. The Project's analytical model identifies three kinds of variables that, as baseline characteristics, may affect the result of various interventions and outcomes following a period of the work incapacity: demographic characteristics, health indicators, and job characteristics.

Not surprisingly, the data show a significant correlation between health indicators and work status after two years (working/not working at T3). In all of the cohorts, subjects who had reported "less pain" and a "better back function" at the onset of the study had a greater chance to return to work than those with a less favorable health status at the start of the study.

The cohorts differed, however, regarding the impact of job characteristics and demographic variables (age, gender, etc.). In the Danish and Dutch cohorts, some demographic characteristics correlated with work status at T3. Thus, younger, higher educated, and male subjects, and persons not living alone, were working more often than older subjects, less educated persons, etc. In the American and Israeli cohorts, on the other hand, hardly any of these characteristics were associated with return to work.

Job characteristics showed another pattern in the cohorts. In the Netherlands and the United States, and also partly in Sweden, the characteristics of the job that the subjects had at the onset of the study were relevant for future work resumption. Physical demands and job strains in the old job affected work resumption for subjects from these countries; the more the demands or strains, the less the chance of returning to work. Since most employees in the Netherlands and Sweden return to work with their old employer, it is not surprising that former job demands affected the chance of return to work. This makes sense especially in the case of the Netherlands, because institutional conditions facilitate return to work with the old employer, i.e. job protection legislation and therapeutical work resumption (job training with benefit compensation).

Looking more specifically at the patterns of work resumption discussed above, that is, continuous resumers, late resumers, relapse resumers, and non-resumers, there were only a few associations with baseline characteristics. A significant correlation with health status at the onset of the study was found in all cohorts for relapse resumers. Subjects who had more pain at the start of the study period and whose back function was more limited had a greater chance of repeated work incapacity in the second year, after having returned to work in the first year. Also, the difference between those who did not return to work at all (non-resumers) and late resumers in all cohorts except the German cohort, which had a very low percentage of late resumers (5%), can be attributed partly to worse health conditions in the former category.

The two cohorts in which baseline characteristics and work status at T3 were frequently related, those from Denmark and the Netherlands, had quite different return-to-work rates. This raises the question whether elements of the social system (health care provisions, benefit arrangements, labor relationships and administrative procedures) are at least as important to the return to work outcome as baseline characteristics.

Health Condition, Medical Treatments and Work Resumption

As noted in the literature review in Chapter 3, the relationship between medical interventions (treatment, rehabilitation) and work resumption has not been established satisfactorily in the past. The data created in the WIR Project studies offers an opportunity to monitor and assess relationships among treatments, health condition changes, and work resumption patterns.

As shown in the previous section, initial health status was correlated significantly with work status after one and two years in almost all of the cohorts. However, there were significant differences in the absolute health status of subjects who returned to work, measured at the same time. For example, the average score on back function one year after the onset of work incapacity (T2) varied considerably. The average score among subjects who returned to work in the Israeli cohort was 52 (on a 0-100 scale, where 100 means the best possible back function), whereas in the Dutch cohort the working subjects scored an average of 73. For subjects not working, the scores ranged from 32 (Israel) to 50 (Sweden). Thus, the self-reported back condition of the subjects who returned to work in Israel was about the same as the back condition of the subjects who did not return to work in Sweden. Cross-national differences in work status in each cohort will be affected partly by differences in back function; however, this characteristic is not an absolute indicator for working or not working in the future. Cross-cohort differences are even more striking regarding pain intensity, indicating that persons with similar health status characteristics may be more likely to resume work in one country than in another. For example, the subjects who did not return to work in Denmark reported less pain than those who resumed working in Germany.

Although a specific repertoire of medical treatments was used for the subjects in each cohort, the core treatments were about the same for all six of the cohorts. Seeing a general practitioner, seeing a specialist, hospitalization and back surgery, pain medication, and physical exercises were common practices in each of the six countries. However, the frequency of these core treatments varied across cohorts. For instance, physiotherapy was frequently applied in all countries; however, a high application rate was found especially in the Dutch cohort. Apart from this more common core repertoire, some therapies had particular application rates in some cohorts. From a comparative perspective, acupuncture was used more in Sweden, whereas medical baths (spas) were hardly used, with the exception of Germany.

One of the major objects of the Project was to assess the effect of medical treatments and interventions on work resumption. It turned out that, with one exception, there was no significant relationship between medical treatments and return to work. The exception was found in the Swedish cohort, where back surgery did have a statistically significant relationship with work resumption. Moreover, the frequency of back surgery in Sweden in the first three months of work incapacity was the lowest among the six cohorts. Swedish physicians seem to be selective in performing back surgery, while at the same time the Swedish subjects benefitted the most from that intervention in terms of work resumption. One effect of medical treatment was obvious in each cohort: in most cases, medical treatment resulted in an improvement of the subject's subjective health status. However, this did not necessarily correspond with an improvement relative to back function and pain intensity, the two health indicators that were most related to work resumption.

Finally, the number of treatments given to the subjects was striking. Even those who did not report a better health status after a year received many treatments. On the one hand, this seems reasonable as their unimproved health condition may have made further treatment more necessary. On the other hand, it seems remarkable that, for any group of subjects, so many treatments and interventions could have no beneficial effect on health status.

Vocational and Other Non-medical Interventions

Apart from medical interventions, a person who is work incapacitated usually is confronted also with a range of interventions from other non-medical actors, such as his or her employer and/or colleagues, benefit providers, or rehabilitation organizations. Most of these interventions are vocational interventions aimed directly at returning the person to work. Another category of interventions arises out of the social security system and the benefit eligibility process. In any event, these interventions should not be evaluated without considering the employment context; for example, changes in tasks or working conditions may be more likely to be offered when the employer faces strong regulations protecting against dismissal.

Among the vocational interventions tracked in the Project, those most commonly provided were training and education, work accommodations, and job services. Training and vocational education were applied most frequently in the cohorts from Denmark and Sweden. Work accommodations were relatively rare in the cohorts from Israel and Germany; in the other cohorts, the application rate was twice as high. Other very popular interventions were adaptation of working hours (temporarily or permanently) and job redesign. The Dutch subjects and, to a lesser extent, the Swedish subjects also received a very high percentage of job training with compensation, which is known in the Netherlands as "therapeutical work resumption." Those subjects returned to their work part time, before they were fully able to perform their job; they received partial sickness benefits during this period, as they were considered still partially work incapacitated. Despite variations in the application of interventions, for all of the cohorts straightforward statements on their impact on work resumption could not be made—as often other factors related to an intervention (e.g. educational level of the subject, duration of the training program) also affect return-to-work patterns.

Another important category of interventions comes from disciplinary measures taken by an employer: warning of dismissal, and dismissal. In this regard, differences in national legislation on job protection during work incapacity proved to be an important source of variation across the countries included in the Project. Whereas in the Danish, Israeli, and American cohorts substantial numbers of subjects were confronted with dismissal, in all of the other cohorts this type of disciplinary action was rare. Consequently, the rates of work resumption, both at the old employer and at a new employer, seemed to be conditioned by the job protection rules in effect in the respective country. This dichotomy between the cohorts reflects the differences in social security and employment contexts among the participating countries, as described briefly in Chapter 2.

A third category of interventions is those initiated by social security institutions. Measures in this area cover the threat and actual withdrawal of sickness benefits, as well as several types of assessments aimed at determining eligibility for temporary sickness benefits and permanent disability benefits. Here also, rules or practices as to the timing of disability assessment proved to be an important determinant of work resumption. As noted in Chapter 8, the intervention significantly connected to return-to-work rates in all of the cohorts was testing of eligibility for permanent disability benefits. Subjects who were tested returned to work to a lesser degree than those did not undergo eligibility tests. Obviously, those who were tested were less qualified for immediate return to work.

Finally, the provision of services was compared across the cohorts. It was concluded that job search and receipt of a job offer, the services that were applied most frequently, were applied less in the cohorts with high rates of work resumption with the original employer. Furthermore, no significant relationship with work resumption rates could be established for well-known and strongly advocated measures such as rehabilitation inquiry and plan. Multivariate analyses, which try to account for the influence of other factors, were made to shed more light on the role of vocational and other non-medical interventions.

Resumers, Non-resumers, and Benefit Receipt

As noted earlier, the subjects in the national cohorts could be classified as falling into one of four patterns of work resumption. Two of these patterns were dominant in all of the cohorts: continuous resumers and non-resumers. Thus, between 73 percent and 83 percent of the subjects in the various cohorts fell into these two categories.

There were considerable differences regarding the benefit status of those subjects who were not working after the second year. Whereas in Denmark, the Netherlands, and Sweden, the vast majority of those subjects (about 90%) received some benefit (e.g. disability, unemployment, social assistance); in Israel and the United States, only a minority received a benefit. At the same time, the data demonstrate that the dichotomy of working vs. receiving a benefit is not necessarily meaningful. Although those who had been assessed for eligibility for disability benefits had a lower return-to-work rate than those who were not evaluated, this did not imply that they did not return to work at all. It is possible to combine working and benefit receipt. Thus, in Denmark, the Netherlands, and Sweden, 15 to 26 percent of the resumers were working with an additional benefit. This focuses attention on the facilitating role of additional benefits as a social political means to maximize the number of people who support themselves to the greatest possible extent.

Not working at the end of the two-year study period was not always due to the original lower back problems. Especially in the Netherlands, reasons other than low-back pain played a large role in not working at T3. Moreover, dismissed employees who did not return to work were not always dismissed due to their health problems. In Sweden, with its strong job protection policies, dismissals were more likely the result of downsizing than caused by the health status of the subjects.

Health Condition, Interventions, and Work Resumption Reconsidered

Overall, the battery of vocational and medical interventions applied to the subjects in the national studies had a limited measurable relation with work resumption, although there were variations across cohorts. Multivariate analysis showed that in each cohort, work resumption was explicitly related primarily to improvement of health condition. Subjects who did not work had, on average, a worse health condition compared to those who resumed working. It also appears that health condition after one year was related predominantly to personal characteristics—age in particular—at the onset of work incapacity.

The role of medical interventions in improving health condition and chances of return to work was difficult to determine. First, some basic interventions were applied so frequently that a statistical analysis could not determine a specific effect. Second, some other interventions were so time consuming that the patients could not return to work early.

Vocational and other non-medical interventions were shown to be associated with work resumption in ways that do not always seem so obvious. Most of these interventions clearly had a positive relation with work resumption in some cohorts, although the real effect could not be analyzed since work-related interventions go together with work resumption. Some vocational interventions, just as medical interventions, could also induce a delay of work resumption, e.g. when testing of eligibility for disability benefits was carried out late or when the intervention was time consuming, as is the case with educational programs. Interventions that were carried out rather late, such as job counseling and job search, had only some relationship with increased chances of return to work in those cohorts, such as those from Denmark and Israel, where a lot of subjects were still not working at T2.

Finally, a striking result appeared concerning the relationship between health improvement and work resumption. In many cohorts, work resumption took place without substantial improvement of health condition. Subjects suffering from chronic back pain returned to work. Work accommodations may, in such cases, be helpful to resuming work. Obviously, health is just one factor and other factors can contribute just as much to return to work.

As noted earlier, job protection is an important factor in stimulating return to work at an old employer. If job protection is limited, as in Denmark, then the benefit system may hinder returning to work with a new employer. Without a good benefit as a financial back up, people are under more pressure to return to work, at whatever salary and whatever health cost. In such cases, the combination of the national system of job protection and the benefit system, with support from adequate vocational interventions, has a major influence on the return-to-work rate.

Additional Conclusions from National Studies

This book focuses on cross-national and cross-cohort comparisons of the social security context, the medical treatment and health care providers involved, the range of vocational and other non-medical interventions applied, and their relationships with work status. National reports were prepared as part of the Project, which focused mainly on the "domestic" cohort. The outcomes of the national studies are discussed in those reports in the context of national policies on social protection, prevention or reintegration.

The national studies may also provide conclusions on determinants (predictors) of work resumption or on the impact of interventions, which may have a validity that exceeds the boundaries of the national study. Therefore, this section presents the most striking outcomes, conclusions, or recommendations that were mentioned in the national studies performed in the six countries. Full citations to the publications referred to in this section are listed at the end of the chapter. A listing of all publications arising out of the Project to date can be found in Addendum B at the end of the book.

Denmark

Findings based on the Danish WIR data suggest that certain vocational and rehabilitation measures, which at first glance appear not to affect the likelihood of returning to work, in fact may help people returning to work. Hence, when the timing of a test of vocational capacity is taken into consideration, Høgelund (1999) finds, in an analysis which included the moment of work resumption, that this measure has a very strong impact on the probability of returning to work.

Germany

Almost all persons coming back to work resumed working in the first year after the onset of work incapacity. This requires the application of rehabilitative interventions as early as possible. Bivariate and multivariate analysis showed that the subjective work prognosis of the work incapacitated worker is a very good predictor of return to work, especially for nonresumption of work.

Utilization of medical and vocational rehabilitation was quite low in the German cohort. This suggests a considerable amount of underutilization. In order to avoid underutilization, the process of accessing medical rehabilitation within the German health care system should be reviewed critically (Weber et al., 1999).

Israel

In Israel, the WIR project has shown quite a good, though late, work resumption rate compared to the "best performers" in the Project. Israel also displayed a relatively high rate of finding new jobs by the many subjects that were dismissed (Gordon, 2000). These findings may be explained by Israel's low rate of granting benefits and by its late and rare rehabilitation efforts.

There is some evidence that earlier rehabilitation might speed up work resumption, especially for those who have to find new jobs. Therefore, it may be recommended to try earlier and broader rehabilitative interventions in Israel.

The Netherlands

The Dutch study showed the importance of the relationship between the employer and the employee for successful work resumption. Work satisfaction was one of the main determinants for return to work. On the other hand, employee characteristics that were favored by employers, such as being younger, being a male, and being higher educated, also determined return to work, especially in the long run (at T3). The employees' and the employers' motivations to continue employment seem to have more impact than vocational interventions. Interventions merely facilitate return to work and do not determine it (Cuelenaere et al., 1999).

Sweden

The Swedish subjects entered the national cohort after 28 days on sickness benefits due to low back pain. Those who returned to work before 90 days had less pain, less functional limitations, and a better quality of life than did those who entered the international cohort for the WIR Project. Generally, they also had fewer treatments. Quality of life (the instrument Euroqol) was the best predictor of work resumption before 90 days, predicting 75 percent of non-resumers correctly (Bergendorff et al., forthcoming).

United States

A number of clearly defined predictors of work resumption were identified in the United States study. Resumers typically were younger than non-resumers, suffered less intense pain, had fewer limitations on their activities and less physical job demands, and were more inclined to live with their families than to live alone. Also, it is noteworthy that over 80 percent of resumers were provided with workplace adaptations and about two-thirds had job training or vocational education (Kearney, 1997).

Outlook for Future Research

The WIR Project produced substantial amounts of data. So far, the data from the national studies have provided a detailed overview of the medical and vocational interventions applied in the countries included in the Project. As to medical interventions, the cross-cohort differences were quite consistent with cross-national differences known from health care studies. There still are many questions for which answers can be found in further analyses of this rich material. The data can be examined further, for example, regarding the selection of persons for various medical treatments (cf. the Swedish data on surgery) and the timing of those treatments.

Further study could also focus attention on the timing of vocational and other non-medical interventions and the detection of specific target groups for which certain interventions are most successful. In general, work accommodations proved to be a relevant supporting condition for work resumption in cohorts with high return-to-work rates. However, the application of this type of intervention requires a willingness and commitment on the part of the employer, which means that this type of intervention is likely to function particularly well when labor relationships are favorable.

Personal characteristics (health condition, age, vocational expectations) play a more limited role in work incapacity and return to work behavior than might be expected. The interrelationship of personal characteristics and labor relationships, including job protection, requires further attention, particularly when one considers that in several cohorts work resumption took place without substantial improvement of health condition.

It also became clear that the weight of "health status" in long-term work incapacity should be reconsidered (cf. the medical paradox, discussed in Chapter 1). Even when measured with international validated instruments, health condition is not an absolute indicator of the probability of work resumption. The model on factors influencing work ability presented in Chapter 10 makes clear that health, work environment, skills, and attitudes are all important determinants of work capacity, itself the variable of focus in return to work. Medical interventions focus on the improvement of health, while vocational interventions focus on the improvement of the work environment and skills. No interventions focus directly on the worker's attitudes, of which "perceived work ability" was the main indicator in this study. Of course, changes in motivation and other aspects of work attitude can occur as a side effect of the interventions undertaken. Relevant issues for further research could be the role of motivation, and ways to influence the motivation of the employee and the employer. Moreover, self-evaluation of health condition and future employment expectations need further consideration (also in the provision of interventions), as the Project also showed that people are more optimistic about return to work than is actually realized.

Finally, due to the research design of the Project, processes that lead to reporting work incapacity and to prolonging absence due to work incapacity of up to three months still are hardly known. In order to reduce psychological barriers to work resumption and to prevent attachment to the sick role, early interventions are being promoted more and more. It would be very fruitful to assess which factors affect the work resumption process during the first three months of work incapacity, and what can be learned to prevent long-term work incapacity.

References

Bergendorff, S., Hansson, B., Hansson, T. & Jonsson, R. (forthcoming). *Prediktorer för återgång i arbete och förändring av hälsotillstånd. Rygg och Nacke 8.* (The Swedish back and neck pain project—Predictors of health status and work resumption). Stockholm: Riksförsäkringsverket och Sahlgrenska Universitetssjukhuset.

Cuelenaere, B., van der Giezen, A. M., Veerman, T. J. & Prins, R. (1999). *Werkhervatting na rugklachten: langdurig zieke werknemers twee jaar gevolgd.* (Work resumption after low back complaints: long term sick employees monitored during two years). Eindrapport Nederlandse studie. Zoetermeer: College van toezicht sociale verzekeringen (Ctsv).

Gordon, D. (2000). *Work incapacity and reintegration - Israel in comparison to five countries: a two years follow-up study* (in Hebrew). Jerusalem: National Insurance Institute, Special research series.

Høgelund, J. (1999). *Bringing the sick back to work: Labor market reintegration of the long-term-sick-listed in the Netherlands and Denmark* (Unpublished PhD thesis). Copenhagen: Roskilde University and the Danish National Institute of Social Research.

Kearney, J. (1997). The Work Incapacity and Reintegration study: Results of the initial survey conducted in the U.S. *Social Security Bulletin*, No. 3, pp. 21-32.

Weber, A. et al., (1999). *Reintegration in das Erwerbsleben bei Dorsopathieen, Abschlussbericht* (Reintegration into working life in clients with back disorders; final report). Frankfurt: Verband Deutscher Rentenversicherungsträger.

Addendum A: Overview of Variables

Various variables have been covered in the three measurement waves of the WIR Project. This overview lists the variables included in the national studies and when they were measured (T1: at 3 months; T2: at 1 year; T3: at 2 years).

This overview does not give specific technical details (e.g. answer categories, scales, values) or empirical characteristics (e.g. distributions, missing values). This technical information can be found in the Technical Guidelines to the WIR International Data Base, which is available at:

International Social Security Association
Research Programme
Case postale 1
CH-1211 Geneva 22
Switzerland
http://www.issa.int

	T1	T2	T3
Patient ID	X	X	X
Country name			
Country ISO code			
Date of reporting sick	X		
Date of questionnaire/interview	X	X	X
DEMOGRAPHIC CHARACTERISTICS			
Age	X		
Gender	X		
Education completed	X		
Born in country	X		
Mother language	X		
Household composition (2 items)	X		X
Pregnancy during T0-T2		X	
WORK AND EMPLOYMENT CHARACTERISTICS			
Occupation	X		

	T1	T2	T3
WORK AND EMPLOYMENT CHARACTERISTICS *(Cont'd)*			
Traveling time home-work former job (T0)		X	
Traveling time home-work present job (T2)		X	
Number of working hours	X		
Job demands:			
Psychological demands (5 items)	X		
Decision latitude (Control) (6 items)	X		
Strain	X		
Physical job demands (3 items)	X		
Social support at work (6 items)	X		
Number of jobs	X		
Employment history last 24 months (4 items)	X		
Company size	X		
NACE branch	X	X	X
Job certainty (3 items)	X	X	X
Attitudes on work (5 items)	X		
Attitudes on benefits	X		
HEALTH			
Number of weeks sicklisted during last 12 months	X		
Number of sickness spells due to backpain during last 12 months	X		
Medical condition at onset: Comorbidity 9 items	X		
Comorbidity: Interference with work resumption?	X		

	T1	T2	T3
HEALTH *(Cont'd)*			
Health problem duration	X		
Back function (Hannover ADL: 12 items)	X	X	X
Sciatic pain	X	X	X
Pain intensity	X	X	X
Perceived work ability	X	X	X
Own work prognosis long-term	X	X	
Work prognosis; moment of resumption	X	X	
General health (5 items)	X	X	X
Social functioning	X	X	X
Vitality (4 items)	X	X	X
Mental health (5 items)	X	X	X
Height in centimeters	X		
Weight in kilos	X		
Passive coping before sicklisting (3 items)	X		
Active coping before sicklisting (5 items)	X		
Social support (3 items)	X		
Quality of social support (who gives what support: 9 items)	X		
HEALTH CARE AND MEDICAL INTERVENTIONS			
Health care: Received treatment before reporting sick?	X		

	T1	T2	T3
HEALTH CARE AND MEDICAL INTERVENTIONS *(Cont'd)*			
Health care: How many doctors (3 items)	X	X	X
Health care: Doctors - frequency (3 items)	X		
Health care: Physiotherapists	X	X	X
Health care: Physiotherapists - frequency	X		
Health care: Physiotherapists - date	X		
Health care: X-RAY	X	X	X
Health care: X-RAY - date	X		
Health care: CT scan			X
Health care: MRI			X
Health care: Hospitalization	X	X	X
Health care: Hospitalization - frequency	X		
Health care: Hospitalization - date	X		
Health care: Operation	X	X	X
Health care: Operation - date	X		
Health care: Other caregivers	X	X	X
Health care: Number of other caregivers	X	X	X
Health care: Other caregivers - frequency	X		
Passive treatments (heat/cold; electric therapy; acupuncture)	X	X	X
Passive treatments (3 items) - frequency	X		
Passive treatments (3 items) - date	X		

	T1	T2	T3
HEALTH CARE AND MEDICAL INTERVENTIONS *(Cont'd)*			
Pain relieving medication	X	X	X
Pain relieving medication - date	X		
Bed-rest	X		
Bed-rest - date	X		
Passive treatments (massage; traction/manipulation; medical baths)	X	X	X
Passive treatments (3 items) - frequency	X		
Passive treatments (3 items) - date	X		
Active treatments (gymnastics and back school)	X	X	X
Active treatments (2 items) - frequency	X		
Active treatments (2 items) - date	X		
Other treatments (walking aids; braces; else)	X	X	X
Other treatments (3 items) - date	X		
VOCATIONAL AND OTHER NON-MEDICAL INTERVENTIONS			
Job training and vocational education		X	X
Job training and vocational education - date		X	
Job training and vocational education - initiative		X	
Job training and vocational education - completed		X	X
General education		X	X
General education - date		X	
General education - initiative		X	

	T1	T2	T3
VOCATIONAL AND OTHER NON-MEDICAL INTERVENTIONS *(Cont'd)*			
General education - completed		X	X
Workplace adaptation		X	X
Workplace adaptation - date		X	
Workplace adaptation - initiative		X	
Adaptation: Transportation to workplace		X	X
Adaptation: Transportation to workplace - date		X	
Adaptation: Transportation to workplace - initiative		X	
Job redesign / Changes of workplace		X	X
Job redesign / Changes of workplace - date		X	
Job redesign / Changes of workplace - initiative		X	
Adaptation of working hours		X	X
Adaptation of working hours - date		X	
Adaptation of working hours - initiative		X	
Sheltered workshop		X	X
Sheltered workshop - date		X	
Sheltered workshop - initiative		X	
Therapeutic work resumption		X	X
Therapeutic work resumption - date		X	
Therapeutic work resumption - initiative		X	

	T1	T2	T3
VOCATIONAL AND OTHER NON-MEDICAL INTERVENTIONS *(Cont'd)*			
Wage subsidy for employer / Exemption of wage payment for employer		X	X
Wage subsidy for employer / Exemption of wage payment for employer - date		X	
Capitalization of benefits		X	X
Capitalization of benefits - date		X	
Warning of dismissal		X	X
Warning of dismissal - date		X	
Dismissal		X	X
Dismissal - date		X	
Threat with negative sanctions		X	X
Threat with negative sanctions - date		X	
Actual negative sanctions		X	X
Actual negative sanctions - date		X	
Contact with colleagues/employer		X	X
Test of vocational capacity		X	X
Test of vocational capacity - date		X	
Work incapacity (re)evaluation		X	X
Rehabilitation inquiry / Rehabilitation plan		X	X
Rehabilitation inquiry / Rehabilitation plan - date		X	

	T1	T2	T3
VOCATIONAL AND OTHER NON-MEDICAL INTERVENTIONS *(Cont'd)*			
Assessment of eligibility for disability benefit		X	X
Assessment of eligibility for disability benefit - date		X	
Assessment of eligibility for disability benefit - result		X	X
Job counseling		X	X
Job counseling - date		X	
Job search		X	X
Job search - date		X	
Job placement		X	X
Job placement - date		X	
Job placement - by ...			X
Activation group / Job club		X	X
Activation group / Job club - date		X	
Daily care for children		X	X
Daily care for children - date		X	
Counseling (welfare, social support)		X	X
Counseling (welfare, social support) - date		X	
Reduction waiting periods in health care		X	X
Reduction waiting periods in health care - date		X	

	T1	T2	T3
VOCATIONAL AND OTHER NON-MEDICAL INTERVENTIONS *(Cont'd)*			
Evaluation of non medical interventions		X	X
Evaluation of non medical interventions - most important		X	X
WORK STATUS			
Still employed?	X	X	X
Type of employment		X	
Has patient worked during last 12 months		X	X
Has patient worked during last 12 months - date of work resumption		X	X
Patient employment history during last 12 months (6 items)		X	X
History of sickness spells during last 12 months - number of spells		X	X
Working hours		X	X
Reason for not working		X	X
Work status (5 items)		X	X
Work status: Benefit		X	
Current work status			X

Addendum B: List of Project Publications

General

Bloch, F. S. & Prins, R. (1997)
*Work incapacity and reintegration: Theory and design of a
cross-national study.* International Social Security Review, Vol. 50, No.
2.

Publications from the Danish WIR Project

Høgelund, J. & Modvig, J. (1998)
*Langtidssygemeldte med rygproblemer - en forløbsundersøglse i 24
kommuner* (Long-term sick-listed with low-back problems - A
prospective study in 24 municipalities). The Danish Institute of Social
Research, Working paper. Copenhagen.

Høgelund, J. (1999)
*Bringing the sick back to work. Labour market reintegration of the
long-term sick-listed in the Netherlands and Denmark* (Unpublished PhD
thesis). Roskilde University and the Danish National Institute of Social
Research. Copenhagen.

Høgelund, J. (1999)
*Reintegration Policies in the Netherlands and Denmark: The Role of
Employers.* The Danish Institute of Social Research, Working paper.
Copenhagen.

Publications from the German WIR Project

Weber, A. et al. (1999)
Reintegration in das Erwerbsleben bei Dorsopathien, Abschlussbericht
(Return to work of patients with low back disorders; final report), VDR:
Frankfurt, 1999.

Weber, A. & Raspe, H. (1999)
*Gelingt die Reintegration in das Erwerbsleben nach
Langzeitarbeitsunfähigkeit? - Zusammenfassung der Ergebnisse der ISSA
Studie in Deutschland* (Is return to work after long term work incapacity
successful? Summary of main outcomes of the ISSA Project in
Germany) in: Die Deutsche Rentenversicherung 4, 219-234.

Weber, A. & Raspe, H. (1996)
Einschränkung der Funktionskapazität bei Dorsopathien und subjektive Arbeitsprognose (Restrictions in functional capacity due to low back disorders and subjective work prognosis) in: Brähler, E./Schuhmacher, J.(Hrsg.): Psychologie und Soziologie in der Medizin, 200-201. Giessen: Psychologische Verlags Union.

Weber, A. & Raspe, H. (1996)
Inanspruchnahme medizinischer Leistungen bei langandauernder Arbeitsunfähigkeit und subjektive Arbeitsprognose (Provision of medical treatments in case of long term work incapacity due to low back disorders and subjective work prognosis) in: Das Gesundheitswesen 8/9 (58), LXVII.

Weber, A. & Raspe, H. (1998)
Langzeitarbeitsunfähigkeit und die Wiederaufnahme der Arbeit-Krankenkassen beteiligen sich an der internationalen IVSS-Kohortenstudie (Long term work incapacity and work resumption: sick funds participate in international ISSA cohort study) in: Die Krankenversicherung 5/98, 145-146.

Weber, A. (1998)
What are the best predictors for not returning to work in Germany? in: Improving Practice by Research, 6th European Congress on Research in Rehabilitation, Congress Proceedings, Frankfurt (DRV-Schriften, Band 10), 247-249.

Weber, A. & Raspe, H. (1998)
Langzeitarbeitsunfähigkeit und die Wiederaufnahme der Arbeit-Krankenkassen beteiligen sich an ISSA-Studie (Long term work incapacity and work resumption: sick funds participate in ISSA study) in: Die BKK 8/98, 404-407.

Weber, A. et al. (1998)
Ist der subjektive Gesundheitsstatus ein guter Prädiktor für die Wiederaufnahme der Arbeit? (Is subjective health status a good predictor or work resumption?) in: Sozial- und Präventivmedizin 4/98, 177-184.

Weber, A. (1998)
Rehabilitation bei Langzeitarbeitsunfähigkeit (Rehabilitation and long term work incapacity) in: Public Health Forum, 6, Nr.21,20.

Weber, A. & Raspe, H. (1998)
Langzeitarbeitsunfähigkeit und die Wiederaufnahme der Arbeit (Long term work incapacity and work resumption) in : Die Deutsche Rentenversicherung 9-10/98, 679-690.

Weber, A. (1998)
Subjektive Arbeitsprognose, Berentungsabsicht und Antrag auf medizinische Rehabilitation bei arbeitsunfähigen Rückenschmerzpatienten - Ein Beitrag zur Diskussion um Rehabedürftigkeit (Subjective work prognosis, desire to obtain a pension, and medical rehabilitation requests in persons work incapacitated due to back pain; a contribution to the discussion on need of rehabilitation) in: Interdisziplinarität und Vernetzung, 7. Rehabilitationswissenschaftliches Kolloquium, Frankfurt (DRV-Schriften, Band 11), 279-280.

Weber, A. & Zimmermann, M. (1999)
Arbeitsunfähigkeit wegen Dorsopathien in Deutschland und Schweden: Bewältigung durch Rehabilitation (Work incapacity due to back disorders in Germany and Sweden: dealing with rehabilitation) in: Grenzenlose Gesellschaft, Kongressband II/1 vom 29. Kongress der Deutschen Gesellschaft für Soziologie in Freiburg 1998, Centautus: Pfaffenweiler, 242-244.

Weber, A. & Zimmermann, M. (1999)
Berufliche Rehabilitation in Deutschland und Schweden (Vocational rehabilitation in Germany and Sweden) in: Seyd, W., Nentwig, A. & Blumenthal, W.(Hrsg.): Zukunft der beruflichen Rehabilitation und Integration in das Arbeitsleben, 342-346.

Weber, A., Weber, U. & Raspe, H. (1999)
Welche Rolle spielt die medizinische Rehabilitation bei Langzeitarbeitsunfähigkeit? (What is the role of medical rehabilitation in long term work incapacity?) in: Reha-Bedarf - Effektivität - Ökonomie, 8. Rehabilitationsissenschaftliches Kolloquium, Frankfurt (DRV-Schriften, Band 12), 147-148.

Weber, A. & Raspe, H. (1999)
Gelingt die Reintegration in das Erwerbsleben nach Langzeitarbeitsunfähigkeit? (Is work resumption successful after long term work incapacity?) in: Die Deutsche Rentenversicherung 4/99, 219-234.

Weber, A., Weber, U. & Raspe, H. (1999)
Langzeitarbeitsunfähigkeit- wer kommt wann und warum zurück an die Arbeit? (Long term work incapacity, who returns to work, when and why?) in: Gesundheitswesen 61, 8/99, A 207.

Weber, A. & Raspe, H. (1999)
Langzeitarbeitsunfähigkeit vermeiden und die Wiederaufnahme der Arbeit fördern -welchen Beitrag können die Krankenkassen leisten? (Prevention of long term work incapacity and work resumption: what can sick funds contribute?) in: Die BKK, 7/99, 356-358.

Weber, A., Weber, U. & Raspe, H. (1999)
Medizinische Rehabilitation bei Langzeitarbeitsunfähigkeit (Medical rehabilitation in case of long term work incapacity) in: Die Rehabilitation, 4/99, 220-226.

Publications from the Israeli WIR Project

Gordon, D. (1997)
Work incapacity and reintegration: international comparative study, second stage (in Hebrew) in: Annual survey 1996/97 of the National Insurance Institute, Jerusalem.

Gordon, D. (1998)
Work or disability? Two years after work injury (in Hebrew) in: Annual survey 1997/98 of the National Insurance Institute, Jerusalem.

Gordon, D. (2000)
Work incapacity and reintegration - Israel in comparisson to five countries, a two years follow-up study (in Hebrew). Special research series, National Insurance Institute Series, Jerusalem.

Publications from the Dutch WIR Project

Veerman, T. J. & van der Giezen, A. M. (1994)
Internationaal onderzoeksplan: werkhervatting na langdurig verzuim wegens lage rugklachten (International research plan: work resumption after long term sickness absence due to low back complaints) Tijdschrift voor Bedrijfs- en Verzekeringsgeneeskunde 2, December, p. 219-221.

van der Giezen, A. M. (1994)
Internationaal onderzoek naar rugklachten en werk (International study on back complaints and work) SURPLUS, Nov/Dec, p. 2.

Prins, R., Veerman, T. J. & van der Giezen, A. M. (1996)
Werkhervatting na rugklachten - Een internationale studie: probleemstelling, opzet en uitvoering van de eerste fase, Deelrapport 1 (Work resumption after back complaints: an international study: central problem, design and operation of the first stage; first report), R96/2, College van toezicht sociale verzekeringen, Zoetermeer.

van der Giezen, A. M., Veerman, T. J. & Prins, R. (1996)
*Werkhervatting na rugklachten - Drie maanden in de ziektewet:
ervaringen van werknemers en hun bedrijfsartsen, Deelrapport 2* (Work
resumption after back complaints – experiences of employees and their
occupational physicians after three months of sickness absence; second
report), R96/3, College van toezicht sociale verzekeringen, Zoetermeer.

van der Giezen, A.M. & Veerman, T. J. (1996)
*Rapport 'Werkhervatting na rugklachten' - Verzuimbegeleiding van
langdurig zieken kan beter* (Report 'Work resumption after back
complaints: supervision and support of long term sick can be better').
College van toezicht sociale verzekeringen Visie 1, p. 16-19.

van der Giezen, A. M. & Veerman, T. J. (1997)
*Werkhervatting na rugklachten - Uitvoering reïntegratie-activiteiten
tijdens het eerste ziektejaar. Deelrapport 3* (Work resumption after back
complaints: reintegration activities in the first year of work incapacity;
third report), R97/2, College van toezicht sociale verzekeringen,
Zoetermeer.

Veerman, T. J. & van der Giezen, A. M. (1997)
UVI verschijnt pas laat op het terrein van de reïntegratie (social security
agency starts reintegration late), College van toezicht sociale
verzekeringen Visie 2, April, p. 9 – 13.

van der Giezen, A. M. & Veerman, T. J. (1997)
*Werkhervatting na rugklachten – Gezondheid en werk negen maanden
na een periode van drie maanden arbeidsongeschiktheid.* (Work
resumption after back disorders: health and work nine months after a
three months period of work incapacity), Deelrapport 4, R97/15,
College van toezicht sociale verzekeringen, Zoetermeer.

Anema, J. R. & van der Giezen, A. M. (1999)
*Weinig communicatie tussen bedrijfsarts en curatieve sector over
belemmeringen voor werkhervatting na langdurige
arbeidsongeschiktheid wegens lage rugklachten* (Little communication
between occupational physician and health care on restrictions for work
resumption after long term work incapacity due to low back disorders)
Nederlands Tijdschrift voor Geneeskunde, 13 maart: 143 blz. 572-575.

Cuelenaere, B., van der Giezen, A. M., Veerman, T. J. & Prins, R.
(1999)
*Werkhervatting na rugklachten – Langdurig zieke werknemers twee jaar
gevolgd. Eindrapport Nederlandse studie* (Work resumption after back
complaints: long term work incapacitated employees monitored during
two years; final report of the Dutch study) R99/2, College van toezicht
sociale verzekeringen, Zoetermeer.

Cuelenaere, B. (1999)
Reïntegratie rugpatiënten: bepalend is relatie met werkgever
(Reintegration of back patients: relationship with employer is decisive)
College van toezicht sociale verzekeringen Visie 3, juni.

Cuelenaere, B., Veerman, T. J., Prins, R. & van der Giezen, A. M.
(1999)
*In distant mirrors. Work incapacity and return to work. A study of low
back pain patients in the Netherlands and five other countries.* College
van toezicht sociale verzekeringen Rapport 99/10, Zoetermeer, 1999.

Cuelenaere, B. & Veerman, T. J. (1999)
Nederland doet het niet slecht (The Netherlands do not perform badly)
College van toezicht sociale verzekeringen Visie 5, Oktober, p. 13-16.

van der Giezen, A. M., Bouter, L. M. & Nijhui, F. J. N. (2000)
*Prediction of return-to-work of low back pain patients sicklisted for 3-4
months.* PAIN (September) (forthcoming).

Publications from the Swedish WIR Project

Bergendorff, S., Hansson, E., Hansson, T., Palmer, E., Westin, M. &
Zetterberg, C. (1997)
Projektbeskrivning & undersökningsgrupp – Rygg och Nacke 1. (The
Swedish back and neck pain project – Study design and population.)
Stockholm: Riksförsäkringsverket och Sahlgrenska
Universitetssjukhuset.

Riksförsäkringsverket och Sahlgrenska Universitetssjukhuset (1997)
*Enkäter till undersökningsgruppen och försäkringskassan. Rygg och
Nacke 2.* (The Swedish back and neck pain project – Questionnaires and
information from local social insurance offices.) Stockholm:
Riksförsäkringsverket och Sahlgrenska Universitetssjukhuset.

Bergendorff, S., Hansson, E., Hansson, T., Palmer, E., Westin, M. &
Zetterberg. C. (1997)
Work Incapacity & Reintegration – Report 1. Stockholm:
Riksförsäkringsverket och Sahlgrenska Universitetssjukhuset.

Hansson, E. & Hansson, T. (1999)
*Medicinska åtgärder för sjukskrivna med rygg- och nackbesvär. Rygg
och Nacke 3.* (The Swedish back and neck pain project – Medical
interventions during sickness absence.) Stockholm:
Riksförsäkringsverket och Sahlgrenska Universitetssjukhuset.

Gerner, U. (1999)
Rehabilitering ur ett individperspektiv. En enkätundersökning bland sjukskrivna i Stockholms, Kristianstads och Västernorrlands län. Rygg och Nacke 4. (The Swedish back and neck pain project – a regional study.) Stockholm: Riksförsäkringsverket och Sahlgrenska Universitetssjukhuset.

Carlberg, P. (1999)
Att återgå i arbete efter sjukskrivning. Vilken roll spelar den psykiska och sociala miljön? Rygg och Nacke 5. (The Swedish back and neck pain project – The role of psychosocial factors at work for work resumption.) Stockholm: Riksförsäkringsverket och Sahlgrenska Universitetssjukhuset.

Goede, C. (2000)
Arbetslivsinriktade åtgärder för sjukskrivna med rygg- och nackbesvär. Rygg och Nacke 6. (The Swedish back and neck pain project – Vocational and other non-medical interventions during sickness absence.) Stockholm: Riksförsäkringsverket och Sahlgrenska Universitetssjukhuset.

Arneson, H. & Bergendorff, S. (2000)
Arbetsgivares rehabiliteringsinsatser – kvinnors hälsa och återgång i arbete. Rygg och Nacke 7. (The Swedish back and neck pain project – Interventions of employers and health status and work resumption of women.) Stockholm: Riksförsäkringsverket och Sahlgrenska Universitetssjukhuset.

Bergendorff, S., Hansson, E., Hansson, T. & Jonsson, R. (2000)
Prediktorer för återgång i arbete och förändring av hälsotillstånd. Rygg och Nacke 8. (The Swedish back and neck pain project – Predictors of health status and work resumption.) Stockholm: Riksförsäkringsverket och Sahlgrenska Universitetssjukhuset.

Bergendorff, S., Hansson, E. & Ghaemian, P. (2000)
Sjukskrivna med ryggbesvär och deras återgång i arbete – Sverige i jämförelse med fem länder. Rygg och Nacke 9. (The Swedish back and neck pain project – Swedish experiences in an international perspective.) Stockholm: Riksförsäkringsverket och Sahlgrenska Universitetssjukhuset (forthcoming).

Hansson, T. & Hansson, E. (2000)
The effects of common medical interventions on pain, back function and work resumption in chronic low back pain. A prospective two-year cohort study in six countries. Spine (forthcoming).

Publications from the US WIR Project

Kearney, J. (1997)
The Work Incapacity and Reintegration Study: Results of the Initial Survey Conducted in the United States, Social Security Bulletin, No. 3, p. 21-32, Washington, D.C.

Wheeler, P., Kearney, J. & Harrison, C. (forthcoming)
The Work Incapacity and Reintegration Study: Results from the U.S. Survey, Social Security Bulletin, Washington, D.C.

Contributors

Sisko Bergendorff is Senior Researcher at the National Social Insurance Board in Stockholm, Sweden. Her main field of research is the evaluation of social security benefits. She has also worked extensively with cross-national comparisons of social security benefits.

Frank S. Bloch is Professor of Law and Director of Clinical Education at Vanderbilt University in Nashville, Tennessee, USA. He is also a consultant to the International Social Security Association on the WIR Project. His main field of research is disability benefit claim processing and appeals. His most recent book is *Social Security Disability Law*. St. Paul: West Publishing Co., 1999.

Boukje Cuelenaere is a Researcher at the AS/tri Research and Consultancy Group in Leiden, the Netherlands. Her main fields of research are disability benefits and return-to-work policy, including cross-perspective studies involving policy makers, employees, employers and social security institutions. Her recent publications include *In Distant Mirrors: Work incapacity and return to work* (with T. J. Veerman, R. Prins, and A. M. van der Giezen). Zoetermeer: Social Security Supervisory Board (Ctsv), 1999.

Dalia Gordon is Director of research on wage replacement benefits and family allowance at the National Insurance Institute in Jerusalem, Israel. Her main areas of research are employment solutions for the unemployed and sole mothers, vocational rehabilitation, and sole mothers and family allowances. Her most recent publication is *Encouragement of Small Business by the Unemployed* (in Hebrew). Jerusalem: National Insurance Institute, 2000.

Elisabeth Hansson is a health economist at the Department of Orthopedics at Sahlgrenska University Hospital in Göteborg, Sweden. Her main field of research is cost effectiveness and cost utility of medical treatment programs.

Tommy Hansson is Professor of Occupational Orthopedics at the University of Göteborg and Head of the Department of Orthopedics at Sahlgrenska University Hospital in Göteborg, Sweden. His ongoing research projects involve pathophysiology, biomechanics, treatment, prevention and epidemiology of back problems. He is widely published in peer reviewed international journals.

Jan Høgelund is a Researcher at the Danish National Institute of Social Research in Copenhagen, Denmark. His main field of research is labor market reintegration of work incapacitated employees. His most recent publication is *Disability Benefit Reforms: Lessons from the Dutch and Swedish Experiences* (in Danish). Copenhagen: The Danish National Institute of Social Research, 1999.

John R. Kearney is the Director of the Division of Disability Research in the Office of Research, Evaluation and Statistics at the Social Security Administration in Baltimore, Maryland, USA. His primary research interest involves the disabled population and return-to-work strategies. He has also published research on the role of social security in alleviating child poverty and on proposals to ensure the solvency of social security programs.

Edward Palmer is Professor of Social Insurance Economics at Uppsala University in Uppsala, Sweden, and Chief of Research and Evaluation at the Swedish National Social Insurance Board. He has also worked as an adviser to governments on questions involving policy and administration of social security. His most recent book is *Changing Patterns in the Distribution of Economic Welfare* (with P. Gotschalk and B. Gustafsson). Cambridge: Cambridge University Press, 1997.

Rienk Prins is Research Director at AS/tri Research and Consultancy Group in Leiden, the Netherlands. He has also consulted on social security policy in Eastern Europe and the former Soviet Union. His main fields of research are social security sickness and disability programs and occupational risks, and rehabilitation and return to work strategies. His recent publications include *A moderate application: interim report on the first experimental year of person-bound reintegration vouchers* (with H. Bosselaar) (in Dutch). The Hague: Ministry of Social Affairs and Employment, 2000.

Theo J. Veerman is Research Director at AS/tri Research and Consultancy Group in Leiden, the Netherlands. His main fields of research are methods of reintegration and employers' strategies relative to sickness absence and long-term disability. His most recent publication is *In Distant Mirrors: Work incapacity and return to work* (with B. Cuelenaere, R. Prins and A.M. van der Giezen). Zoetermeer: Social Security Supervisory Board (Ctsv), 1999.

Andreas Weber is a Researcher in the working group of rehabilitation and prevention research of the faculty of sociology at the University of Hamburg in Hamburg, Germany, with primary responsibility for all research projects of vocational and medical rehabilitation. His main field of interest is the reintegration of disabled persons into the labor market.

Jockel Wolf is a Researcher at the IEA Data Processing Center in Hamburg, Germany, where he was responsible for creating the international database for the WIR Project. His main field of research is multimedia in the classroom.